The DOCTOR, The MURDER, The MYSTERY

The **Doctor,**
The **Murder,**
The **Mystery**

The true story of the Dr. John Branion murder case

by Barbara D'Amato

The Noble Press, Inc.

Printed in the United States of America

Library of Congress Cataloguing-in-Publication-Data

D'Amato, Barbara
    The doctor, the murder, the mystery : the true story of the Dr. John Branion murder case / by Barbara D'Amato.
        p. cm.
    ISBN 1-879360-13-6 : $20.95
    1. Murder—Illinois—Chicago—Case studies.   2. Homicide investigation—Illinois—Chicago—Case studies.   3. Branion, John—Trials, litigation, etc.   4. Afro-American physicians—Illinois—Chicago—Biography.   5. Fugitives from justice—Illinois—Chicago—Biography.
    I. Title.
    HV6534.C4D35   1992
    364.1'523'0977311—dc20   91-51217
                                                                   CIP

Noble Press books are available in bulk at discount prices. Single copies are available prepaid collect from the publisher.

The Noble Press, Inc.
213 W. Institute Place, Suite 508
Chicago, Illinois 60610
(800) 486-7737

▪ TABLE OF CONTENTS ▪

· ACKNOWLEDGEMENTS ·

So many people helped at so many stages of the work on Dr. Branion's case that it is difficult to name them all. I would particularly thank Professor Thomas Geraghty of the Legal Clinic at Northwestern Law School, Professor Jon Waltz from Northwestern Law School, and the late Professor James Haddad from Northwestern Law School, who gave freely of their time and great expertise pro bono. Thaddeus Aycock of the Northwestern Traffic Institute drove the Branion route many times and analyzed the distance and time issues. Dr. William Buckingham of the Northwestern University Medical Faculty evaluated Dr. Branion's prison medical records and gave advice about what care he needed. His recommendations led to Dr. Branion being supplied with a low-salt, low-fat diet in prison. Dr. Douglas Shanklin of the University of Tennessee at Memphis spent hours analyzing the autopsy, inquest, and trial records, and made himself available to Michael Niederman from Columbia College in Chicago for his television documentary and to "Unsolved Mysteries" for their television program on Dr. Branion. Michael Niederman helped Dr. Branion both by producing his documentary, and by turning up new evidence during his interviews. Similarly, the professionalism of director John Joseph and producer Kris Palmer of "Unsolved Mysteries" made it possible to attract national attention to Dr. Branion's plight, and resulted in several witnesses coming forth with information that had been buried for twenty years. Betty Nicholas gave freely of her advice during the time Dr. Branion's supporters marched at the State of Illinois Building. Rob Warden, then editor of *Chicago Lawyer*, obtained interviews with difficult-to-reach people involved in the case and also provided me with the benefit of his experience.

Rebecca Taniguchi, attorney Martha Conrad, Joann Garcia, cinematographer Ron Boyd, William Hooks, Pauline McCoo, Alicia McCariens, and Joe Mahr provided much welcome help. Members of the Court Reporters' Office lent a hand in an attempt to trace old memos. Members of the Chicago Police Department made me welcome, rooted old documents out of a retired file, permitted me to sit at a desk in their office to study the documents, and even printed up old photographs that made it possible for me to be more accurate in describing the crime scene than I could ever have been from written reports. That so many people are interested in finding truth is heartening, and meeting them has been one of the great rewards of my work on the Branion case.

· INTRODUCTION ·

Truth and the murder of Donna Branion

Most Americans think that a trial in the case of a major crime proceeds quite rationally. We see television shows and movies in which the hard-working detective pieces the case together into a consistent picture of guilt. Then the prosecution takes this evidence and presents it to the jury in a way that makes sense, and the defense tries to refute it, bringing all available ammunition to bear. That was what I thought happened.

I was naive. In the course of researching the book you are about to read, I found that prosecutors do not necessarily even try to paint a consistent picture. Police detectives overlook obvious evidence. Defense attorneys miss important testimony. Juries may not try to make sense of it all, either. And judges may summarize the case in slanted ways by distorting un-controverted evidence. One of the most distressing aspects to me was a growing awareness of how small a portion of the facts in a given case are actually heard by the jury.

Juries have a hard job.

Even under the best circumstances, juries are trying to decide what really happened at a time in the past and a place far removed from the courtroom. Plea bargaining in criminal cases is so prevalent today that it is primarily the most difficult criminal cases, with the most balanced proof of guilt or innocence, that come to trial. It is estimated that in the majority of jurisdictions, over 90 percent of criminal cases are plea bargained and never reach a jury. The defendant simply pleads guilty to a lesser charge than the one the prosecutor threatens to try him on. In first-degree mur-der cases, and especially in capital cases, plea bargaining is generally not permitted, but many cases that might be tried as first-degree murder are reduced to a lesser charge like manslaughter and then plea bargained.

Therefore, juries by and large are hearing only the hard-to-decide cases. They are trying to find *real truth* in very difficult circumstances. As the prosecutor in the trial of Dr. John Branion told an interviewer, the same case with the same attorneys and the same evidence in the same courtroom, but with two different juries, could come up with "guilty" in one instance and "innocent" in another. My own belief is that, if they reach the truth eighty percent of the time, they would be doing very well.

The jury system is probably the fairest system of justice yet devised. But it is a system of humans and is not infallible. We should use it and be glad of it, but be aware of its potential errors.

This story began on December 22, 1967, when Donna Branion, the wife of Dr. John Branion, was shot to death in their Chicago apartment. Dr. Branion was eventually convicted for the crime of murdering his wife after a trial by jury. I first became involved in Dr. Branion's case eighteen years after Donna Branion's death, when his second wife, Shirley, approached my husband, Anthony D'Amato, for help. Tony is a professor of law at Northwestern Law School. Although Shirley Branion maintained that John was innocent, there was very little evidence available, and John himself had forgotten much of what had happened the morning his wife was killed. We all decided that I would do some research, see whether there was enough data to use to write an article about the case, and then see if there was enough for an appeal through the courts.

Dr. Branion was essentially a forgotten man, despite the interest in the case when the murder occurred in 1967. Worse, there was very little information available to tell me why he had been convicted. The state of Illinois had lost both the trial transcript and the physical evidence. This is not supposed to happen, because it makes it virtually impossible for the convicted person to appeal. Even if important new evidence turned up, without a trial transcript an attorney would be hard-pressed to show a court how it would fit in.

At first, I was only curious. His family insisted he was innocent, but most guilty felons insist vigorously on their innocence. After some research into the time sequences of what Dr. Branion purportedly did on the morning that Donna Branion was murdered, I began to have strong doubts about his guilt. I am a mystery novelist and time alibis are a mainstay of mystery novels. I became fascinated with the question of whether it was possible—in real life, not in a mystery novel—to reconstruct a day that had taken place eighteen years before. The more evidence I collected from police reports and witnesses, the more complicated the facts seemed and the more frustrated and outraged I became. When we finally found a copy of the trial transcript, it was obvious that the errors in the Branion case went far beyond a few problems with the time sequence. Important witnesses who knew Dr. Branion was at the hospital when the murder must have taken place had never been called to testify. Significant evidence had been lost. After a year of work, I was astonished to discover that even the prosecutor doubted that Branion could have been in the apartment when his wife was killed.

A few people you meet change your life. When I first saw Dr. John Branion Jr. he was in prison and likely to spend the rest of his life there. He was about to turn sixty and was serving only the third year of a twenty- to thirty-year sentence for murder. For most of every day he was in a state of controlled fear, because he was claustrophobic and yet had to spend much of his time in a cell. "My greatest terror has always been suffocation," he told me, after I had known him several months. "I wake up in the night in here, sometimes, thinking I can't breathe."

But he was describing, not complaining. Despite his situation, John Branion had mental energy and strength to spare. He was interested in everybody he met—and he'd give them advice, too. He would tell young men in his cell block how they did *not* need to wind up back in prison after their release. He'd tell the older men not to eat so much salt and fat. He was interested in his family, in the political condition in the United States, in what was happening to old friends.

For more than four years, John Branion and I talked on the phone at least once a week. I enjoyed our conversations because of the range of his interests and his genuine concern for the people around him. He opened up the world of prison life to me, and eventually the world of the criminal justice system. Courts and judges would never look the same to me again.

Getting to the bottom of the Branion murder became an obsession with me, partly because Dr. Branion was in prison and ill, but partly because I was so angered at the irrationality I found in our criminal justice system. The research took five years, thousands of hours of interviews, and hundreds of trips to courts, prisons, and government offices.

Meanwhile, Dr. Branion became a friend. Many times I went to visit him at the prison, either with members of his family or by myself. He got to know my children's voices on the phone and spoke with them if he happened to call when I wasn't there. Always the doctor, he asked frequently about our weight, our blood pressures, and any health problem any of us might be having.

Dr. Branion was a complex person. He had done things he was ashamed of, like divorcing his second wife, Shirley. He had done things, such as keeping loaded guns in his home, which he now believed terribly foolish. Like all of us, he had good characteristics and bad characteristics.

He had enormous energy and breadth of interests. I got to know, for instance, that he would never telephone at a certain time of the evening because he was watching the "MacNeil/Lehrer News Hour."

Dr. Branion's story ranges across the entire sweep of American life. His wife's family was wealthy, and the milieu in which they moved in the middle decades of this century was a class of educated, professional, wealthy black Americans that at the time was largely invisible to white America. Dr. Branion was hunted through Africa during his thirteen years as a fugitive, and he passed through more than a dozen African nations at a time of unusual political turmoil. When he was at last returned to the United States, the passage of his case through the courts is a chronicle of the way judges make decisions that determine the fate of human lives.

I should include a note on method. In the account of Dr. John Branion's actions on the day his wife was murdered, all factual details for events between nine that morning and noon are taken from official papers, such as police reports, or have been related by someone other than Dr. Branion himself in affidavits, interviews, or other documents. The only parts of the story that rest on Dr. Branion's unsupported word are his own opinions or feelings, and these are in every instance attributed to him.

Certain conversations between John Branion and people now dead are reconstructed from his memory. In no instance does the question of John Branion's guilt or innocence turn on the content of these reconstructed conversations. They are included as illumination of his world.

▪ PART ONE ▪

Murder

· CHAPTER ONE ·

The last day of normal life Dr. John Branion would ever know was Thursday, December 21, 1967.

He enjoyed that morning at work. He almost always enjoyed work. In fact, he enjoyed practically everything he did. John Branion was a tall, burly black man, now forty-one, with a hundred enthusiasms. He walked fast, talked with verve, cooked gourmet dinners and ate with gusto, rode horses, and raced cars. And he loved being a doctor. He had been trained in Switzerland, but had come back to the States to work in his home neighborhood in the Hyde Park area of south Chicago.

He saw a dozen patients Thursday morning, including a man near his own age, who wheezed like an asthmatic, was sweaty and clammy-skinned, and could hardly walk across the tiny examining room without stopping to rest. The man was very worried.

"It's my heart, isn't it?"

Branion sat down to talk with the man. He usually stopped and talked with patients, especially the fearful ones. "Jimmy, your heart sounds are perfectly normal. Your EKG's normal. Blood work's normal. What you are is too fat."

"You're not just a shadow yourself, Doctor B."

It was true. Branion liked food. "I am fifteen pounds overweight," he said. "You are a hundred and ten pounds overweight."

"Uh-huh."

"It's going to kill you."

"My wife's a cook like — like, it's an art, Doctor B. She says taste this. Taste that. I taste it."

"You didn't get this fat by tasting. You got this fat by eating."

"Okay. Yeah."

Nurse Betty Adger had come into the room and was standing quietly near the door. This was her signal that he was taking too long on one patient. She knew Branion's tendency to go on chatting and chatting.

Branion said, "Come back in four months or so. Let's see how you're doing."

"'Preciate it, Doctor B."

Dr. John Branion left the hospital at noon, waving goodbye to two friends, the pharmacist, LaHarry Norman, and the lab technician, Robert Wadley. He was taking the afternoon off, going Christmas shopping with his wife and another friend. There were just three shopping days to Christmas.

John was half an inch under six feet tall. He carried some extra weight, but like many former football players he carried it in his shoulders and chest, so it looked like power. His face was light brown and gave two separate impressions. The features were lively, smallish, constantly in motion. They looked Irish, and when he had an especially good idea for fun, he looked rather like a leprechaun. Above the mobile features, though, was a forehead so high and broad that it dominated his face.

His specialty was obstetrics and he loved delivering babies.

He told Betty Adger, "Don't worry. I'm going to put in a full day tomorrow."

But as it turned out, he would not have the chance.

The weather was the kind that makes Chicagoans proud of their ability to survive.

Yesterday had been pretty much the average for Christmas week, barely edging above the freezing mark in the middle of the day, then falling to twenty degrees overnight. But today, Thursday, everything had gone wild. It was already sixty degrees at noon and a wind that felt almost hot hurled slashes of rain diagonally across the pavement. The heavy raindrops pinged on John's car as he got in. Then abruptly the rain died and a warm, dead calm fell over the street.

In southern Illinois the unstable air and violent hot updrafts were giving birth to tornadoes, usually a spring and early-summer phenomenon in the Midwest.

He left the hospital that Thursday noon, still carrying one of his morning patients in his mind. Mrs. Rawly was two months pregnant. She had previously suffered an ectopic pregnancy, in which the embryo had implanted in the fallopian tube, not the uterus. Untreated, such pregnancies are usually fatal. Discovered in time and surgically removed, as he had done with her first, they carry a death rate only slightly higher than caesarean section. Ectopic pregnancies occur in one of every two hundred pregnancies. But in a person with a previous ectopic pregnancy, the chance of another is between 10 and 25 percent.

Well, he'd asked her to come back in two weeks. And she knew how to get hold of the clinic by phone, day or night.

By the time he got to his home, it was raining again, but the wet didn't dampen his mood. He liked changes of weather and this heat was interesting, because it was so unseasonable.

John picked up his wife, Donna, for the Christmas shopping expedition. They went to get their friend, Bill Hooks. Usually Donna liked to shop at Marshall Field's, Carson Pirie Scott, or Bonwit's in downtown Chicago. Bonwit's was her mother's favorite. But today they were breaking with tradition. There was a new phenomenon in merchandising—the shopping mall. John, Billy, and Donna were going to drive out to a shopping mall and see what it was like. John wanted to get a slot car racing set for his four-year-old son Joby.

John wasn't going to let on that he had already decided on Donna's Christmas present. She'd be starting to ask for hints. He'd be very casual and keep her guessing.

In the news that Thursday, presidential hopeful George Romney told the press he was optimistic that a solution to the Vietnam War was just around the corner, while in Oakland, California, singer Joan Baez had been ordered to jail for forty-five days for taking part in an anti-war demonstration. District Attorney Jim Garrison in New Orleans was probing John F. Kennedy's assassination. And in Cape Town, South Africa, a man named Louis Washansky had died eight days after the world's first heart transplant surgery.

Locally, *The Graduate* had opened at Loop theaters and was doing well, but its years ahead as a perennial cult film were far in the future. Polk Brothers appliances advertised clothes dryers for $109.95. Dominick's Finer Foods was selling eight 16-ounce Pepsis for 68 cents. And Walgreen's had one-pound boxes of Whitman's Samplers all boxed for Christmas for $2.25. If you wanted to opt for a big-ticket item and bring home a car for Christmas, the new Buick Skylark retailed for $2,664. In the comics, Snoopy was going to the Olympics in Grenoble, France.

That evening John and Donna were going to her brother's house for dinner.

"I'll go out and get the scotch," said Nelson.

"No, no, I'll go," John said.

"I am the host, and I have run out, so I ought to go," said Nelson.

Bill Hooks said, "I'll go."

The ladies—Donna Branion, Sonja Brown, Maxine Brown, and Bill Hooks' wife—laughed and laughed at the heroes, offering to go out into the storm. The heat wave of the day, the rain, and the tornadoes were gone. In one of those lightning Chicago weather changes, the temperature had fallen forty degrees in six hours. It was now twenty degrees and the temperature was still falling. Eddies of snow were blowing across the street outside and making hazy the outlines of the bare trees in Drexel Square across the street.

Nelson Brown was Donna Branion's younger brother. They were children of realtor/banker Sydney Brown, one of the richest and most powerful black men in Chicago. Nelson was an attorney, and the apartment where he and his wife lived on South Drexel was big and lavish. It was a condominium, facing directly on the park named Drexel Square, and Nelson owned two apartments of three rooms each, one above the other, connected by a spiral staircase.

Nelson was a lanky, good-looking man who liked to tell stories and keep a party lively. Bill Hooks, big, jovial, and deep-voiced, liked to tell stories, too, and so did John Branion. The ladies had fallen into fits of laughing over and over through the evening.

Maxine Brown was there without an escort. She was married to Donna's cousin, Oscar Brown, Jr., the entertainer, composer, and writer, but they were separated. Oscar's father and Donna's father, Sydney Brown, were brothers. Maxine was petite and vivacious. She giggled a great deal and called everyone "hon," but Donna, who was her great friend, believed that underneath the cheerful front Maxine kept up she was very depressed about the separation.

Maxine lived in the same building as John and Donna. She had come to the party with them, and would drive home with them.

"I'm firm on this," said Bill Hooks. "*I'll* go out for the scotch."

"Oh, it's cold out. We don't need it that badly," John said.

But Bill was out the door.

Sonja had laid out a big buffet, with cocktail sausages and open-faced sandwiches for hors d'oeuvres, and then a huge bowl of spaghetti and meat balls and another huge bowl of salad. She knew these men; they would eat. She offered beer, scotch, or bourbon to drink, and cognac with dessert. She had not noticed that her supply of scotch was nearly gone, though, until someone tipped the bottle up and found there was just an inch left.

Bill was back in a matter of minutes, dusted with snow. There were always all-night places open. Everybody applauded the returned hero.

"When's the skiing trip?" Donna asked Sonja and Nelson.

Nelson said, "We leave the twenty-fourth."

"Doesn't give you much of a Christmas Eve."

"We're having skiing for a present."

John said, "Oh, you know, Santa Claus can find Vail just as easy as Chicago."

"John and I are going to go to the Bahamas," Donna said. "But a little later."

Nelson said, "When?"

"Oh, after the holidays. The holidays are for the children."

Donna said to Maxine, "Come on over to lunch tomorrow. We'll get John to take us to lunch, and then you and I can go Christmas shopping."

John groaned. "*More* Christmas shopping!"

"Now listen, we might even get *you* something."

"Okay, okay. I take it back. I don't mean it. Come on over, Maxine."

"If I can get off work—"

"I'll pick you up on my way home at noon."

"Okay."

They ate and drank and talked, all old friends who had known each other for years, having a casual party, informal and comfortable. There was nothing out of the ordinary about the evening. There was no anticipation that they were twelve hours from disaster.

The party broke up late, but the guests did not have far to go. They all lived within a few blocks of each other. They shouted goodnights and ducked, giggling, out into the cold. Pellets of snow tickled their faces.

Maxine's apartment was upstairs in the same building as the Branions', but her entrance was adjacent. They walked her there to see her safely inside and said goodnight. Donna and John let themselves into their apartment, where their daughter Jan, now thirteen, was babysitting their son Joby, who was four. The children were asleep, which was a good thing. They had to be in school tomorrow, the last day before Christmas vacation.

· CHAPTER TWO ·

Friday, December 22, 1967.

On the final morning of her life, Donna Branion rose about seven. She dressed as soon as she had washed. She did not enjoy slouching around the house in robe and nightgown. She hadn't been raised to be sloppy. Today she decided to wear a new beige sweater with a brown and white skirt, and gray stockings with a pattern of small squares. But for comfort she kept on her slippers.

She started a skillet of sausage and then decided on bacon, too. While the meat was sizzling and John was showering she ran a batch of biscuits into the oven, then went into the master bedroom and made the bed. She'd get around to the kids' beds later.

Back in the kitchen, which was large and contained every type of equipment needed for gourmet cookery, she turned the bacon, called to Jan to make sure she knew it was past seven-thirty, and then went to help Joby dress.

When she went back to the kitchen with Joby in tow, John was taking the bacon out of the pan, putting it to drain on paper towels. John liked to cook, and some days he fried up leftover meat—roast beef or ham—with spices, for breakfast. But he didn't have as much time this morning as usual, because he had to take Joby to nursery school.

"You're not going to forget to pick him up?" Donna said.

"Oh, come on. Forget my boy?" John said, pinching Joby's nose lightly between his index and middle fingers.

"When are they supposed to be done with the Corvette?"

"I don't know. I'll call this afternoon."

"If they keep it past today—"

"Yeah, I know. There won't be any mechanics on tomorrow, because it's Saturday. Then Sunday. And Monday is Christmas. I wouldn't be able to pick it up until Tuesday, probably afternoon at that."

9

"Still—I guess there's no point in taking it back if there's a problem that isn't fixed."

"Well, I'll just have to use the Buick, however long—"

"And don't forget to pick up Maxine."

John laughed. "My mind is not a complete sieve."

Jan would walk to school at Shoesmith Elementary, which was only a few blocks away. Since it was the last day before Christmas vacation, school would let out at noon.

John picked up the morning paper, *The Chicago Tribune*. It headlined a mystery: JOHNSON ON SECRET TRIP. The subheadline announced "Plane May Be Headed for Thailand or Viet." In other news, the state of Michigan had rejected an open housing law intended to prevent realtors and municipalities from keeping African-Americans out of certain neighborhoods. John grunted with a kind of half disgust, half confirmed expectation.

The movie made from *Valley of the Dolls* had just opened, starring Sharon Tate. In the comics, Snoopy came home after trying to reach Grenoble, France, for the Olympics.

The paper was choked with advertising for last-minute shoppers. It was three days before Christmas, but the next to the last shopping day.

Donna had the biscuits and sausage on the table. The phone rang. Donna went to answer it. John got the toast when it popped up. The table was loaded with dishes; the Branions liked a lot of breakfast.

John knew from what he could hear of the conversation that it was Donna's sister, Joyce. Joyce called once or twice most days.

"I could babysit about—oh, midafternoon," Donna said. "Not before—"

Joyce had a young baby.

"Well, I'll tell you what *I* bought." Donna lowered her voice for a few moments. "No, he hasn't said—but I know what I *think* it is."

They were talking about Christmas presents. After a pause, Donna said, "I had this wonderful idea. We'll talk later."

Jan came in and sat down. Joby was eating sausage. Joby ate anything that wouldn't bite back. Donna ate slightly less than the rest of her family. She was never especially inclined to gain weight, but she had noticed that a few pounds had crept on after she passed forty last year, and she was being just a little bit cautious. John liked everything and ate everything. He used up a lot of energy in a day. But he had a real tendency to gain weight. He had had a mild heart attack a few years before, so he, like Donna, was trying to keep the pounds off.

John tickled Joby, who was smashing his sausage. Joby giggled.

"Do you know why we call you Joby?" John said.

"No," said Joby, who had heard the story before and knew perfectly well.

"Well, now, your name is John Marshall Branion the third, and the first two letters of your first name are J - O - "

John drew a big J and a big O on Joby's tummy. Joby giggled.

"And your last name starts with a B!"

John drew a big B. Joby patted John's hand.

"And that spells JOBY!"

After breakfast Donna bundled Joby into a jacket, boots, and mittens. The unusually warm weather of the day before had gone without a trace. It was ten degrees and there was snow on the ground. The forecast was for still more snow. John had left $500 on the nightstand for Donna to use for Christmas shopping. The mall the day before had been interesting, but there were still presents to buy.

"I left you money in the bedroom, babe," he said.

"Maybe Maxine and I can shop after lunch."

"What about Joyce?"

"I'm not going there until later."

Jan, John, and Joby went out, Jan to walk to Shoesmith Elementary School which was just a couple of blocks away, John to drive Joby to nursery school in the car.

"Think about where you want to take Maxine for lunch," John said, the last thing before he left. Joby waved to his mother.

Donna turned back into the house. Sometimes Maxine dropped in from upstairs in the mornings to gossip. Donna was in the habit of leaving the back door unlocked for her. But Maxine had started work at a realty office in September, so she wouldn't be dropping by today.

It was a big apartment, a hundred feet from front to back, with three bedrooms and two sun parlors. Donna decided to get some of the housework out of the way. She collected the breakfast dishes to wash later. Then she went to make the beds.

It was about 9:00 a.m. and snowing lightly when John dropped Joby off at the Hyde Park Neighborhood Club nursery school. He arrived at the Ida Mae Scott Hospital at 9:15 to take clinic duty. The Ida Mae Scott Hospital was a small, neighborhood hospital with a large turnover of clinic outpatients. The clinic ran on a first-come-first-served basis. There were always people waiting; there were several there already. John was the only doctor taking clinic duty today. From the moment he arrived he was plunged into an unceasing parade of ailments.

He and his nurse, Betty Adger, worked together, she admitting the patients, taking their names, finding their charts for medical histories, scheduling the patients, and placing them in examining rooms as Doctor Branion finished previous patients. He worked three examining rooms in rotation, all down one side of the hall. Betty and John were a good team, experienced, and each had confidence in the way the other worked. For the two hours and fifteen minutes John was there that morning this rotation continued, and he stopped only long enough to make three phone calls from the office, which was in the same area. That morning he would see exactly thirteen scheduled patients, and one emergency patient at the end.

John called home a little after ten. He always called home a couple of times a day.

"Decided where you want to go to lunch, babe?" he asked Donna.

"No, but I'm thinking about it."

"Well, I have to work this afternoon. The clinic is full of people. I can't do a two-hour lunch."

At 10:15, Donna's sister Joyce called Donna again. They chatted a while, casually, and Joyce said later that Donna had sounded just as she always did.

At 11:05, Donna's next-door neighbor arrived home with groceries. Theresa Kentra had seven bags of food, which she carried from her car into her kitchen. Her back porch and the Branions' were connected, and their living rooms shared a common wall. Theresa Kentra had been born in Yugoslavia. She was the same age as Donna, forty-one, and like Donna she had children whom she expected home when the schools closed at noon. She had a few presents as well as food in the bags, and she wanted to hide them before the children came running in.

At about 11:15, John called home again, to see whether Donna had made up her mind where to eat. She didn't answer, but he was not at all alarmed. Probably she was in the shower. He phoned American Airlines to try to arrange tickets for a doctor friend who was going on vacation. Then he went back to work.

At about 11:20, while Theresa Kentra was moving around her apartment putting away presents and groceries, she heard strange noises. There were three sharp sounds and a crash as if something heavy had fallen. Thinking at first that it was a truck dropping boards in the alley, she put it out of her mind.

John's last scheduled patient was Robert Jordan. John entered the examining room to see Jordan at 11:27. The other patients in the waiting room had been told that the clinic was closing for lunch. That moment—11:30 a.m.—would be of the utmost importance to John Branion for the rest of his life.

After seeing Robert Jordan, John walked across the corridor to the clinical laboratory to ask about a test result for one of his regular patients. In the lab he found the hospital technician, Robert Wadley, and the pharmacist, LaHarry Norman. John asked about the test results and the three men talked a few minutes. John was in the habit of letting Norman, the pharmacist, know when he was leaving for lunch, because when John stopped seeing patients, patients would stop coming to the pharmacy for medicines, and Norman himself could then go to lunch. In fact, about once a week Norman went home to lunch with John.

John was about to leave when the nurse, Betty Adger, hurried in. Betty was bouncy, plumply pretty, and extremely sympathetic to patients in pain.

"Oh, I'm glad I caught you," she said.

"What's up?"

"Kenneth Morris just came in. He's a long-time patient here. He's in acute distress."

"I was just about out the door."

"I don't think he should have to wait around."

"I have to pick Joby up at school."

"Morris is in pain and if he doesn't see you, we don't reopen again for an hour and a half."

"Okay. Okay. You're right."

But the doctor's examining rooms were either not cleaned or still had patients getting dressed to leave. Adger decided to put Morris in the office of the dentist, Dr. Moore, which was open, and John examined him there.

Morris was in great pain, but John thought a painkiller would be enough for now and prescribed morphine. Adger noted the prescription, gave Morris the painkiller, and recorded the morphine use and time in the drug book.

Meanwhile, John was starting to run late if he was going to pick Joby up at nursery school at 11:45.

John walked quickly through the laboratory the second time. "I can't stay to talk," he said. "I've got to pick up Joby and it's too cold for him to wait outside."

Both Wadley and Norman thought he had spent about five minutes with the emergency patient. They would have chatted longer, but John said he had to go. The time was about 11:37.

As he was leaving the hospital, John ran into the hospital administrator, Leonard Scott, whom he called Bub.

"I'd stop and talk, Bub, but I'm in a hurry," he said. "I've got to pick up Joby at nursery school."

"How's Donna?"

"Oh, fine, fine. We're going to go to lunch later."

Usually Donna picked Joby up at nursery school. John thought that the children would be put out on the street when the school closed at 11:45 and Joby would be left standing in the cold. Actually this was not so; the school kept the children indoors in a common room until the parents collected them. His misunderstanding would cost him a great deal of anguish later.

It was bitterly cold outside after the warm hospital. The skies were overcast as he walked to his car, and his feet skidded a little on the powdering of snow that whitened the blacktopped area behind the hospital—his own fault, he thought to himself; he never liked to wear rubber boots.

He had parked in the rear of the hospital. Donna's maroon Buick coughed a couple of times before it decided to start in the cold. John had a moment of worry that they might have to get through the Christmas holidays with both cars in the shop.

He drove down the alley, waiting at the end for a stream of pedestrians, then turned into 51st Street. 51st Street is a major east-west artery in the area, and it was particularly crowded today, three days before Christmas. He passed Provident Hospital on his left and Washington Park on his right, then Drexel Square, where Donna's parents and her brother Nelson lived.

It was a mile and a half to Joby's school, through a crowded area of small shops and larger stores, all of them bustling with Christmas business. Pedestrians loaded with packages made runs across the streets against the lights and in the middle of blocks. There were even more cars than usual, half of them looking for parking places. John worried that it was taking too long to get to Joby, but there was nothing he could do about it.

The Hyde Park Neighborhood Club nursery school was on Kenwood, and he had to drive around three sides of the block because of one-way streets. When he pulled up outside the school at about 11:43, the children were not standing outdoors. He found a parking place, turned off the radio, and waited a few moments. Then he saw parents going into the building, and got out of the Buick, went inside, and asked where the children were. A woman directed him to the "all-purpose room" where he found Joby waiting. The boy was wearing only his indoor clothes.

"Hiya, Tiger."

"Daddy!" Joby giggled.

"Hold still a minute, Tiger, and let's get you dressed. It's cold out there."

John took off his own jacket because the school was warm, and helped Joby into his coat, boots, and mittens.

"You are just about the wiggliest thing I have ever seen."

Joby giggled again and wiggled harder, just for show.

It was now about 11:47.

John walked Joby to the car, helped him inside, then locked the car door so he wouldn't fall out. John drove to Maxine Brown's office at 1369 E. 53rd Street, just a few blocks away through busy streets. On the way, unknown to them, at 54th and Dorchester they passed an acquaintance of John's, Cottrell R. Meadors, who had just returned home from a Christmas shopping trip. Meadors waved, but John did not notice him. He was talking to Joby.

John and Joby drove on to the building where Maxine Brown worked, Apartment Homes, Incorporated. John again parked the car, extricated Joby, and went in, taking Joby with him. He asked for Maxine. When she came out from the back offices, she was wearing indoor clothes.

"Where's your coat?"

Maxine said, "I'm sorry, hon, but my boss came up with two errands he wants me to do."

"But we've got a lunch date. Joby here's planning a big date with his girl Maxine."

Joby giggled and swung on his father's arm.

"Hon, I can't get the time." She lowered her voice. "My boss just won't give me that long."

"I'm sorry."

"Joby, every time I see you you're two inches bigger."

Joby smiled.

"Well, let's do it soon," John said.

"Sure. Give me a raincheck."

"Over Christmas, maybe."

John walked with Joby back to the car. By then it was past 11:50.

The two drove on home. John remembers that as he took Joby out of the car near their house, a woman he and Donna knew was passing on the street and he stopped and talked with her, but he has never been able to remember who it was. The events of the next few minutes would drive her name and face forever out of his mind.

They walked up to the door, Joby pulling and skipping.

"Can we go to lunch anyway?"

"Let's see what your mother thinks."

"We can go ourselves. Can't we?"

"I sure don't see why not."

"Yes, yes, yes, yes!"

Joby was excited about Christmas coming, and the excitement spilled over onto everything else in his life.

"We're home, babe!" John called, and he gave his special whistle, one all his close friends knew.

Somehow, the house looked subtly different to him. The lights were on in the living room, though it was broad daylight. There were places on the carpet where the nap was scuffed up in long streaks. John whistled again; then he called for Donna.

"We're home, babe!"

There was no answer.

"Where's your Mom?"

"Maybe she's hiding under the sofa," Joby said, and he scrunched down, laughing, to look.

John was vaguely uneasy. Surely Donna was here some place. She was expecting to go out for lunch with him and Maxine. Donna was extremely reliable and she would never have forgotten about it. Joby caught up with his father.

John and Joby, holding hands, went looking, and calling out for Donna. She was not in their bedroom nor in the bathroom washing.

One of the sliding doors of their bedroom closet was leaning off its track.

They walked back down the long hall from the bedrooms into the living room, turned right and right again into the kitchen. She wasn't there. But one of her slippers was lying on the floor between the kitchen and the utility room beyond. This was a tiny room containing laundry equipment and some of John's gun collection. John could see something on the floor in there, almost like a pile of clothing.

He walked over and flicked on the utility room light. For a moment he did not comprehend what he saw. Donna was lying on her back, slightly turned onto her right side, feet toward the door, utterly still. Her skirt was pushed up, showing her legs, and her sweater was up around her breasts, showing her abdomen. Her skin was a terrible grayish color. Her beige sweater was soaked with blood. There was blood all around her in a shiny pool.

He went half a step closer, feeling as if he couldn't breathe. She had fallen with her left side up against the wall and her head half into a paper shopping bag near a chair. There was an electric iron cord twisted around her arm. The room was deathly quiet and her abdomen did not move with any breath of life.

Donna was dead.

▪ CHAPTER THREE ▪

For an unmeasurable instant John did not move. Then Joby's hand contracted in his, and he thought, "Don't let him see."

Instinctively, he flicked off the light, but simultaneously realized how foolish that was. He had to get Joby away from here and not let him carry in his mind forever the picture of his mother lying dead and her skirt and sweater pushed up. In life she had been so modest, so proper.

He scooped the boy up in his arms and turned and ran into the kitchen. Joby was very rigid and quiet. Desperately, John thought, where could he take him? He had to call the police.

First he would get Helen Hudson. She was Donna's cousin and lived upstairs. She would take care of Joby.

John started screaming "Helen! Helen!" while he was still in the kitchen. He ran out the kitchen door onto the back porch, which the Branions shared with the Kentras next door, still calling "Helen!" and careless of the cold and snow.

She heard him and came running down.

"Something terrible's happened to Donna!"

"What? What's happened?" She could see that he was near panic. He felt as if he might faint.

"I've got to get Joby out of here!"

"Take him up to my place. The back door's open."

John pounded up the stairs with Joby in his arms.

Meanwhile, Helen Hudson went to look at Donna. It was possible whatever had happened wasn't as bad as John thought.

But when she saw Donna's body, it was obvious. She ran out the front door of the apartment and up to the third floor to get Dr. Helen Payne, who lived there with her mother. Dr. Payne's brother William was in the apartment visiting. Helen Hudson told them both that something had happened to Donna, and they all ran back downstairs to help. John had left Joby upstairs with Helen Hudson's husband, Edsel. When William Payne

17

got downstairs, he found John standing in the kitchen in a state of barely controlled hysteria.

William Payne said, "Do you want me to call the police?"

John did not seem to understand him. He was hyperventilating and pale. "Shall I call the police?"

Payne had to repeat himself several times. "John. John, do you want me to call the police?" Finally, John said,

"Yes. Call the police."

Payne went to the telephone in the Branion apartment and dialed. The police dispatcher logged the call at 11:57. The nearest patrol car was 2114, containing Officer William Catizone, star number 9563, who worked out of the 21st District. He was in the vicinity of 51st Street and Lake Park. At 11:58, he picked up the message on his car radio.

At 12:00 noon, Catizone was at the Branion home.

John was dazed and unable to function, so William Payne took Catizone to the utility room.

As a uniformed officer, not a detective, Catizone's job was to find out what had happened. If a person were sick, or injured in an accident, it was his job to get an ambulance to respond. If the victim was dead, he had to call for a doctor or coroner, and if it looked like a crime had been committed, call the area center for detectives and the crime lab.

Catizone acted by the book. Although he believed that Donna Branion was obviously dead, he tried to get a pulse. He found none. He called for the lab people and the detectives from Area One homicide.

Early in that first half hour, Catizone discovered that Helen Payne was a doctor. It is proper procedure to have a doctor pronounce death, however obvious death may be, so that the officer at the scene does not have to call an unnecessary ambulance. Then, after the initial investigation, a squadrol may transport the body directly to the morgue. Catizone asked Dr. Payne to pronounce Donna dead, which she did, and he noted the time as 12:20.

Catizone's call to headquarters had summoned Sergeant Cleary and Officer Alvin Kersten, who for seven years had been in the mobile unit of the crime laboratory. The job of the mobile unit is to search the scene of a crime for physical evidence and transport the evidence to the crime laboratory. Kersten arrived, carrying his photographic equipment, about ten minutes after Dr. Payne pronounced Donna dead. He knew at a glance, as soon as he was within two feet of the body, that Donna was dead. He immediately began to take photographs and collect evidence. Catizone made notes of what they found.

Donna Branion had suffered multiple gunshot wounds. At that moment the officers thought there were twelve in the head, neck, and shoulders and a cut in her right eye. They found four spent 9 mm shells and three pellets underneath her body. Cleary and Kersten took charge of them.

Meanwhile John, who was in a state of alternating anxiety and paralysis, had become worried about Jan. School let out at noon for the holidays. Edsel Hudson had come down to the Branion apartment and Helen had gone up to look after Joby. When John said, "We've got to do something about Jan!" Edsel offered to go pick her up by car. John agreed that was a good idea.

"You can—Edsel, you'll prepare her, won't you?"

Edsel could start to break the news to her gently. She must not just come walking up the street and see the police cars in front of the house. Better to have someone she knew with her.

Edsel Hudson left, but other friends and relatives, alerted by phone, began to arrive. Someone telephoned the office of Donna's brother Nelson. He was in probate court and his office called him there. The bailiff at Probate Court in the Civic Center found him and gave him a cryptic message that "something had happened" and that he should call his office.

William and Dr. Helen Payne waited in the apartment with John. John sat and stood and sat again, in the sun parlor, surrounded by friends, occasionally being asked questions by the police.

John's thinking was sometimes rational, sometimes disoriented. As the policemen tramped back and forth, tracking in snow that soon melted on the floor, John rose from his seat. He had taken half a step forward when he realized that he was about to tell them Donna wouldn't like that. She kept a spotless house and wouldn't want water tracked all over the floor.

He sank back down. What had he been thinking of? Donna would never see the water they tracked in. Or any mess they made. Or even Christmas. It didn't matter any more.

If Donna had died as suddenly as this but of natural causes, he thought, along with the disbelief and shock there would be friends and consolation and quiet and respect. Along with the grief there might be peace. But this was murder, and the result was that John found his grieving had to take place in the midst of strangers. Donna did not belong to him, she belonged to large men carrying clumsy equipment, and John did not even have the right to sit with her.

Area One homicide personnel were beginning to arrive. The first were long-time veterans Detective Charles McMullen and Detective John Norris. McMullen at that time was starting his twenty-eighth year with the Chicago Police Department and had been a detective for eight. Norris had been a police officer for twenty-seven years and had become a detective in 1956, eleven years earlier. Sometime after McMullen and Norris, two other Area One detectives arrived, Michael J. Boyle and James McGreal. Boyle, ambitious and a fast-rising star in the force, had been a policeman seven years and a detective two years. McGreal had been with Area One homicide for four years. Catizone showed them Donna's body, and they made notes that it lay face up, head to the east, in the utility room. The four set about taking statements, looking for witnesses, and directing Kersten and Cleary in their search for physical evidence.

The homicide detectives made their own catalogue of the wounds they could see: "Two gunshot wounds left side of neck, one gunshot wound right side of head (base), two gunshot wounds right side of neck, two gunshot wounds right arm pit, one gunshot wound back of neck, one gunshot wound top of right shoulder, one gunshot wound top of left shoulder, one gunshot wound upper right back, one gunshot wound upper left back." Twelve in all. There was also what appeared to be an abrasion on Donna's right eyelid which the pathologist later found to be another bullet wound.

Cleary and Kersten took a blood sample near the body. There were also two small round pools of blood on the floor in Donna and John's bedroom. They took a sample of one, in a vial. There was a smear of something reddish brown that looked like blood on the kitchen wall. They took a sample of that, too.

Then they photographed the crime scene.

Cleary and Kersten made photographs of only two parts of the apartment, the bedroom and the utility room where Donna's body lay.

The master bedroom was tidy and clean. The bed was neatly made. A shoehorn had been left out, but other than that the only items out of place were the signs of murder. The bedroom closet had two sliding louvered doors. The right-hand door was smashed off its track and leaned diagonally backward into the closet at an angle, held there by the clothing hanging behind it. On the bedroom floor directly in front of the damaged door were the two small round pools of blood.

In the utility room where Donna's body lay, there was more evidence of violence. A long heavy table with a wooden top and metal legs, the type that might be used to sort clothing, had been knocked over on its side. One pair of the table's metal legs had been broken completely off of the table and lay on the floor. An ironing board lay on its side. There were blood spatters on the floor and a large pool of blood under and around Donna's body.

Cleary and Kersten took two photographs immediately, before the body had been handled very much, though Catizone had picked up Donna's hand to feel for a pulse and Dr. Payne had examined her sufficiently to officially pronounce death. In these first two photographs, Donna's head was not entirely visible, being partly covered by a shopping bag which was wedged against a chair. It was as if she had fallen down with her back against the wall, her head falling on the side of the bag, which then partially collapsed over her face. To take the next photographs, one of the officers pulled the chair and shopping bag away from Donna's head. In doing so, her head and arm were moved and a cartridge casing rolled to a spot perhaps seven inches from her right hand.

Directed by the homicide team, Cleary and Kersten fingerprinted the doors of the apartment.

Detective McMullen tried to talk to John, who was pacing around the apartment. John walked back and forth in the living room. McMullen spoke to him, but John hardly heard and walked away down the long hall. McMullen thought he was leaving, so he walked up to him and spoke to him again. John said, "I can't talk to you now," and went to the sun parlor and sat down on a chair. He said he couldn't talk, he was too upset.

At some point, one of the officers asked John whether Donna was careless about letting people in. John said, "She was careful about who she let in."

"How could somebody gain access to the apartment, then?"

"I don't know."

John was questioned off and on by one officer and then another. They asked him when he had arrived home. He couldn't remember, exactly, and it seemed unimportant to him now. In Catizone's report, handwritten that evening, Catizone said John thought he had arrived home about 11:40. In the typewritten Area One homicide report filed that evening by Boyle, McMullen, Norris and McGreal, they said that he thought he arrived home about 11:45.

Finally, the squadrol arrived. John stood in the sun parlor, rigid and numb. Two attendants loaded Donna into a body basket, covered her, and moved out of the utility room, down the hall, and out through the front door to the street. He watched as they pushed her into the wagon. One foot was exposed. Snow was in the air. He was upset that they were letting her foot get cold.

It was now about 1:15.

Donna's body was taken to the Cook County Morgue by squadrol 2171. By 1:35, Deputy Coroner Tragarz was notified of the death.

· CHAPTER FOUR ·

The empty cartridge casings that had been found under Donna's body were stamped "9 mmk" on the bottom, meaning they were nine millimeter short ammunition. In John Branion's den there was a display case of rifles and antique guns. There were other guns displayed around the apartment. It was obvious that Dr. Branion was a gun collector.

"How many guns do you own?" one of the detectives asked.

"About thirty, I guess."

Thinking that the murder could have been committed with one of those guns, Detective Norris asked, "Do you have a nine millimeter?"

"Yes, I think so."

John looked around and found a nine millimeter Colt Commander, which he handed to Norris.

About 2:00, Detective Boyle came to the chair where John sat in the living room.

Boyle asked, "Is there anything missing around the place?"

"What?"

"Is anything missing? Anything stolen?"

"I don't know. I guess not." He hadn't looked.

At 2:30 Donna's brother Nelson arrived. For some reason, after leaving Probate Court, he had stopped at his parents' house and talked with his father before going on to John and Donna's apartment. This was rather typical behavior for Nelson and Donna, whose father still exercised great control over them. They were in the habit of checking with him frequently.

"My God, what happened here?" Nelson said, throwing his arm around John.

"I wish I knew."

Nelson could hardly hear him.

"How are you doing? How are you holding up?"

Again he could hardly hear John's reply. He wasn't even sure whether

John had answered or just sighed. John, he thought, was near collapse. He sat him back down in a chair.

John started asking about Jan and Joby. Where was Jan now? Should he find her and talk? Was Joby still upstairs at the Hudson's? This was the time he usually took his nap. Did the Hudson's know that?

"Let them take care of Joby for a while. You're not in any shape."

Sergeant Harry Anderson, a tall, balding black man from Area One homicide, had arrived sometime during the afternoon, though John had not noticed him come in. Now he and Detective Michael Boyle approached John.

"We'd like you to come down to the station and give us a statement." They were referring to the Washington Park District Police Station not far from the house.

John said, "All right," not caring very much.

There were several relatives in the apartment who could stay with Jan and Joby. The sooner he got it over and got back, he thought, the sooner he could decide what he and the children would do about tonight—stay in the apartment or go to relatives.

Nelson and John rode to the Park District Police Station in the detectives' car with Detective Norris. But when they got to the station the detectives all disappeared and Nelson and John were left sitting in an interrogation room. John sat, not even restless, just drained.

They waited and waited. Ten minutes. Half an hour. The place had the smell of all Chicago public institutions in the winter, a combination of coffee that had been kept hot too long, Lysol, sweat, and wet wool clothing. John and Nelson stayed in the small interrogation room where Norris had put them. In the outer lobby policemen tramped in and out, bringing along little showers of snow that melted immediately on the floor.

They waited an hour. Nothing seemed to be happening—no questions, no activity.

Nelson said, "Are they just going to leave us here?"

"I have to get home," John said, thinking about the children.

None of the policemen who had been at the apartment appeared. "I suppose they're taking care of other details . . . " John began, wearily.

"Sure. Filing papers. Talking with neighbors. Who knows?"

"Why are they keeping us waiting?"

"I don't know. Try to rest."

John and Nelson had been sitting for over an hour when Sgt. Anderson, Detective McGreal, and Detective Boyle came in, three large men in dark blue pants, light blue shirts, and guns in leather holsters. Their presence filled the room.

"Okay, we want you to tell us where you went today."

"I was at work. At the Ida Mae Scott Hospital."

"Address?"

He gave it to them.

"What time did you get there?"

"About nine, I think. I had to drop Joby off at school."

"Why was that?"

"Um—I had Donna's—my car was in the shop, so I had to take my wife's car to work, so I dropped Joby off and picked him up."

"Address?"

The questions went on and on.

"How many patients did you see, doctor?"

"About a dozen, I guess. My nurse would have the list."

"When did you leave the hospital?"

"About 11:30."

"Where did you go from there?"

"The nursery school first. I picked up Joby and then I—"

"What time was that?"

"About—I don't know. It must have been about a quarter of twelve."

"Then where did you go?"

"To Apartment Homes, Ltd. A friend of ours who works there was going to come to lunch with us."

"Name?"

"Maxine Brown."

"Address?"

"1369 E. 53rd St."

"You picked her up?"

"No, her boss had some errands for her, so she couldn't make it."

"Then where did you go?"

"Home." John shuddered. But the questions went on.

"Which door did you go in?"

"The front door."

"Was it locked?"

"I think so. The back door wasn't."

"Wasn't locked?"

"No."

"What did you do when you walked in?"

"I called for Donna—for my wife. There were lights on, and they shouldn't have been. I whistled. I suppose I called again. She didn't answer."

Quite suddenly, one of the policemen got up and left. Then another, then the third, saying, "Wait here."

Nelson and John waited. Again, nothing seemed to be happening. No one came in. By now John was aware that they suspected him of killing Donna, but it seemed ridiculous, and he didn't worry about it much. The detectives would soon find out he hadn't. From John's point of view, he had been hurrying that morning when he left the hospital, picked up Joby, stopped by Maxine's and got home. Since he immediately called neighbors down when he found Donna dead, and since several people saw him before he left the hospital and two or three others as he left the hospital, it seemed to him there was just no extra time to play with. No time to kill Donna. It was just a matter of waiting until the police detectives had talked with all the people at the hospital and along the way and at the apartment. Then they would know he was innocent.

He was worried instead about the children.

"I wonder if they'll remember Joby's snack when he wakes up from his nap," John said.

"Of course they will."

"What if they don't—"

"If they don't, Joby will tell them himself."

"Jan didn't have lunch."

"Oh, come on, John! Maxine and Helen are both there. All your friends are there. The women are sure to be trying to feed the kids. Women always feed kids."

"I guess you're right."

Still they waited. Finally, Nelson got exasperated and went out in the hall to nose around. He found Sgt. Anderson, the only black man on the police team.

"Listen, how long do we have to wait here? Doctor Branion has his children to think about."

"Just a few more minutes."

Nelson shrugged and went back into the small room with John. It was more than a few minutes when the detectives came to the door, but didn't enter.

"Nelson Brown? Could you come out here a minute?"

Nelson left John sitting in the little room.

Detective Michael Boyle said, "We think Dr. Branion killed his wife."

"That's impossible."

"We want to ask him some more questions and we want him to take a lie detector test. I know you're an attorney. We'd like you to advise him to co-operate."

Nelson had heard stories of serious errors with lie detectors. He was very uneasy about the idea. "Dr. Branion didn't do it. You're wasting investigation time even suspecting him. I want you to find out who killed my sister."

"We're trying to, Mr. Brown."

Another detective said, "Will you advise him—"

"I won't advise him to do anything."

"Well, at least don't tell him what we've talked about. Okay?"

Nelson agreed, for the moment. He was thinking hard. He was not really John's attorney, just his brother-in-law. If he said or did the wrong thing, it could prejudice John's relationship with any future attorney and possibly lead to legal problems if John was arrested. But on the other hand, he wouldn't *be* arrested. He was innocent. He'd been at work when Donna was killed, and even if it had happened another time, when he was home, he wouldn't have killed Donna. So maybe it didn't matter.

Nelson decided to wait and see what the detectives did. He went back in the room with John. John was so apathetic that he didn't even ask what the officers had wanted to talk about. Nelson didn't say anything about the police suspicions or the lie detector test, and he and John simply sat and waited some more. The window was darkening, though it was only mid-afternoon. Yesterday, December 21, had been the shortest day and longest night of the year.

After a time, one of the patrolmen ducked his head in and said,

"You'd better stay in here with the door closed. The place is swarming with reporters."

News of the murder was out.

John and Nelson went on waiting in silence.

McGreal, Boyle, and Anderson came back.

"Okay, let's go over this again."

John sighed. He nodded; he did not consider refusing to answer. He remembered years later that the detectives at this point became more aggressive. They took him through his morning.

"When *exactly* did you get to the nursery school?"

"When *exactly* did you leave the hospital?"

"When *exactly* did you get to Maxine Brown's place of business?"

"When *exactly* did you get home?"

John didn't know, exactly. "I wasn't watching the time every minute. I knew I had to get Joby at 11:45, and I was worried about being late. But he was waiting when I went by, so it must have been by then."

"How long does it take to drive from the nursery school to Maxine Brown's?"

"I don't know. Two or three minutes."

"How long from Maxine's to your home?"

"About the same, I think."

"How long from the hospital to your house?"

"Maybe five or six minutes."

McGreal, Boyle, and Anderson all fired questions—sitting, standing, leaning over John, trying to shake him up. McGreal was taking notes.

"All right, we'll go on to something else. You come home. You walk in the door. You call for your wife. Then what?"

"Well, when she didn't answer I went to look for her."

"Were you worried?"

"No, not at first. She could have been in the shower or something."

"Then what?"

"Well, she wasn't in the bathroom or the bedroom, so I went into the kitchen. I saw her slipper lying in the door between the kitchen and the utility room. So I went and looked and—um—saw her."

"What did you do?"

"I think I flicked the light on. And then I flicked it off."

"Did you examine her?"

"No."

"Did you go to her aid?"

"No."

"Why not? You're a doctor."

"I could see that she was dead."

"How?"

"She was cyanotic."

"What does that mean?"

"Well, I could see her legs. It was her color—the skin color changes." John gestured, feeling the skin of his upper arm. "The blood isn't getting any oxygen, so it gets bluish. Sort of a livid color."

Cyanosis is the bluish or livid hue skin takes on after death or in severe oxygen deprivation. In the case of Donna's light brown skin, as cyanosis developed the color would go from a warm brown to a cold grayish-blue brown. Lividity refers to a pale or bluish discoloration of the skin. Physicians will often call bruises "livid", and Donna was certainly bruised. But pathologists and policemen usually use the term "lividity" as a shorthand for "postmortem lividity", the sinking of blood to lower parts of the body after the heart has stopped beating. This pooling of the blood in the lower parts of the body begins immediately after death and may be visible in as little as half an hour, but more often is not visible for over an hour, then becoming more and more pronounced for several hours.

The police officers were familiar with the term "postmortem lividity" and not with "cyanosis," Branion thought later. It was the word that was familiar to them that would stay in their minds.

In fact, Joby was the actual reason John did not linger after seeing that Donna was dead. John did not think to explain that to the policemen. He was not functioning very well. Donna had been part of his life for twenty-seven years. It was hard for him to remember a time when he had not known her. He just answered whatever questions they asked.

Finally, the detectives left the room again.

Nelson was still in a dilemma. He could tell John not to answer any of these questions, but he wasn't John's attorney, and anyway, it might look bad to refuse to answer. Who could tell what would look bad to detectives? Nelson was confident that a little research would show that John had been at the hospital. And meanwhile, how could it hurt for John to tell them where he had been?

While they were alone, he said, "You know, they asked me to advise you to take a lie detector test."

"Well, okay."

"I don't know, John. How do you know whether those things really work? What if all they do is show you're upset?"

"I don't know. I don't know anything about them."

"Well, I've heard some real horror stories about them. I advise you not to do it."

But he was uneasy, and after waiting still longer, he went out into the hall, saying to John, "I'm going to find out if we can go. This is ridiculous."

After a little looking, Nelson found Sgt. Anderson. Nelson asked the detective whether they could leave now. Anderson told him that they had been taking a statement from the Branions' neighbor, Theresa Kentra, and her testimony exonerated John. Sgt. Anderson said they could go home.

Nelson was pleased.

"You're all set, John."

"What do you mean?"

"Mrs. Kentra heard shots while you were still at the hospital. It's okay. We can go."

"Oh. Well, okay."

It didn't bring Donna back.

Nelson went out again to ask one of the officers if the reporters were still hanging around. The officer said they were gone. Nelson peered out the door to the street to be certain. The street was clear. A sharp wind was blowing and the night was dark and very cold. He and John left the station.

They returned to an apartment filled with friends and relatives. Somebody had brought in food. Joby was back from upstairs.

CHAPTER FIVE

The Branion apartment was full of friends who had come to help, bring food, and sympathize. John decided to stay there, reasoning that it would be even harder for the children to come back to the house if they were away for a while.

At 8:00 that night Detectives Michael Boyle and John Norris arrived. Boyle asked, "Do you have a .380 handgun?"

The Chicago Police Department ballistics expert had told them late that afternoon that a .380 firearm could have fired the 9 mm ammunition, because the two calibers, while not identical, were close in size.

John did not have the heart to deal with it. He had a .380 somewhere, he thought, but he couldn't find it right off. He asked Donna's brother Nelson to look for it and gave him the key to the gun cabinet. He told Nelson to let the detectives look around for whatever gun they wanted. Nelson found a .380, which he handed to Boyle.

The detectives left. After that night, the police would never again ask to talk with John, nor would they telephone him, nor inquire whether he later found anything missing from the house, nor ask for another guns, nor have any contact with him at all beyond a glance and a nod at the inquest, until a month after Donna's death.

The police firearms expert had not completed his study of the markings on the spent pellets and empty cartridges to determine what make of handgun fit these characteristics. It would take several days to develop this data. First the ballistics markings on the spent pellets had to be categorized. The number of lands and grooves in a gun barrel differs among guns, and this determination would narrow down the types of gun that could have fired the pellets. Then the ballistics expert would examine where on the base of the cartridge the firing pin had struck. This, too, differs among guns. Finally, they would hope that the particular combination of markings on the pellet and on the cartridge was specific to only one type of gun, so that they could say "This is the type of gun that shot Donna Branion."

Nelson Brown stayed on after Jan and Joby had gone to bed and all the other friends and relatives had left. John started looking around the apartment to see whether anything was missing. The $500 he had left on the nightstand in the bedroom for Donna's Christmas shopping was gone. Then he went through the other rooms, eventually working his way to the den. His Walther PPK was missing. An antique gun worth about $1,500 was gone, too. He told Nelson.

"What'll I do? Call the police and tell them specifically what's missing?"

Nelson said, "I don't know. It might make them suspect you."

"No, it won't. I was at work."

"I don't know, John. Personally, I'd advise you not to do it. White cops; they're always gonna pin it on the black guy."

Whatever gun was used in the murder—John's or someone else's—it would never be found.

Nelson stayed until the early morning hours, keeping John company. During this time, Nelson had talked twice by telephone with Sydney Brown. Donna's parents, with their concern for respectability and their horror of negative publicity, had decided to leave Chicago for a few days. They had not come to the Branion apartment, nor had they offered to take the children.

"They're going to Cleveland," Nelson told John.

"Why?"

"So reporters can't get to them."

"What does it matter?"

Nelson didn't answer this directly. He said, "They want you to go away, too."

"Why can't we all just lock our doors and not answer the phone?"

"John, Sonja and I are going to Vail for Christmas. I'm sure we could squeeze you and Jan and Joby in some place."

"I don't feel like it."

"You won't feel any better here."

"How can you go off on a vacation when your sister has just been killed? How can I?"

"For the kids' sake. You want them exposed to questions and publicity?"

"No. No. I don't know."

John said he'd think it over. He found it hard to think at all right now. About 3:00 a.m., Nelson went home.

The next morning, Saturday, December 23, John woke up to a terrible world. He could not take it in that just yesterday they had all eaten breakfast together. They had all been looking forward to the Christmas holidays. Jan had been excited that vacation was coming. Two weeks with no school. Joby had been excited about Christmas presents.

What would he do about Christmas now? What was he going to do with the children on Christmas morning? They'd hardly be able to run in happily and pull presents out of stockings, knowing that Donna was not there. And what about the presents Donna had bought them—and the presents he had bought her? What would happen when the children opened presents from their mother who was now dead?

The day outside was gray. It was fourteen degrees and there had been a little more snow during the night.

Nelson called. He repeated to John again all the arguments he had used the night before that John and the children should get away. He and Sonja belonged to a club of skiers called the Twisters, and the club had reserved accommodations eleven months before in Vail, Colorado—a new ski resort that had been open only five years. They were leaving the next day, Christmas Eve. Would John and Jan and Joby come with them?

"The family thinks you should go," Nelson said, almost capitalizing the word "family." "Besides, it'll give you time alone with the children. Off by yourself, you can talk with them. And get them out of the apartment, where—you know."

Where their mother had been murdered.

This gray, cold morning John began to think Nelson was right. There could be no funeral until after the autopsy. No one had told him when the autopsy would be. He and Donna had always said they wanted to be cremated, with no special service. But even that had to wait. They were all just waiting. He said they'd go with Nelson.

It would turn out to be a bad decision.

That same morning at the Cook County morgue, an old building now gone, Dr. John Belmonte was performing the autopsy on the body of Donna Branion.

He found not twelve but thirteen gunshot wounds on her body. What had looked like an abrasion on her right eye was the entry wound of a bullet. One bullet had remained in her upper right arm, near the shoulder. The others had passed through. There were four wounds in her upper chest at the base of the neck. The carotid arteries and jugular veins had been pierced. One of these shots had pierced the aorta. There were three wounds in the upper arm, near the shoulder. One at the rear base of the skull and four in the upper back. He noted that the back wounds seemed to be exit wounds.

Donna's lip was split, her elbow and left arm were bruised, and there were other upper body bruises. Surprisingly, she had also been half-strangled. There was a groove three-eighths of an inch deep and seven inches long around the front of her neck. But it was not the cause of death. The gunshot wounds had killed her.

The split lip and bruises indicated that Donna had struggled with her killer. So he took clippings of her fingernails and scrapings from under the nails. This is routinely done in cases where the killer and his victim are likely to have been in direct physical contact. The intent is to find bits of the killer's skin, makeup, clothing fibers, or hair.

Dr. Belmonte packaged the fingernail evidence. Later that day, December 23, Sergeant Smith and Technician O'Malley picked up the fingernail clippings from the morgue, along with an oral swab, some of Donna's head hair, and blood samples, and took them to the Crime Lab at the Chicago Police Department. The receipt, signed "Sgt. D.E. Smith, #1185, at 1230, 23 Dec 67," said "received from Dr. Belmonte the following material in the case of Donna Branion—head hair—nails—oral swab—blood."

And there the fingernail scrapings and clippings vanished. The other evidence was analyzed, but the fingernail material never turned up in any evidence analysis, nor in any testimony at the inquest or the trial. There is no record that Boyle, the officer in charge, ever asked to have the clippings microanalyzed. They have since been lost.

· CHAPTER SIX ·

Some time during that first week of the investigation, possibly the first day, the police dropped John as a suspect and started to look elsewhere. As *The Daily Defender* newspaper said, summing the case up a month later: "During the early stages of the investigation, police stated that Branion had an 'air-tight' alibi and throughout their investigation there was no evidence to point a 'questionable finger' at the slain woman's husband."

At this time, Chicago had five operating major daily newspapers, the *Sun-Times, Daily News, American, Tribune,* and the black daily, one of the country's oldest, established in 1905, the *Defender.* There were literally hundreds of area and specialized papers, such as *The Hyde Park Herald,* which covered the neighborhood where the Branions lived. All the major newspapers carried stories on the Branion case. In the course of their coverage, some very strange facts and non-facts emerged. And some strange insights into police thinking.

On December 23, the day after the crime, the *Tribune*'s article was headlined: "Doctor Finds Wife Slain in South Side Home." The article reported that the "police said the back door was open." The remark is not ascribed to any particular policeman, but it is interesting in light of later events that the *Tribune* got this information from a police source.

The *Defender* gave the Branion murder story more prominence than the other papers did, not unreasonably, since the victim was from a well-known, socially prominent black family, but all the papers got mileage out of Donna Branion's death. By Tuesday, December 26, four days after the murder, the *Defender* called the police "baffled," and in a headline big enough for World War III asked, "Who Murdered Mrs. Branion?" To add to the interest, the sub-head explained, "Victim Daughter of Prominent Southsider."

Sergeant Anderson told one of the papers: "We are completely baffled in this investigation but we are going to continue working around the clock. We cannot allow this type of crime to remain unsolved and if it is humanly possible, we will get the killer."

The *Defender* reported that Sydney Brown wanted results. "Slain Socialite's Father Urges Quick Solution," shouted the January 3 headline in two-inch bold type, with the subhead: "Police Probe Continues in Pitiless Crime." There are some oddities in the report. The first paragraph quotes "Sydney Brown, prominent Chicago attorney" as urging the Chicago Police Commission to "Ferret out and find the slayers"—plural—of his daughter. There had already been talk that more than one assailant was involved. Indeed, there was ample fuel for this opinion in the autopsy report. Sydney Brown himself seems to have picked up on this, possibly from the policemen. The article says Sgt. Anderson, "heading the murder investigation team," admitted that "the probe had not revealed any evidence thus far." But a few paragraphs on, Maxine Brown is described, then her date to have lunch with the Branions, then her questioning by the police. Then Anderson is quoted as saying Mrs. Brown had been interviewed in an effort to learn whether she had noticed "anything unusual" at the Branion home, which is strange since presumably she had not been there that day. One paragraph about the murder weapon intervenes, and then: "The latest theory which police are still investigating is that Mrs. Branion might have been killed by a woman.

"A member of the investigating team said, 'A woman usually kills the way Mrs. Branion was murdered. It was a very vicious murder and women can be very vicious when they get mad enough.' The officer said that although they are strongly considering the theory, they are not ruling out the possibility of a man. It's just that the killer could have been a woman well-known to Mrs. Branion."

Who was the unnamed "member of the investigating team"? No name is given, though present at the Washington Park homicide headquarters for the news conference were Chicago homicide commander Frank Flanagan, Washington Park homicide commander Lt. Edward Landis, and Sgt. Harry Anderson. And the story quotes Sgt. Anderson again a paragraph later:

"'Nothing was taken from the apartment and there's nothing to indicate someone forced their way into the victim's home. This simply means that Mrs. Branion admitted her killer into the apartment because she knew her slayer well.'"

By the time the "Big Weekend Edition" was published, Maxine Brown was looming larger in the headlines. On the front page of the *Defender* was the headline, "Quiz Oscar Brown Jr.'s Wife In Baffling Branion Murder," and the text reported that Maxine had been questioned "for over an hour" by homicide detectives. The paper was bringing increasing pressure on the police for a solution. The inquest had not yet been held and the paper asked repeatedly why it was taking so long.

In the January 6-12 "Big Weekend Edition," the lead headline shouted, "Defender To Give Reward For Donna Branion Killer." There were two subheadlines. One said "14 Long Days." The other "Offer $1,000 For Arrest And Conviction Of Slayer." Under the second headline the *Defender*'s editor, John Sengstacke, who was a long-time friend of Sydney Brown's, wrote, "Women are terror-stricken in their homes. Mothers are afraid for their children to walk the streets . . . Every available police officer should be pressed into service to solve this crime."

Between the two subheadlines was a cartoon. It showed a Chicago policeman asleep with his feet on his desk, cobwebs all over him, while the Branion murder case casts a shadow on the wall—a silhouette of a horrible man in a lumpy hat, his hands dripping blood.

An editorial, presumably by Sengstacke, asked: "What gives in a city of 3,466,000 when the violent deaths of Negroes is looked upon with seeming indifference? . . . How thoroughly is the Police Department delving into all the circumstances of one of the most bizarre cases in Chicago's infamous criminal history? The Daily Defender believes that there should be no double standard for people who live in Chicago . . . One is forced to ask about the sensitivities of a community which, in 1968, responds with such indifference to violence in the ghetto. This is the same community which, in time of racial crisis, spreads its Pilate clean hands and asks 'why?'"

With this sort of newspaper attention, the police were under pressure to do something. The *Defender* was pushing hard. But the first result of the reward offer seems to have been a time-waster.

On January 9, the *Defender* reported, "First Branion Murder Clue A Hoax." What had seemed like a real lead had fizzled, the paper said. "According to the police they received information from a close relative of the slain woman who informed them that a patient at the Chicago State Hospital told him she had information that might help police in their investigation of the case.

"Police were dispatched to the hospital but after questioning the woman, they learned that she actually knew nothing about the case other than 'what she had read in *The Daily Defender*.'"

To add to the outcry from the *Defender*, the University of Chicago may have been privately urging the police to find the killer quickly. The University of Chicago is located in Hyde Park, on the south side of the city in an area, just a few blocks from the Branion apartment, that is largely black. The University of Chicago exists in an uneasy truce with the surrounding neighborhood. There is both a kind of pride that the racially mixed Hyde

Park neighborhood has survived—in fact, foreign vistors to Chicago are often toured around the area to show how well integration works. At the same time, there are sporadic flare-ups of anger. Students have repeatedly accused the university of trying to fence out the neighbors, and the neighborhoods occasionally accuse the school of paternalism or hostility. The school is very sensitive to bad publicity about the immediate surroundings, and to any suggestion that it is a dangerous place for students to live and work. Hyde Parkers say that the university routinely tries to play down crime reports in the area.

It is impossible to know for certain whether the police had initially taken the case less seriously because the victim was black. However, the investigation proved to be casual or even sloppy, and the fact that they may have regarded it as a black-on-black crime is a plausible reason. It is equally difficult to prove that the community outcry as given voice by the *Defender* caused the police to push harder for an arrest as time went on—after it was too late to find evidence that might have been collected at the time and had since been lost. But it must have had some effect. If this was really the sequence of events, the result would be tragic for John Branion.

While John was in Colorado with his children, the mechanism of the state was chewing through the facts of his life. Sgt. Joseph DiLeonardi, supervising the homicide investigation, assigned detectives Rodney Dawson and M. Langhart to find out exactly what Dr. John Branion had been doing from the time he left home the morning of December 22. Dawson and Langhart talked with Leonard Scott, the administrator of the Ida Mae Scott Hospital. They thought Scott was a doctor, because he wore a white coat, but he was in fact not a physician. Scott told them John had arrived at the hospital around nine or five after nine and left about 11:30. Scott arranged for the policemen to look at the hospital daily log book. John was initialed for treating thirteen patients, beginning with Fletcher Barr, aged fifty-seven, at 9:15. The last entry in the regular log was Robert Jordan, aged thirty-five, at 11:30.

The emergency patient, Morris, was not in the regular log.

Mr. Scott told the officers that he met John as John was leaving the hospital for lunch about 11:30 and the two had a conversation. They talked about John having to pick Joby up at nursery school and John's plans to go out to lunch with Donna.

Two detectives interviewed the clinic nurse, Betty Adger. She told them, "Dr. Branion and I worked together in the clinic from approximately 9:15 a.m. until he closed and left at approximately 11:30 a.m. About three or four minutes later an old known patient by the name of Kenneth

Morris came in to be seen, as he was in acute distress. Not wanting him to be around until the clinic reopened, I went to the lab and stopped Dr. Branion to check the patient.

"Since all exam rooms were occupied, Dr. Branion examined the patient in the dentist (Dr. Moore's) office, where I had him wait. He (Dr. Branion) ordered morphine and left the clinic about 11:50 a.m. I had to record the time in the narcotics book. Dr. Branion was in a hurry to pick up his son from nursery school."

11:50 is probably the time she recorded the morphine order, not when John left the hospital, which must have been several minutes earlier, or he would not have had time to pick up Joby and go to Maxine's place of work before heading home.

Other officers had been canvassing the buildings across the street and to the west of 5054 S. Woodlawn, looking for anyone who had noticed anything suspicious. They also questioned all the tenants of the building the Branions lived in. On Christmas Eve they reinterviewed Mrs. Kentra, the next-door neighbor who had heard noises. On Christmas day they found a teenaged boy named Oscar Gray, who lived in the same building, although, because the entryway was separate, it was called 5052 S. Woodlawn. Gray thought he had seen Dr. Branion in front of the building the day of the murder, before the police arrived. He did not see Joby with his father.

They talked with William Payne, who told them about coming downstairs to the Branion apartment at Helen Hudson's call. He told them that they had all gone to look at the body, and that John Branion was so upset it took several repeated questions before he told Payne to go ahead and call the police. Detective Boyle estimated that all the rushing around up and downstairs in the apartment before the police were called would have taken about five minutes.

On December 24, Boyle and McGreal visited Dr. Helen Payne, who lived upstairs from the Branions and had come down that day in response to Helen Hudson's call. They asked her whether the body was still warm when she examined Donna and pronounced her dead at 12:20. Dr. Payne said it was, and the police included the fact in their report. This is unfortunate, if it suggests the police and prosecutor's office believed it was important in the time frame of the Branion murder. In fact, as a result of certain biochemical changes, most dead bodies do not start to lose heat until half an hour to forty-five minutes after death. In addition, there are many causes of death that actually *raise* the body temperature after death. Cerebral stroke, strangulation, brain injury, cholera, typhoid, and strychnine poisoning all do. In any case, a body normally clothed in an average room loses about two to two and a half degrees Fahrenheit per hour.

The detectives also asked Dr. Payne whether she noticed any signs of lividity on the body. In their report they record that she said no, but it is not clear whether she said she did not notice any or that there were none.

Also on Christmas Eve, the officers interviewed Mrs. Joyce Kelly, who was thirty-three years old and an assistant nursery school teacher at the Hyde Park Neighborhood Club nursery school. She told them John had arrived about 11:45 to pick up Joby, and that the children were never allowed outside the school alone.

Three days after Christmas, December 28, detectives talked with Maxine Brown. She told them an odd mixture of things. John, she said, had called her the night before the murder to ask her out to lunch. In fact, she said, he called late, about 11:00 p.m. She had apparently forgotten about being at Sonja and Nelson's that evening and about Donna and John both asking her to lunch. She told the detectives that Joby and John had both come to her office the next day, the day of the murder, but that at the last minute she could not go to lunch. She also said it was "common knowledge" that John had a girlfriend named Shirley Hudson.

By New Year's Day Boyle and McGreal were at Shirley Hudson's door. They were lucky to catch her there; Shirley had spent the last couple of days getting ready to move. She told McGreal and Boyle that she had been seeing John for six years, that John had no plans for divorce, and that she and John had no plans to marry.

While John was in Vail with the children, the story started to go around that he had flown off to Vail with his girlfriend—Shirley—just two days after Donna's murder. The rumor found its way into the newspapers.

It was here that John Branion's flamboyant lifestyle began to haunt him. People who did not know him well but knew that he owned horses and raced cars could believe that he might run off skiing with a woman friend just after his wife's murder. Reporters claim that Shirley told the police that when they talked with her after the murder, but in fact the written report of their two conversations with her say no such thing.

Several other rumors, however, were apparently started by the police. Detective Michael Boyle seems to have told newsmen that both of Donna's hands were pierced by shots. Why he would have put this out is not clear, unless Boyle was uneasy about reconciling the number of wounds on the body with the number of spent pellets he actually found. At any rate, neither the first police reports, the inquest testimony, the autopsy photographs, nor the pathologist's report, show any wounds in Donna's hands whatsoever.

Another rumor possibly traceable to Boyle was the claim that Dr.

Branion headed an abortion "ring." Yet another was that Mrs. Kentra, the next-door neighbor, had seen Branion's face *before* he came out on the back porch with Joby, and he did not look distressed. However, neither Mrs. Kentra's police station statement, nor any other testimony from her, ever makes that claim.

By now the detectives had received the copy of Dr. John Belmonte's autopsy protocol. They would have known from the facts that Donna's lip was split, her elbow was bruised as if someone had gripped her tightly by the upper arm, and her neck was deeply dented by cord marks, that some considerable time had elapsed in the commission of the murder. Evidence in the photographs of the apartment pointed to a prolonged struggle—the closet door smashed off its track, the blood spots in the bedroom a hundred feet from the utility room where the body was found, the slipper lost in the kitchen, the table tipped over in the utility room. They knew John Branion had been at work at least until 11:30, and that he was home well before 11:57, when the police were called. They had talked with the people in the apartment building and had been told about John rushing out on the back porch, running upstairs to get the Paynes, and so on before the call. They knew John had gone both to the nursery school and to Maxine Brown's place of business between leaving the hospital and arriving home and had to escort a child in and out of the car and drive through crowded streets. In addition, Mrs. Kentra had always tended to think she heard the shots around 11:20. It was quite reasonable at this point for the police to tell the newspapers they did not suspect Dr. John Branion.

But if John appeared not to have killed his wife, other leads were starting to peter out. The police searched John's friend Bill Hooks' apartment for the murder gun, for example. He says they "tore the place apart, made a mess of it," and found nothing. The greatest pressure from the newspapers and the community was coming now, at just about the time when the police began to realize they had no real suspects. There simply was not much evidence, altogether.

The effect of missed opportunities early in the investigation could not be corrected now. It was too late to go back and ask the pathologist to try harder to trace the direction of the bullets through the body; the body had been autopsied and released to the family and cremated. It was too late to fingerprint surfaces in the apartment that had been overlooked; they had all been handled by the family and friends. It was too late to go back and diagram the position of each pellet and cartridge casing. It may have been too late to analyze the scrapings from under Donna Branion's fingernails to see whether she had scratched one of her killers. They appear to have been destroyed.

It was not too late to go back and check the walls of the utility room for ricochet marks, but for some reason that was never done. It would certainly have been possible, too, to go into Mrs. Kentra's apartment and find out what sorts of sounds in the Branion apartment could have been heard from the Kentra's. It would have been especially valuable to know whether she could hear shots at the Branions' from her kitchen, which was contiguous, and not from her bedrooms, which were not contiguous.

The police were forced to fall back on one of their many truisms. Only a few days before, they had stated the truism that women killed with great violence, just the way Donna was killed. Now the one they were calling on was: if a wife is killed, it's usually her husband who did it.

This was a horrible period of time for John and his family. Jan went back to junior high school, Joby went back to nursery school, and John went back to work at the hospital, where his coworkers were supportive of him.

But their home felt cold and empty. The police didn't seem to be getting anywhere. Puzzling it out, John believed that what had happened was essentially a random crime—that some intruders had rung the doorbell, maybe a couple of teenagers looking for Christmas money. A lot of people who wouldn't ordinarily keep money in the house would make an exception at Christmas time for last-minute buying. Perhaps it had just been their tragic misfortune that the Branion home was struck.

John was depressed, and his grief was compounded by his embarrassment over the rumors that he had taken Shirley Hudson to Vail. More and more he felt he was the object of other people's curiosity and suspicion. Worse, he realized that the police had to be thinking of him as the possible killer. But he was still not worried that he could be considered a serious suspect.

At Area One homicide, a net of suspicion was slowly closing on John Branion.

Prosecutors in criminal cases like to show the jury that the defendant has lied. The fact that a person lies makes everything else he says sound suspect. Also, there is a feeling that if someone is willing to lie, he may be willing to commit more serious transgressions. Police detectives and state's attorneys are eager to develop early in an investigation places where a possible defendant may have lied.

At this time it was still not clear what would be useful during a trial. Nevertheless, the investigators were certainly trying to trap John Branion in lies. By the time of the trial, they would have developed three that they considered important: the "gun lie," the "lividity lie," and the "Joby lie."

Neither the Colt Commander John had handed to the detectives in the afternoon when they asked for a 9 mm, nor the .380 automatic that Nelson found for them that evening when they asked for a .380, proved ballistically to be the gun that had killed Donna. Now, three weeks or so after the murder, the detectives seem to have become convinced that John had intentionally misled them about the fact that one of the other guns he owned was a Walther PPK, which is a nine millimeter but could fire some kinds of .380 ammunition.

Generally speaking, American handguns are calibrated in fractions of an inch and European guns are calibrated in millimeters. Thus, for approximately the same diameter barrel, an American gun might be called .380, meaning three hundred and eighty one-thousandths of an inch, and a similar European gun might be called a 9 mm. These are not exact equivalents, however. Nine millimeters converts to .354 inches. Therefore, .380 ammunition would not necessarily work in a 9 mm gun. Dr. Branion would not necessarily think of the two types as equivalent.

The average citizen may not know which calibers are metric and which are measured in inches. However, neither did the officers on the scene—a fact that did not come out until much later, under oath.

It must be said in fairness to the police officers that in 1967 the attempt to convert to metric measures in the United States had not begun and metric measure was not taught in the schools. But their confusion would be disastrous to Dr. Branion. Once informed about the ballistics, they would decide that John intentionally deceived them about which guns he had.

The detectives were also beginning to reinterpret some of the other data from the day of the murder. Part of the problem was faulty record-keeping. Detective Charles McMullen later said, "My partner, Norris, asked Dr. Branion questions about any guns he might have. Dr. Branion turned over some guns to my partner. I don't remember what caliber gun it was, but it is inventoried. Those guns were inventoried. I can't recall right off hand their caliber. I don't recall if anyone asked me for a 9 mm gun. No one told me to seek a .380 caliber gun. No one in my presence asked Dr. Branion for a 9 mm gun."

Norris said, "I asked the defendant for a weapon capable of shooting a

9 mm shell. I received a weapon from the doctor when I asked for it. I saw the defendant Dr. Branion [later, in the evening]. There were quite a few people present at that time, all friends of Mr. Branion. They were throughout the apartment, living room, kitchen, and so forth. I spoke to Dr. Branion at that time and asked him if he had another gun in the house capable of firing a 9 mm shell. He said he thought he did and went into this utility room where there was a little cabinet that was locked. They had to look around for a couple of minutes and they located the key and he opened the cabinet. I don't know who [opened the cabinet], it might have been Dr. Branion himself. Everybody was looking for the key. I don't know who found the key. I received a gun from the cabinet, I think from Dr. Branion. I am not sure. I think it was Dr. Branion who gave me that gun. It could have been Attorney Nelson Brown, I don't know. I don't know but I think it was Dr. Branion. It may not have been. I inventoried it. I never asked Dr. Branion for a Walther PPK. I did not ask him whether or not any weapons were missing from his home."

But Detective Boyle believed *he* asked John for the gun and that they were asking about a .380 that night, not a 9 mm as Norris thought: "I asked Dr. Branion if he had any .380 caliber weapons. He told me he had only one and told Mr. Nelson Brown where it was. Mr. Nelson Brown then went into this utility room and obtained a .380 caliber automatic pistol from a cabinet there. He got the key to the cabinet at Dr. Branion's directions."

If they asked for a .380 that evening, John probably thought they *meant* a .380. Most likely, since the officers at the time were not really aware of the meaning of the terms, their questions were confused and confusing, and John—busy with his bereaved children and surrounded by grieving friends and relatives with whom he had to cope—just handed them, out of his collection of thirty, one of whatever gun they seemed to be asking for at the moment.

He should have stopped to ask himself right then whether there were any other guns in the house that could possibly be what they were looking for. But it was a devastating day for him. After that evening, the police never asked him again about any gun. The confusion was well on the way to becoming the basis of what later became known as the "gun lie."

Much of this confusion could have been avoided if the detectives had made sure that the questions and answers at the Branion home and during those two interrogations at Area One headquarters the afternoon of December 22 had been properly recorded and transcribed.

McGreal, Anderson, and Boyle interrogated John at headquarters that afternoon. McGreal, who apparently was taking some sort of notes, was later never able to remember whether he was the only one doing so, nor did he call a stenographer. "I don't recall if anyone else was taking notes. Yes, there are stenographers employed at Area One homicide. I suppose that there were some around that day. No, I did not bring a stenographer into the room where Dr. Branion was."

Boyle later said: "I didn't take any notes at the police station. I took notes at the apartment. Detective McGreal took notes. There are stenographers employed there. No, we did not bring one in."

Donna's brother Nelson Brown would say that, at the police station, "Detective Boyle took notes."

And Sgt. Anderson would say, "To my knowledge there were no stenographers present in the building that day. I say to my knowledge because I'm only in one section. I had no need to inquire as to whether a stenographer was available as I had no use for one. There was no occasion to have a stenographer. To my knowledge none of this conversation at the police station was reduced to writing. I do not recall Detective McGreal taking notes. I didn't notice that. I don't recall anyone taking notes."

The result of the sloppiness is that no one really knows what was said, about the "gun lie" or about two other topics the prosecution would use against John Branion.

The second was the "lividity lie." The detectives who interrogated Dr. Branion at the police station on the day of the murder came to believe he said not that Donna was cyanotic and her color livid, but that she showed lividity. They would infer from this that he claimed that she showed post-mortem lividity when in fact she did not.

The third was the "Joby lie." Detective Boyle's summary of the case, written on January 22, 1968, when the decision had been made to arrest John, says that John told the investigating officers that he "drove to the Hyde Park Neighborhood Club nursery school to pick up his son who was waiting out in front of the school." These are Boyle's words, not John's. He considered that this statement was contradicted by the facts—the "Joby lie." Boyle says the nursery school teacher, Joyce Kelly, told police that Dr. Branion "came into the school building and helped his son dress." In fact, Joyce Kelly said that John came into the school, asked for Joby, was directed to the all-purpose room, went in, took off his own coat, helped Joby on with his coat and possibly boots, and then escorted Joby back out to the car.

Nelson Brown, who was present at the interrogation, later said, "Throughout the questioning I never heard Dr. Branion state that when he went to pick up his son Joby, that he was waiting outside for him. I do recall what Dr. Branion said relative to picking up Joby. He said that he left the hospital, went by the Hyde Park Neighborhood Club and his son was ready."

Sgt. Anderson heard it rather similarly: "I was there when he was asked about picking up his son from the Hyde Park Neighborhood Club. The nearest I can recall, he said he picked up his son at the school."

Possibly John actually said only that he went to the nursery school to pick Joby up and the boy was ready. Possibly he said he went in, but the police simply wrote "went to nursery school," or "wnt to nurs. schl.," something like that. Or possibly, because John had never picked Joby up at school on a snowy day before, and because he was so worried when he left the hospital that Joby would be standing outside in the cold, that thought was all that remained in his mind after the catastrophe of the murder blasted every other consideration away.

At any rate, the "gun lie," the "lividity lie," and the "Joby lie" were being interpreted among the police and prosecutors as throwing suspicion on Dr. Branion for the murder of his wife.

CHAPTER SEVEN

Like so many American blacks—separated from kin by slavery, then made rootless by political upheaval—John Branion knew his ancestry only two generations back. Family tradition tells the story that somewhere in the southern United States at the turn of the century there lived a childless Jewish couple and the black woman who was their housekeeper. The housekeeper died and left a baby boy. No one knows how old the little boy was when he lost his mother, whether she died at his birth or later. The childless couple adopted the boy.

The boy's name was John Marshall Branion. He was named John Marshall after the great jurist John Marshall, who served for thirty-four years on the Supreme Court. No one today even knows whether he was named by his mother or whether the couple named him themselves after a personal hero of their own.

He was a bright child. When it came time, his adoptive parents sent him to Rust College, a small Methodist-run school in Holly Springs, Mississippi. John Marshall Branion graduated high in his class. There, too, he met and married his wife, Annie.

After graduation he decided to go to law school. With his name, the decision was perhaps not a great surprise. Possibly his adoptive parents urged it. Maybe he felt destined by his lost mother to be an attorney. But it is surprising that he decided to go from his small, rural school in the deep south to the University of Chicago.

It must have been an enormous change. From the quiet of rural Mississippi he had come to streets densely packed with pedestrians, carriages, produce carts, noisy elevated trains, saloons, public bath houses and elegant hotels. The winters were bitter. Winds off Lake Michigan could reach sixty miles an hour. Temperatures in January often plunged to twenty degrees below zero. Snowfall was fifty and sixty inches each year. Amazingly, at the end of his legal training he decided to stay. He may have felt freer in the less obviously segregated, less obviously racist North. He may have liked the turmoil or the opportunities or the challenge that the brawling, turbulent city provided. And yet, as a man, he is remembered as quiet, gentle, and rather shy.

He became a public defender. He would hold that position thirty-four years—coincidentally the same length of time his namesake was a justice of the Supreme Court.

In 1926 he and his wife had a son who would be their only child. They named him John Marshall Branion, Jr. John senior, who was a big, bear-like man, loved the baby beyond anything in life. He played with him, read to him, took him downtown to his office to meet the other attorneys and the secretaries, and even took him to see the court building where he tried his cases.

John junior went to McCosh grammar school in the Woodlawn neighborhood, where they lived at that time. In the 1930s there was a black ghetto in the area, but a very small one, extending from South Park, which is now Martin Luther King, Jr. Drive, to Cottage Grove, and from 63rd Street to 67th Street. To get to McCosh school, John had to walk from 60th to 63rd, through the white area. John described it in an understated way: "The white kids would give you a hard time."

John remembered the first time he realized he was black, though he could see later he had been getting hints from his mother. "I was about eight. Every summer my father took a two-week vacation. We all went, my dad, my mother, and me. Fishing. We were heading for a small place in Minnesota, between—I think it was—New York Mills and Perham.

"We'd been driving all day from Chicago, probably four hundred miles, and all of us were exhausted. We were going to spend the night in Minneapolis and go on the next morning. But this was the first time we'd been to Minneapolis and Dad didn't know exactly how to get there.

"My mother asked him, 'How far is it?'

"'I don't know. I'm looking.'

"Time passed. We were getting hungry.

"I said, 'Let's ask that man,' and pointed to a white man on the sidewalk.

"Dad said, 'We'll see.'

"We kept on driving. I pointed out more people and Dad wouldn't ask them for directions. It must have been miles and miles later, my mother said, 'There's a Negro over there.' Dad drove right over and asked him for directions.

"This was my father, an attorney, the star public defender in Chicago, a man I later realized scared the hell out of prosecutors, and he could not get up the nerve to ask a white stranger for directions!"

The Branion family didn't have much money, because the public defender was a civil service employee. Branion senior did not make big fees the way an attorney in private practice might. John remembered his father as loving his work and not being concerned about financial things, cars or home furnishings or clothing. His father was tidy, but beyond cleanliness did not care what he wore. His mother, on the other hand, wished her husband would make more money.

"One Christmas when I was very little, I wanted a cowboy outfit—you know, chaps and a cowboy hat and six-shooters. My parents had to sacrifice to get it for me. And on Christmas Eve, during the day, somebody broke into the basement where they had the Christmas presents stored and stole it! My father went out. It was late on Christmas Eve by then and he hadn't any cash. He borrowed money from somebody, and finally found me one. The outfit was there on Christmas morning.

"My mother was dissatisfied because he didn't make very much money, but he was happy to play bridge with her and he worked very, very hard on his law practice. They went to church together, and that was their social life."

The public defender was a different job then. In the 1930s, if a person accused of a crime could not afford to hire an attorney, he went to trial with no defense except his own efforts. It was not until 1942 that the Supreme Court forced the states to appoint an attorney for an accused person, and then it was only for capital offenses. Twenty-one years later, in the famous case of *Gideon v. Wainwright*, the Supreme Court required the state to appoint an attorney to defend any indigent person accused of a felony.

But even in 1930, courts at their discretion could appoint a public defender in certain cases that were of general public importance or involved an important point of law. And Cook County was one of the most progressive counties in the nation; it provided a defense for all people accused of felonies decades before this became a national standard. This was the sort of law John Branion, Sr. chose to practice.

Chicago was a rough town to do it in and the thirties were rough years, even for Chicago. It was the era of prohibition, the mobs, and gang wars in the streets. John Branion, Sr. was seated in his office one gray afternoon at the end of a successful defense. He had defended a man he knew nothing about, except that his physical appearance did not match the description of the eyewitnesses to the crime he was accused of committing. Branion had argued the discrepancy and the man was acquitted. Late that day, a stranger knocked on his door and entered the office. He handed Branion an envelope. Branion opened it and found it contained two hundred dollars. He did not know what it was for, but he knew it looked wrong. He folded it closed and said to the messenger, "I can't accept this. I'm already paid by the county to defend people." The man left.

Several days later, the same man appeared with another envelope. This time, when Branion opened it, he found five hundred dollars. This was a fortune to him at the time. Again, firmly—and maybe thinking to himself he'd better not tell Annie—he handed it back.

A week later, he was walking down the courthouse steps when he was approached by two men in dark topcoats. "Come with us," they said, and they pointed him toward a long dark car at the curb. He followed them, wondering whether he was going to be kidnapped by the mob.

One of the men swung open the back door of the car. The occupant, overweight and overdressed, with a round, pale face and pouting lips, leaned out and took Branion's hand. "I thought," he said, "I'd like to shake the hand of an honest man." Then the door slammed and the car pulled away, leaving Branion standing amazed on the sidewalk.

It took Branion several seconds to realize that the man was Al Capone.

Branion senior was famous in Chicago for his defense cases. When he was in court, law students from the Chicago area law schools like Northwestern and the University of Chicago would come to hear him speak. As his reputation grew, there was talk about appointing him First Public Defender. But no black person had ever been appointed to this post. Rumors flew. Some said he would *have* to get the job; he was clearly the best man; this time the politicians wouldn't be able to think of a way out of it. Even the family came to believe it was possible.

The announcement came at last. Another man—white—was appointed First Public Defender. A new job had been created just for John Branion. He would be First Assistant Public Defender.

CHAPTER EIGHT

"I can still remember the first time I ever saw Donna," John Branion told me in 1986. "I know it hardly seems possible that I could. It was forty-six years ago! It was when we had both just started at Englewood High School. Freshman year. Ninth grade. 1940. She would have been fourteen. I must have been fourteen and a half.

"She was perfect. I don't remember what she was wearing, but it was the *way* she looked. She was so perfectly put together. Every pleat in her skirt was perfectly pressed. She was beautifully groomed. Girls didn't wear much makeup then, but she was—every hair in place—you know. Donna was small and well-built and beautiful.

"Then when I talked with her, I was even more attracted. She had such a soft voice, and perfect diction. Beautiful manners. Warm-hearted but shy. Graceful. Outside of school, she was studying modern dance and ballet. And she was smart! I mean, it all went together! I told her I had just made the football team, and she thought that was wonderful.

"I must have just walked right up to her and introduced myself. It was really love at first sight."

John courted Donna in conversations at the drinking fountain, long talks sitting on the school steps, and by doing heroic acts on the football field. He was not the biggest boy on the team, but he had a lot of what coaches call desire, and he made left tackle. He laid every victory at Donna's feet.

After a few weeks of this, John saw Donna heading down the school stairs between classes one day. He caught up with her.

"Donna, as far as I'm concerned, you and I are going together."

Donna smiled. The other kids were streaming past.

She said, "All right." Then she ducked her head to hide the fact that she was happy, and she ran down the steps.

Going steady. This made it official.

John and Donna were in love the way teenagers are, the first time, to the total exclusion of all the rest of the world. But they lived in the real world and in a flow of history that would sweep them along with it.

At this particular time, the early 1940s, black Americans were beginning to pull apart into two groups: those who wanted to go along and get along with the system, and those who wanted to challenge it. It was as if two bitterly opposing armies on parade marched down two separate streets, all unaware that some distance ahead the two streets met at the same corner.

The explosion lay twenty years in the future. But for John and Donna, they belonged to families marching on two parallel courses, and their Montague and Capulet situation threatened their future.

In 1900 the city of Chicago was mostly white. The few blacks, about 40,000 all told, were scattered across the city and a handful of suburbs. But beginning in the early years of the century, a stream of black migration moved out of the south and away from the poverty and racism there. A favorite route was along the Illinois Central Railroad line to Chicago. Former sharecroppers and servants from Arkansas, Alabama, Louisiana, and Mississippi, they owned absolutely nothing whatsoever.

By 1920, Chicago's black population had more than doubled. By 1930, it was nearly a quarter of a million.

The city responded by isolating them in an area of about three dozen blocks on the South Side called the Black Belt. When blacks ventured into the rest of the city, they found restrictions. In movie theaters they were confined to separate sections. Many restaurants would not serve them. Like previous immigrants—and later immigrants as well—they were criticized for the crowding, disease, and vice among which they lived.

They performed jobs without futures: janitors, porters, cleaning women.

Donna's father, Sydney Brown, had come to Chicago in the early years of the century from Arkansas, and her mother, Vivian, from Alabama. They were from families determined to succeed, and the world in which they had to do it was the white world. They resolved to succeed on terms defined for them by whites.

Sydney and his older brother Oscar got law degrees. They began to practice law, and slowly and determinedly, they started investing their earnings. Oscar went into real estate; Sydney went into banking. With a friend, Sydney opened the first black-owned bank in Chicago, the Illinois

Federal Savings and Loan. Sydney was honest but unyielding, a shrewd investor who made sure he got all the value he should for each dollar. The bank prospered.

By the time Vivian and Sydney's three children were born, in the 1920s, the Brown family was already wealthy and respected. They owned their own home on South Indiana Boulevard. Later they moved to the Hyde Park section on the southern side of the city, not far from the Black Belt, filled with beautiful Queen Anne homes built in the late 1800s, huge stone mansions from the early 1900s, and enormous mansion-flats in solid old buildings with high ceilings and soundproof walls. The Brown home was a luxurious building on Drexel Square. Drexel Square is a small, green, rectangular, old-fashioned park, full of trees and grass, very formal and Victorian in appearance. It is surrounded by elegant stone and brick Victorian houses with beautiful woodwork and magnificent front steps and front doors. Vivian Brown shopped at Bonwit's and Marshall Field's. The black news daily, the *Defender*, covered the Brown family parties, christenings, clubs, charities, births, and deaths. They were watched and talked about in the black community in a way that blacks in Chicago today, with a wide diversity of origins—the Bahamas, Africa, Latin America—and wide dispersion in the suburbs, would hardly understand.

The Browns had become one of the richest black families in Chicago, and they were determined not only to be an upper-middle-class family financially, but to maintain respectability, the *appearance* of an upper-middle-class family. Like so many blacks at that time, they valued lighter skin and straight hair. The more like "white" a person was, the better. They were deadly serious about raising their children in an appropriate upper-middle-class way. Vivian made certain that the three children, Donna, Nelson, and Joyce, were always meticulously dressed. She carefully inspected the other children they played with. She monitored their behavior. They were to walk, not run, speak softly, not shout. They were not even permitted to chew gum. Nelson loved to work with his hands and wanted to be a carpenter when he grew up. The Browns said that was out of the question. Nelson would be a lawyer. Donna, who was a genuinely talented dance student, wanted to become a famous dancer some day, but the Browns refused to let her try. She could study classical ballet for now, they said. It would be good for her grace and poise. But then she must go to college to study physical education and become a teacher. In any case, it hardly mattered. She would work as a teacher only until she married, they said. After marriage, it was not proper or necessary for a woman to work.

Vivian Brown was a tall, stately woman who carried herself as if she were a queen. And in her home and in Drexel Square society she *was* queen. She had filled her house with antiques, some of which were extremely rare and valuable, and she collected porcelain, especially blue-and-white Delft.

Vivian Brown was in control of her home. She always knew what she thought, and what was right or proper in any situation. The children did as they were told. If they objected to the fiats their mother laid down, they were wise enough to keep it to themselves.

Donna's father Sydney was shorter than Vivian, strongly built and autocratic. He was not a handsome man, more like a little brown bull. He was utterly devoted to Vivian. Apparently he was fond of his children, too, but both he and Vivian had very clear and very limited ideas of what was respectable. Their children were going to be respectable—or else.

"Sydney was a cold man," John said. "He had a chilly nature, standoffish. He never seemed to have any time for the kids. But he was a hard worker."

In the community outside their home, he was a very major power.

Naturally, Vivian and Sydney inspected Donna's new boyfriend very closely. There were pros and cons to John Branion, Jr. His father's profession, the law, was perfectly respectable, though the office of the Cook County Public Defender was a public one and therefore not quite as desirable from the Brown point of view as a lucrative private practice. The fact that John Marshall Branion, Sr. was revered for his defense of the poor did not make up for the fact that he did not earn much money. The Branion apartment was small. And who could tell what the boy John junior would grow up to be?

All his life, John believed he was accepted, however grudgingly, in the Brown household more because he had straight hair and light skin than because of his father's profession or any accomplishments of his own.

Donna belonged to an informal club of girls her age, and John to a boy's club. Some afternoons the clubs would get together at the apartment of one or another to dance to records. The clubs had names, exciting at the time, since forgotten.

"I remember one time I took a new friend to the Browns'," John said. "I think it was an afternoon when we were going to listen to records. This boy was very black, and his father was a painter who was often out of work—not the sort of person the Browns wanted to see in their home. Well, they didn't say anything while he was there, but later Vivian took me aside and she told me not to bring him back."

John laughed. "I thought at the time—well, you know how it is when you're young and you think you can change everything right away. I got the clubs together, the boys' and girls' clubs, and we all decided to reject the values of the older generation. We were going to avoid all narrow values and be open-minded and logical all our lives."

He succeeded in making an issue of it, and antagonized the Browns in the process. The last thing in the world they were ready to permit was Donna questioning their values.

"You know, you can't entirely blame them. They were narrow-minded, sure. But then they'd faced a lot of prejudice in their lives. And it had taken them a lot of hard work to get to where they were. They were determined to hold on to what they had.

"And you know, they really believed that if they could do it so could other blacks. If some other family wasn't making it the way the Brown family was, it was because they didn't work hard enough, or didn't save their money enough. Because Sydney and Vivian had made it, they just weren't able to believe that any of their success was due to plain luck. Or that anybody else could have bad luck, or bad health, or not be scholarly, or just run into so much prejudice again and again that they got discouraged.

"And then, it *was* harder for the people who were darker skinned. The Browns in a sense admitted that. Tacitly. They preferred to associate with lighter-skinned black people and wanted their kids to associate with lighter-skinned black people. They *knew* it was an advantage. But still, if you asked them they'd say anybody could make it if he worked hard enough."

John was confrontational and completely outspoken; if he believed he was in the right he would argue the point, and he wouldn't give up. And he was stubborn. The Browns were using a psychology doomed to failure when they made it clear they objected to him. If anything, the Browns' increasing antagonism had the effect of increasing his devotion to Donna.

By senior year he was captain of the football team. Like football players everywhere, he was considered a catch as a date, but he was Donna's and she was proud of it. John was elected president of the student body, a major accomplishment in a high school that was still over 50 percent white. He was the second black president the Englewood student body ever had; the first was the man who would many years later defend him against the charge of murder, Maurice Scott.

The Browns became more and more opposed to the relationship between Donna and John, insisting that they stop seeing each other. By graduation time, events in the world outside were also converging on their lives.

It was 1943. John had been accepted at the University of Wisconsin. He intended to major in one of the sciences and then go on to medical school. The University of Wisconsin was also one of the finest physical education schools in the country, and Donna wanted to go along with John and major in dance and gym. But Sydney and Vivian Brown refused to let her go to Wisconsin. They sent her instead all the way across the country to the University of Southern California. That was about as far from John as they could possibly send her and still keep their daughter in the United States.

At this time USC was segregated. Donna was in physical education, but she was not allowed to swim in the USC pool. More than that—she was not allowed to play golf or tennis. As a black student, she could not even live on campus, but instead had to live a few blocks away with an older female student and friend of the family.

John said, "Fight it. Make an argument."

"How?"

"Ask them how you're going to get a meaningful degree in physical education if you can't even compete in any sports. Go to the student paper. Make an issue of it."

"I don't *want* to make an issue of it."

"Donna, come on. Stand *up* for yourself!"

"No, I'll be better this way."

The world was engulfed in war, and after only one semester at Wisconsin, John was drafted. He completed basic training. Then, bound for the Pacific and not knowing whether he would survive or be killed, he was routed through southern California.

He went to USC and found Donna. They married there, hastily, just before he went overseas.

He was in the Pacific on Okinawa, when he received a batch of papers. They were worse than a Dear John letter. They were legal documents from the Browns claiming Donna wanted an annulment. "I felt helpless," he said. "I felt that there was nothing I could do. It said that *she* wanted the divorce. Here were all these legal things. Papers. I think I was angry at her, too. How *could* she want a divorce? And of course, it turned out later she didn't want it. But that was the way it was put to me, and her family being so efficient in the law. . . . I didn't fight it. Maybe I felt I had no right, I don't know."

John was a T-5 corporal in a segregated unit of a segregated army. In 1946 he received an honorable discharge. By this time, first through mutual friends, then from writing to Donna, he had discovered that she had never wanted the annulment. She just wasn't very good at resisting Vivian and Sydney Brown all by herself.

"When I came home, this was in 1946, I went to the Brown house. It was the first time I'd been inside it since those days before graduation from high school, and I said to her father, 'Look, Donna and I are going to get married, and we would like you to participate.' And he said, 'Okay.' There was nothing else he *could* say at that point.

"Sydney Brown went right to my father and said, 'What are we going to do?' He meant what are we going to do financially. He wanted us to live in a way that maintained his middle-class image. The family image was the most important thing to Sydney.

"My father said, 'John is going to go to school on the G.I. Bill.' He had faith that I'd work it out. I worked as an air-hammer operator for a while to get the money to buy Donna's wedding ring. I worked on Michigan Avenue breaking up pavement right out in front of the jewelers, Peacock's, and the other stores—the very stores Vivian Brown liked to shop in! They were chagrined! Some of my friends were embarrassed, too. They'd walk right by, pretend they didn't know me, the laborer. I collected my checks, and then one day I just walked in, I think I was wearing my work clothes, and signed over the checks to Peacock's and bought Donna's ring."

The wedding was big and elaborate. Donna was carried by limousine to the church. The only unusual aspect was that she did not wear white or a veil. Vivian Brown had decreed that white was inappropriate because Donna and John had been married previously in California—even though the marriage was annulled. John liked what Donna wore, anyway.

"She wore a sort of—a satin, or a silk—a beautiful satiny silk in a gray eggshell color. Below the knee. It wasn't a long dress, but it was below the knee. She was beautiful. The Browns invited all the people from the upper-class black community. Donna had even registered her wedding patterns at the best place, Peacock's, naturally—the china and silver—which was not traditional for blacks at that time. Everyone came. All the Browns, without exceptions."

After they were married, John and Donna went down to the University of Illinois at Champaign and lived in a small house with a relative of Donna's. John studied and worked part-time. After three and a half years, the G.I. Bill ran out. John got permission from the University of Illinois to take his last credits at Northwestern and Illinois Institute of Technology in Chicago. Money was short, but they managed by living with Donna's parents. John earned money working eight hours a day at Michael Reese Hospital for a gastroenterologist named Dr. Nicholas, and he took his pathogenic bacteriology at IIT and parasitology at Northwestern at night.

He was up until three and four o'clock every night studying during that year.

"I think that was the only period where Sydney Brown kind of got close to me, because we were living in their house and he realized how hard I was working. He couldn't sleep well at night; he had painful arthritis. And he'd get up and find me working."

But after graduation John wanted to go to medical school and discovered it was nearly impossible. Thousands and thousands of young men had put off their education through the war years and were trying to make it up now. The schools were full. "I had a B-plus average, but a B-plus average was not enough if you were black. It would be now, but not in the early 1950s."

John went to graduate school at the University of Illinois Medical School, but in the Department of Pharmacology, not medicine. Still, he went into it with optimism. Something would work out.

Then he received a surprising letter from his cousin, Jordan Scott. Scott had been accepted at medical school in Paris the previous year. John wrote back to him with a dozen questions. John had never given up the desire to go to medical school. He wanted to be a doctor; even as a teenager he'd never had any doubt. Not even his father's professional success or his love and pride in his father had steered him toward law. John and Donna talked it over. Donna was strongly in favor of going to Europe. She had always wanted to see France and she wanted John to become a doctor. They quickly made the decision to go to Paris. But how were they going to pay for it?

John said, "Now you have to understand that just then, in 1952, my father and mother had bought their *first* house. After all those years of work. He was fifty! He hadn't even been able to afford a car of his own until 1941. They had just got into the house when we started talking about going to France. They were able to pay twelve thousand dollars for the house. And they had to pay cash! Banks did not give credit to black people. He was making some minuscule salary as Public Defender. But he volunteered to split the cost of our going to Paris with Sydney Brown—to support me halfway. I don't know what sort of sacrifices they had to make, but they didn't want the wealthy Sydney Browns to do it all.

"It was so cheap over there! Food, clothes, tuition, everything. Fortunately! Because we had nothing extra to spend. We went over in April. We got there in the middle of exams. I didn't know any French and I wanted to learn before starting classes. All my American friends were taking exams, and all of them failed! Well, two buddies from New York were there, and one of them was the only one who passed. He said the way the French teach, you have to learn to regurgitate the book word by word, which meant that your French had to be impeccable. They would not accept errors in grammar *at all*. He said I should go to Toulouse because the classes were smaller and the attrition rate was less. The freshman class in Paris was fifteen hundred people, and all but five hundred failed the first year, even the French kids.

"Donna and I went to Toulouse. I was accepted. We happened to get there—I'll never forget!—in the middle of the flea season. And we'd wake up in the morning covered with bites and fleas. The whole place was full of fleas! We got out of there in a hurry and went back to Paris.

"In Paris I met a friend from Canada named Jack Swartz who suggested that we go to Switzerland. There was a good medical school in Geneva. I said, 'Can we just go?' Jack said, 'Bring all your records and we'll try.' So that's what we did.

"Jack and I and another man went to Geneva. In Geneva they said the class was full, but they said, 'Why don't you go to Fribourg?' This was Fribourg in Switzerland, not Freiberg in Germany, but you know, they speak both German and French there. Well, I'd taken some French lessons at Alliance Francais, but I wasn't great at French. I didn't have any German at all. We went to Fribourg, and in Fribourg some of the classes are taught in French and some are taught entirely in *German*. The dean, who was their physiology and chemistry professor, asked us in English with a heavy German accent, 'Do you speak French?' I said yes in English. Then he said 'How's your German?' I said, 'Not too bad.' In English. So he accepted us. I figured I had a few days to get a working idea of German.

"And find a place to live. There was an apartment house being built in a beautiful neighborhood. It was almost done. I went up to the builder and asked whether I could rent one and he said sure! I couldn't believe it! I was from the United States and black and here was somebody saying I could just rent anywhere I wanted. They didn't give a damn what your color was! It was the first time in my life I felt really free."

John's attitude toward Europe, even toward the difficulties, was positive. This was fun, and the world was an adventure. He liked trying something new. And he was willing to work to make things happen.

By the time classes started, he had a rough but working grasp of German.

Donna was quite a different sort of person from John. John was optimistic almost to the point of rashness. Donna's reticence seemed inbred. She dressed meticulously and spoke softly. She was careful in the presence of people she did not know well. Donna Brown Branion was a young woman who took no risks. Marrying John had been her one act of rebellion.

In her own way, Donna liked Europe. But in the five years they spent in Switzerland, where German, Italian, and French are all spoken, she never learned any European languages at all. To learn a new language on the spot, among native speakers, takes a certain amount of outgoing enthusiasm, a willingness to make mistakes, even foolish mistakes, and to let other people laugh at you and correct you. Donna was never able to do that. She could not expose herself to ridicule. John could, easily. He would rush right in and try the new words. If he made a mistake, and of course he did, constantly at first, he'd smile about it and store the correction away in his memory. Donna and John had one of their few real disagreements about it.

Donna made some friends among the Swiss people they met, because many of them spoke English. Her principal way of relating to the European cultures was through food. While John was in school, she shopped for groceries with English-speaking friends and learned to cook the local dishes.

John was taking two degrees at once:

"In Switzerland, if you show a certain interest and aptitude, you're allowed to work on a graduate degree and medical degree at the same time, so I did that."

During the fourth year John was in Switzerland, he and Donna became friends with another American who was just beginning medical school, C. Rogers Wise, called Roger. Roger Wise was coping with being an American abroad, just as John had been four years before.

"John was their top student," Wise says. "He did things that just amazed the faculty, John coming from abroad and not knowing the language at first. He was at the top of his class. It really made you feel good to be an American to have him ahead of you in school, making that kind of impression."

John said, "We were in Switzerland five years. While we were there we had a baby. Donna had trouble conceiving, and then later one of the professors there gave her an ovarian hormone to induce labor—an amount we'd consider criminal today. We know now it could have caused uterine rupture. But then it was what they used. Anyway, we had a beautiful baby girl, Jan Elizabeth. Donna picked the name Jan. I don't know where she got it from; neither of us knew anybody named Jan. Or Elizabeth. But it was what she wanted. Donna's mother even came over to see her and be with Donna."

Two of their Swiss neighbors became Jan's godparents.

"As I got to the end of medical school, we started to talk about where we would go. In 1956, Ghana was the first country in Africa to get its independence, and Donna and I were both interested in going there. We were so compatible in so many ways—Donna was a homebody, and I—well, I wasn't—but still." John was aware that he was a socially and politically outgoing person. And he was aware that the woman he had married was not. But they seem to have developed a way of life that worked for them both.

"We thought we couldn't go to Ghana until I had gone back to the States for an internship and residency. I wanted to go into surgery, I loved surgery; it was exacting and you were doing something with your hands. But the residency in surgery was too long—I just couldn't afford it. I had a dear old friend who encouraged me to go into gynecology. I came back to the U.S. and went to Cook County Hospital. Ken Anderson was the first black to get a full residency in OB/GYN at Cook County, then Jimmy Jones, and then myself."

At Cook County during this period, a young woman named Shirley Hudson was in nurse's training. She was one of the few black nurses training there, and she noticed John Branion, one of just two black residents. But she did not meet him. The interweaving of their lives lay a little way in the future.

At Cook County Hospital John joined AIMS, the Association of Interns and Medical Students, an organization dedicated to improving working conditions and treatment of these young professionals and about-to-be-professionals. AIMS wanted better facilities and pay and greater acceptance of minority groups as students. During this period John's political thinking leaned toward socialism. Outspoken, he got into political debates with anybody who wanted to talk.

But mostly, John worked. He was away from home long hours. Money was short. For recreation, both he and Donna cooked. They had accumulated recipes and techniques from all over Europe, and they cooked Italian, German, French, and Swiss specialties for themselves and their friends. They loved having friends over for a special dinner. Once Donna's uncle Oscar Brown asked John and Donna to cook for a dinner meeting of the 1,500 members of the Chicago Negro Chamber of Commerce. The headwaiter was Oscar Brown, Jr. They were paid for making the dinner, and with the money they earned they bought a gourmet stove—a Chambers—which they had always wanted but had never been able to afford.

Donna and John gave up the idea of going to live in Ghana. Sydney and Vivian were very much against it. They were growing older. Vivian was not well. Sydney's arthritis was worse. They wanted their daughter and granddaughter near them. And they were afraid of Africa. There were too many unknowns there—poverty, strange diseases, the political situation. It was too risky, they said.

John didn't fight that view, because he felt the time had come for him to start earning some real money. He had been just scraping by for too long, first on the G.I. Bill, then on school money from his father and Sydney

Brown. He had worked at part-time jobs almost continually, but it was time now to provide, *really* provide, for Donna and Jan.

After one year of internship and three years of residency at Cook County Hospital, John was accredited. In 1962, at the age of thirty-six, Dr. John Marshall Branion went into the private practice of obstetrics and gynecology.

▪ CHAPTER NINE ▪

The black population of the United States existed in many ways separate from and partially parallel to white, mainstream American life. Blacks lived here and worked here, but usually in low-paid jobs of a service nature; they were citizens, but were not admitted to full participation in civic life. Much of their lives were invisible to the white population. Television ads were all white. The heroes on television programs were white. With a few exceptions, such as the broad comedy "Amos 'n Andy" and Jack Benny's man of all work, Rochester, virtually all the people visible on television were white.

By the time John Marshall Branion, Jr. returned from Europe in 1958, he was an oddity—a Swiss-trained obstetrician/gynecologist who spoke four languages and happened to be black. He interned one year at Cook County Hospital, then put in three years of residency. By that time it was 1962 and he was thirty-six years old. He went into private practice and was on the staff of Columbia Hospital, a Catholic hospital in Chicago. He was optimistic, hard-working, cheerful, and personable. People liked him. It looked as if nothing but financial success and personal accomplishment lay ahead of him.

John had in his life two examples of extremely successful black men, his father and Sydney Brown. Sydney was cold, ruthless, determined, hard-working, careful, and except where his wife Vivian was concerned, penny-pinching. He had succeeded in a white world by becoming richer and more powerful than most whites, but he was very cautious and very middle-class in behavior. John Marshall Branion, Sr. was warm, humane, but hard-working and even single-minded about his job, a crusader *within* the system, and in person very retiring, low-profile, and cautious.

Dr. John Marshall Branion, Jr. was one of a new young breed of black men. Like both Sydney and John senior, he was hard-working—but he played hard, too. He was warm with people and a soft touch for a hard luck story. He spent money—on his family, friends, even strangers. He had a reputation of being a womanizer. But the biggest difference was that he did not keep a low profile; he was not concerned about what sort of image he was creating. The cars, the horses, the boat—all looked like showing off. As a friend of Donna's said many years later, "He'd just go right ahead. Say what he thought."

Other people in the black community felt that John's lifestyle was a problem, not just to him but to them as well. "You couldn't just do that, attract attention like that. Some people didn't like the way he went around, 'There goes Dr. Branion.' It wasn't smart." There was a certain amount of envy of John in the black community. And to a certain extent, it was justified. But it was equally true that John put time and effort into issues of social justice. John believed if something was wrong in the society he had a right to say so. And he was stubborn enough to go on saying so. He was *not* cautious.

Given the tenor of the times, he may have been an arrest looking for a chance to happen.

John and Donna Branion seemed to have embarked on the American dream in the American way, through hard work, persistence, dedication and strong values. John had fought for his country, then put in fifteen years after graduation from high school learning his profession. He had applied flexibility and imagination in finding a medical school, and he had paid his dues as an intern and resident.

Donna had reached all the goals a woman of her station was supposed to have: she had attended college, married her childhood sweetheart, produced a child, and now devoted herself exclusively to home and family. She had followed her parents' wishes—she lived near them, in a building they owned; she kept her house clean and herself and her child well dressed. By 1962, they began to reap the rewards of their industriousness. In the American way, they started to accumulate possessions.

They bought a Corvette. They bought an Owens cabin cruiser, which they berthed in Jackson Park Harbor and used on Lake Michigan. Friends came over on weekends to go for a ride. And—shades of the small boy who wanted a cowboy outfit for Christmas—John bought two horses, a sorrel trotter and a palomino quarterhorse. He kept them on a farm in Indiana. Several days a week, he got up at 4:00 a.m. and drove to Indiana to train them. He even fed and groomed them, and enjoyed it. And he drove back to Chicago in time for work at the hospital.

His father had given him a book called *The Black Cowboy*. Maybe his father remembered the child who wanted chaps and a ten-gallon hat for Christmas. John started to collect guns, cowboy guns like Colt revolvers, then some hunting guns—rifles and shotguns. After a while he became interested in antique guns and bought several that were quite valuable. He said much later, "It all seems so mercenary, looking back at it—all those possessions!" But he had worked hard, and he must have felt it was time to enjoy what he had earned. And in a way, it was not the possession of things but the fun of it all that appealed to John—studying the characteristics of antique guns, learning how horses responded to training. For a while he even tried racing his Corvette and did the maintenance work on it himself to keep it in racing trim.

Donna was not an outdoor person. She would occasionally spend time with John and friends on the boat, using it as a kind of far-removed out-door porch to serve picnic meals, but she didn't enjoy cruising on choppy water. When John raced his Corvette, she stayed home. When John and his father went fishing, she stayed home. She even stayed home when John went to a concert. John was accustomed to her retiring nature, and they didn't argue about it the way they had over her refusals to learn French or fight the racial restrictions at USC.

Their apartment at 5054 South Woodlawn was large and elegant, in a neighborhood of huge old houses and roomy well-built apartments near the University of Chicago. In the 1920s, the area was so racially segregated that even the janitors in the large apartment buildings were required to be white. By the 1960s, joint efforts by the community, the churches, and the University of Chicago had produced a largely integrated neighborhood. Within a couple of blocks at this time lived the president of the University of Chicago, the cartoonist Bill Mauldin, and the leader of the Black Muslims, Elijah Muhammad.

The Branions lived on the first floor of a three-story, twelve-flat build-ing. They had eight rooms and two enclosed sun parlors, one in the front and one in the back. The entire apartment from front to back was 105 feet in depth. The living room was twenty-six feet long. John had knocked down the wall between the living room and dining room to make one big space which, laughing, they referred to as the ballroom. Inside the front door was a long foyer opening into a large hallway from which the bed-rooms and study led off.

John had the kitchen and living room remodeled for Donna in a French provincial style. There was a built-in barbecue in the kitchen where Don-na could entertain. John liked to cook on it, too, when he had the time. The kitchen and utility rooms were floored with real brick. The hall, foyer, and Jan's bedroom were carpeted, Jan's with pink plush, but in the living room, study, and other bedrooms Donna had kept the polished hardwood floors and displayed area rugs on them—a style she and John had come to like when they were in Europe.

"Donna had just beautiful taste. I was so proud of everything she did with the apartment. The living room was white. In fact, she used light colors throughout the whole apartment. The hall carpet she chose was gray. The hall was wallpapered in a gray and white stripe. The foyer was gray with a black enamelled table. The master bedroom had gray striped paper too, wide and narrow stripes. Quite Victorian. She wanted my den to be different, sort of masculine, so she chose beige walls and a tiled floor, an oak gun cabinet and an oak desk.

"Donna's 'den' was the kitchen. That was where she worked, where she expressed herself, where she excelled. She had a brick floor, oak cabinets, and a big bulletin board where we left messages to each other and she kept current recipes she was trying.

"We were still remodeling what had been an extra closet and bathroom into the utility/laundry room when—well, in 1967."

After they had adapted the apartment to suit themselves, it was a big, sunny, happy-looking place. The Browns, concerned about their daughter's place in the community, approved of the new home.

Through the Browns, John began to meet important figures in the national African-American community. Composer-entertainer Oscar Brown, Jr., now a rising star, introduced John to show business people. And the Browns knew sports figures, political figures like Roy Innes, the head of C.O.R.E., and others.

There was one major disappointment in John and Donna's world. Donna had not been able to conceive again. But in 1963 they adopted a baby boy. They named him John Marshall Branion III, and called him Joby for short.

John became medical director of the Ida Mae Scott Hospital. It was a small, community-based hospital with a few wards of beds and a large outpatient service, including a technical lab, pathology lab, pharmacy, and a dental service as well as medical services. It was about ten minutes from home, which pleased him.

John loved people, and he loved talking with people. The Ida Mae Scott Hospital took its outpatients on a clinic system, a first-come-first-served arrangement. The waiting rooms were often very full, but John didn't rush people through. The nurses, putting people into the examining rooms, were constantly after him to hurry up. Betty Adger, his long-time nurse and assistant, said, "The patients loved him. He treated every patient as if he or she were the only patient. He'd sit and ask them why they let themselves get sick, why they couldn't lose weight, whatever. He'd talk and he'd listen to them talk. I used to go try to hurry him up. I'd go in the examining room and just stand there—not saying anything—and then walk out, so he'd know I wanted him to hurry. And like as not, I'd have to do it again five minutes later. They all liked him, and they wanted to just sit there and talk with him."

Not long after he switched to the Ida Mae Scott Hospital, John began to notice one of the nurses there, Shirley Hudson. She had trained at Cook County Hospital, like John, and he recognized her Cook County nurse's cap. Hospitals all had their own distinctive signature caps, which were awarded at graduation. Cook County's was an unusual style, a sort of tiny white organdy puff that perched on top of the head.

Shirley looked like Diahann Carroll. "She was so beautifully perfect," John said. "Beautifully groomed, her uniform perfectly pressed. Maybe I have a weakness for tidiness in women. But she wasn't just pretty. She was cool and serene. And independent."

Shirley had seen John once or twice at Cook County when she was training and he was a resident. "The Ida Mae Scott Hospital was different from Cook County," Shirley says. "Cook County is huge. Scott Hospital was small and everybody who worked there knew everybody else. It was warm and friendly, like a family. I hadn't met John yet, but I knew who he was.

"I was making out charts one day and he just walked up and said, 'You have the most beautiful hands.' Well, I thought he was being *too* friendly. A lot of the doctors I knew were pretty much on their high horse. They'd give orders, but they didn't chat. They were too important. But people told me, no, Branion is always friendly like that. Not stuffy, and he loves to talk.

"It wasn't too much later he asked me out for a drink after work. We went to a sort of pub. It was a nice place, but I didn't drink and I didn't dare say I didn't. It seemed important to act more sophisticated—you know how it is when you're young and you want to act older. So we had one drink. And John was asking me questions and telling me about things, when suddenly the bartender came over with champagne. I thought John had asked for it, and I surely didn't want another drink, but he was already saying, 'What's this?'

"The bartender said, 'The gentlemen at that table sent it over.'

"We looked and neither of us knew the man at the table, but he raised his glass and toasted us.

"The bartender said, 'He told me he wanted to drink to two people who were so much in love.'

"Well! I thought 'What does that man know that I don't know?'

"A week or two later John asked me out for a drink after work. He was going to pick me up at the desk, I think, but he didn't show up. That wasn't like him. He was a responsible kind of person. But I assumed he had an emergency surgery.

"I didn't see him except in the hall for several days. Then he came up one day and said, 'Listen, I've got to talk to you.'

"I said 'sure' and we went out for coffee.

"He told me then. He said something like, 'I should have said this before. You've got to know that I'm married.'

"I thought, how could I have made such a blunder? Why didn't somebody tell me? But there wasn't any real problem. All I had to do was not see him any more.

"Except it wasn't that easy."

"What was it about John? He was different from any other man I'd ever met. More alive. He had a dozen interests at any one time, and the way he talked about them and the way he showed them to you, you got interested in them, too. Fishing. I hadn't gone fishing before, never *wanted* to fish before, but he made it fun. I wasn't really very much interested in civil rights until I met him. And then I was.

"And he was strong. About what he believed in. He did what he thought he should and he didn't care what anybody thought of him. I knew the Browns didn't want him to be involved in civil rights. They didn't believe upper-class blacks did things like that. He was too—just too *up front* for them.

"He was strong and self-reliant. What a man ought to be. He just had more life than anybody else."

In any marriage, there are imbalances and trade-offs. The time John spent with Shirley must have detracted from his marriage. Just the fact that the time was not spent at home would be a problem, aside from the knowledge that he was with another woman. It must have been embarrassing for her. On the other hand, John seems to have wished that Donna would go out with him more, to political events, to sporting events, and so on.

Donna had become more and more a homebody. They had sold the boat; Donna didn't really enjoy it. Donna was not career-minded. And she didn't like socializing, except in gatherings with close friends and relatives. But she and John had plenty of both. They entertained at home, both of them doing the cooking.

As it evolved, when John wanted to go out, he ended up going out with Shirley.

John's father liked to cook, too, especially meats. Sometimes the whole clan would get together and they'd all cook, each one his specialty. John and his father had always been close, and these times with the grandparents and children—Jan and Joby, Annie and John, Sr., Donna and John, Jr.—were for all of them some of the happiest of their lives.

Then one day in 1965, it ended. "John called his folk's home one day," Shirley said, "just to check in, like he did every couple of days. He got his father on the line. John said, 'How you doing?' or something like that and his father said 'Fine. But I thought I might not go to work today.' Well, you have to know, he *always* went to work. That man never missed a day, no matter what. He loved his work.

"So John said 'Oh?' sort of casually, and finished the conversation sort of casually, and put down the phone and tore out of the house and jumped in the car and zoomed right over to his parents' house.

"His father was there in a chair with his legs all swollen. John said to his parents, 'Why didn't you tell me? I'm a doctor!' but really, there wasn't much to tell. It was a malignancy in the colon, and it was too late; there wasn't anything that could be done about it.

"Well, John and his father'd gone fishing together every year. *Every* year. At this place in Canada near Lake of the Woods where a black man who had left the United States and lived up there had married a Canadian woman and opened a resort. A lot of U.S. blacks would go up there to fish. There were Indian guides who would take you back into the lakes and you could get muskelunge, or crappies, or bass. The guide would take along potatoes and salt and pepper and butter and so on, and you'd fish all morning and then the guide would light a fire and cook your fish and some potatoes and maybe biscuits and you'd eat lunch. Then you'd fish the rest of the afternoon and take those fish home for dinner.

"John was determined that his father would have that last fishing trip. John usually went just with his father, the two of them, but this time—I don't know what it was, maybe he had such a hard time facing the fact that it really *was* the last time—he loved his father so much. Anyway, he wanted somebody else along. Donna wouldn't go. Donna never went fishing. She didn't like it. She didn't like tents or cabins or any of that.

"So he asked me to go. I didn't know how it would work out. It was awkward. But I said, 'Sure.'

"He told his father he was bringing a guest, but it wasn't until they stopped by to pick me up that his father knew who it was. He looked at me out of the car window, when they stopped for me. He looked a little doubtful. But he could see how it was, and he was nice. He bought me candy bars every time we stopped for gas.

"We got to the cabin and there were two bedrooms. One for Bunion.

John always used to call his father 'Bunion.' It was sort of a joking pet name. Anyway, Bunion took the one bedroom and John and I had the other.

"John's father was weak and tired a lot, though. He couldn't really fish, but he sat in the boat. He'd watch John fish. He loved John. They were so close. I think he had a good time. As much as he could, in the circumstances."

John said, "It's funny, the way the human mind works. He knew he was dying. He *knew* it. But just before we left to go fishing, he bought himself a brand new pair of fishing boots."

"Donna knew about Shirley," John said, "but she never mentioned it. Maxine Brown told me she knew. We had all settled into a routine and Donna seemed happy. Except I know that what you put into one relationship you take away from another relationship. I don't deny it. The time I spent with Shirley I wasn't spending with Donna. I know that.

"I've wondered how she felt about it. If she had lived, we might eventually have talked about it. I don't know—it seemed she was drinking a little more. She never drank too much, but Maxine did, and Maxine would come downstairs to gossip and they'd have a drink.

"I just don't know."

Donna did not want to go fishing, or sit outdoors at the automobile racetrack, or train horses, or hike, or take boat rides on Lake Michigan in rough weather. Shirley did. John had far more energy than Donna, and Donna may have been rather glad that she was not going to be pressed into all the vigorous sports that John loved.

"I think maybe, once I had found Shirley, I was easier on Donna. I didn't try to change her so much. Or am I just trying to make myself seem better? I don't know. But I had always been sort of trying to expand Donna's horizons.

"I'd ask her to a meeting, civil rights or something, and she wouldn't want to go. I guess there was probably a period where once in a while I said it was her duty. Here she was a wealthy black woman. In a way she owed it to the poorer blacks to stand up for equality. But Donna wasn't like that. And I think after I met Shirley, it didn't bother me so much.

"I loved both of them. People can believe that or not, but that's the way it was. I loved them both."

As a member of AIMS, one of John Branion's goals had been the admission of more minority students to medical programs, so that they would not have to deal with the discrimination he had faced in being admitted to medical school. But he had never been very active politically. He never had the time, in the long years of working and going to school. Now that he had more time, he became deeply involved in the civil rights movement.

On January 26, 1966, the Rev. Martin Luther King, Jr. moved from Alabama into a top-floor walk-up apartment at 1550 S. Hamlin Avenue in Chicago to begin his civil rights campaign in the north. King had won the Nobel Peace Prize in 1964, but most of his activities had been concentrated in the South. His nonviolent civil rights movement had made progress with voter registration and desegregation in both transportation and the schools—in the South.

But the north, more subtly segregated, was a different problem. There was more crime and more despair in the north and, King felt, less community spirit. In moving north he wanted to achieve two main goals: to replace apathy with hope, and to open up Chicago's heavily segregated housing.

Not all local black leaders were enthusiastic about King. After all, there was an obvious criticism in his coming to help them achieve what they had not achieved on their own. Before his arrival, black ministers and politicians held a press conference at which they expressly invited King—to stay away. Dorothy Tillman, who is now alderman of Chicago's Third Ward, was a teenager on King's staff at the time. She recently told the *Tribune*, "We were rejected by most of the black leadership. Dr. King could hardly get into a church to speak. But I think we changed a lot of mindsets. I think we set the stage for change."

White leaders were nervous, too. By 1966, Mayor Richard J. Daley had been in office for eleven years. In 1955, when Daley, then a Democratic committeeman from the Eleventh Ward, first ran against two other democrats in his Democratic primary, it was the black vote, as much as anything, that pushed him over the top. He actually did better in black wards on the south side than in his own. Primarily this was a result of the strength of the Democratic Party machine in these wards. Since the 1930s and the Roosevelt administration, blacks had mostly been Democrats. The black wards on the south side of Chicago had a strong precinct organization at every level and blacks in many positions of authority.

Daley believed he was the leader and champion of Chicago blacks as well as whites. He thought he was making progress in race relations. And like a number of the black ministers, he didn't believe an outsider like King knew anything about how Chicago worked.

But the black population of Chicago was nearing one million, and most were packed into sections of the south and, increasingly, west sides. Here, overcrowding in crumbling buildings was the rule. Outside this area, housing discrimination on racial lines held fast.

For some months Daley and King sparred, Daley trying to defuse the increasing tension by praising King, the Nobel laureate, at every turn, and holding meetings at which Daley or his aides explained privately to King how much they were accomplishing. Meanwhile, nothing really changed.

The summer of 1966 was the third in the series of long hot summers that were altering the course of United States society. The first was 1964 and the riot in Harlem. The second was 1965 and the even bigger riot in Watts, a black suburb of Los Angeles. In Watts, property damage was $50 million; 3,500 people were arrested; nearly 900 were injured and 35 killed.

Feeding into the accelerating violence was the resistance of white, middle-class young people to the draft. The civil rights movement and the antiwar movement were gathering force, sweeping away political apathy.

1966 was a summer of 100-degree days in Chicago. On the tenth of July, in shimmering heat, 40,000 people gathered at Soldier Field to hear King speak. Then they marched after him to City Hall. There, Martin Luther King, Jr., like his namesake, nailed a list of demands to the door.

On July 12, the temperature was 102. Some black children were playing in the spray from fire hydrants on the West Side. Firemen pulled up in a truck and turned the water off. This act set off three days of rioting.

Meanwhile, King's organization was collecting evidence of housing discrimination, which Daley maintained did not exist. By the simple technique of sending black couples out to ask for housing at real estate offices, they were able to document widespread violations of the city's toothless fair housing ordinance.

On July 21, Jesse Jackson and James Bevel from King's coalition led a protest march to a real estate office in white Chicago Lawn. They were met by a crowd of white hecklers. The police were called. They arrested the marchers, not the hecklers.

On July 24, this time with police protection, both blacks and whites from King's coalition, singing hymns, marched again into Chicago Lawn, a Polish and Lithuanian area of Chicago around Marquette Park, south and west of the Loop. They were met by rocks, knives, sticks, bricks, gasoline-filled bottles, and cherry bombs, hurled over the heads of the police into the marchers. White youths flipped over cars and threw cherry bombs into the gas tanks. There were hundreds of injuries.

On July 27, President Lyndon Johnson established the National Advisory Commission on Civil Disorders to look into the causes of urban rioting. Among the ten committee members, he appointed Edward Brooke, U.S. Senator from Massachusetts, and Roy Wilkins, Executive Director of the NAACP, both black but both very moderate. He appointed Governor Otto Kerner of Illinois chairman of the commission.

On August 5, King led a march to Marquette Park. Now there were radio, television, and newspaper reporters among the marchers. In Marquette Park, King himself was hit on the head by a rock. He was knocked down and lay there for a moment. Then he got up. "I've been in many demonstrations all across the South," King said, "but I can say that I have never seen—even in Mississippi and Alabama—mobs as hostile and hate-filled as I've seen in Chicago."

King's basic tactic was the nonviolent march. And he insisted that his followers be strictly nonviolent. In Chicago, he recruited young men who were members of street gangs and converted their anger into energy for change. One of his early strategies was to appoint them marshals of the marches. It was their job to keep the peace. When glass bottles and bricks and rocks rained down from the rooftops at the marchers, the gang-members-turned-marshals caught them as a ballplayer would catch a pop fly, and then laid them gently on the ground.

Another of the strategies of the King lieutenants was to line up physicians and nurses to march with King. In case King or any of the other marchers was seriously injured—and with bricks hurled off rooftops several stories above, there was always the specter of very severe or fatal injury—these physicians could give immediate, skilled first aid.

Dr. John Branion marched with King in the Cicero and Gage Park marches. Shirley Hudson marched with him. Bottles shattered around them in the street. Some bricks found their targets in spite of the marshals. Stones, pieces of mortar, tin cans, chunks of metal—it was terrifying walking through the rain of hate. Shirley and John made on-the-spot decisions. They treated some of the injured and sent others to hospitals for stitches. They patched what they could while still walking.

"I remember," John said, "how frightened Martin was. It's one thing I'll always remember—how frightened he was about the marches in Chicago. He was actually terrified. But at the same time he was so brave that you'd have to be close to him to realize it, because he would smile and he would carry himself well. But he was always physically aware of all the violence around him. And I remember on one march when rocks began to fall and I fell on top of him to protect him, he was trembling. I was amazed; I could feel him actually trembling. But that's what courage is, isn't it? To go ahead even though you know the risk and even though it frightens you.

"And he was so *commanding*. It was unbelievable. From the first syllable! He was like Paul Robeson used to be. The minute he opened his mouth, that was *it*."

John spoke to civil rights groups and medical groups occasionally. *Muhammad Speaks*, the official mouthpiece of Elijah Muhammed's Nation of Islam, quoted some of his remarks. He had been asked about the physicians' strikes in Canada and Belgium. He answered that he did not think they would occur here, because of the power of the AMA. He had earlier been quoted in the same publication as saying he "had travelled to Switzerland to study for his medical degree because of the quota system imposed against Negroes in many medical schools in America." These remarks were abstracted and placed in a file that was being opened on John Branion in the United States Department of Justice.

Twenty years later, it was still difficult to obtain these files. A request under the Freedom of Information Act brought me a few pages, with large areas of the pages blacked out as if, all that time later, there was sensitive information here, or agents still in place who had to be protected.

That year, 1966, John began to be visited by injured blacks who had been beaten or shot by the police and did not want to go to Chicago hospitals for treatment. Some had escaped while being taken to jail. Some were Black Panthers who didn't want the hospitals to report them to the police. Some were simply terrified of officialdom.

Doctors are supposed to report gunshot wounds to the police. John didn't. He could not bring himself to call the police down on a black man who had already been shot fleeing from them.

John was not a Black Panther. But he was one of a handful of Chicago physicians, black and white, who treated Black Panthers during this period. In 1966 there were five doctors in Chicago, four men and a woman, who were known to be willing to treat gunshot cases and not report them. In the black movement, the names of these doctors were supposed to be held secret, passed on only to those who needed medical attention, and not written down. But of course word always leaks out, especially in situations where it isn't possible to verify the reliability of everyone who might need a doctor. John Branion's name was coming to the attention of the Chicago Police and the state's attorney's office.

After some months of this, John began to receive telephone calls, at home, not at work, purporting to come from the state's attorney's office and threatening him with reprisals if he didn't stop treating Panthers. They said, "Give it up, doctor." Or, "Don't do this to yourself; these people aren't going to thank you later."

During this period, large amounts of federal, state, and local money was going into identifying Panthers and anybody connected with them. In addition, governments were fearful of more civil rights and antiwar violence. Police departments were stockpiling riot equipment—machine guns, tear gas, grenade launchers, flak jackets and mace. The long hot summers of 1966 and 1967 would prove to be only the beginning.

In late 1967, events were building toward their climax. In the autumn of

1967, Dr. Martin Luther King, Jr. was seven months from assassination. John Branion was three months from his own personal disaster. And the fury surrounding King's death would add its weight to the calamities that overtook John Branion. Dr. Branion believed in the American dream, and he believed people were reasonable. He thought that bringing injustice before the American people as a whole would cause the people to respond and build a new, more just society. He was an optimist, but the American dream is an optimistic view of the world.

He had no idea what trap fate had laid for him, just around the bend of time.

· CHAPTER TEN ·

T here comes a point in the investigation of a major crime when the emphasis shifts subtly from trying to discover who could possibly have committed the crime to trying to prove that a certain person actually did commit it. At this point the investigators may, with the best will in the world, start to narrow their focus. They may also try to make the evidence fit the theory.

The narrowing of focus has several effects. First, peripheral investigations tend to fall away. Less and less attention is given to looking for outside suspects: if two teenagers are caught breaking into apartments in the area of the original crime, or if a home invasion with murder takes place farther downtown, less effort will be made to find these cases and to connect them up.

Second, facts about the prime suspect that don't quite fit with his guilt will start to appear less important.

Third, ambiguous information will begin to be interpreted in ways consonant with guilt.

There is another development that is not a product of the narrowing of focus, but which exacerbates it. It is a by-product of the record-keeping process itself.

What happens during an investigation is a slow hardening of information. This is a product of the reporting method, in which investigators lower in rank explain to their superiors what they have discovered. It is a result of the simple process of condensation as the facts are passed along up the chain of information, combined with a desire on the part of the investigators to demonstrate to their superiors that they have accomplished something.

The vague memories of many hours of interviews, imprecise comments, and partial observations of investigators on the scene become shortened, and certain "facts" begin to sound surer and firmer as they move from an oral report to a written report, to a summary, to inquest testimony, to trial

77

court decisions, and eventually to the abbreviated and definitive conclusion of a higher court.

Soft facts become hard facts and then turn to stone, building a wall of apparently solid evidence.

This process was taking place in several areas of the Branion investigation: for example, the matter of the doors in the Branion apartment. When the police arrived, several people had already entered both the front and back doors. John believed he had found the front door locked but not barred and the back door unlocked. The police noted there were no signs of forced entry—no breaking or splintering of the doors themselves. The New York Burglar Bar, an extra lock on the back door, was in the open position, and everybody agreed Donna often left it open.

The first report, Officer Catizone's, said that the back door was unlocked. So did the newspaper accounts, quoting the policemen. The second report, by Detective Boyle, said the locks were secure, apparently meaning unbroken, with no sign of forced entry. It did not state whether they were locked or unlocked. By the time of the inquest, "secure" would be reinterpreted as "locked."

Interpretation was working on the policemen's attitude toward John Branion's verbal testimony. They themselves had any number of confusions about who had said what, who had received this or that gun, who had taken notes, and so on. In fact, one of them would testify at the trial that the initial investigation at the Branion house the day of the murder had been conducted by Boyle and his regular partner Detective Mannion, although Mannion actually did not get back from furlough until after the New Year. And the policemen were confused despite the fact that they were doing their usual job in their usual way—one they had all done for years—under no emotional stress. Had John Branion been clearly innocent, his guess that he had arrived home about 11:45, off by three to five minutes, would have been considered the minor error of a distraught man. Now it was beginning to be viewed as intentional deception.

Then there was the sixteen-year-old boy who lived across the hall from the Branions, named Oscar Gray. When the detectives first questioned Gray, he had told them he had seen John out in front of the building on December 22. When? Well, he had been sleeping, but three friends of his had come over about 11:15 and gotten him up. Some time after that, he had looked out the window and seen Dr. Branion standing in front. The officers asked Gray whether Dr. Branion had his son with him. Gray said no.

Boyle noted that this "contradicted" Dr. Branion's statement that when he arrived home he had his son with him. It went into the record that way.

However, Gray never suggested that John was running or hurrying.

Since the police view was that John sped home, let himself hurriedly into the house to avoid being seen, shot Donna, and left as secretly and as quickly as possible so that he could pick up Joby with no time lost and then come back home and discover the body later, Gray's statement is not consistent with the police picture of the way the crime was committed.

Boyle did not ask Gray whether John was talking with someone out in front, or whether Joby could have been playing under John's supervision but out of Gray's sight. Nor did he go to Gray's room and look out to see how much of the yard could be seen from his window. Nor did Boyle ask John whether he had come home for lunch the day before. And he was in the habit of coming home to lunch. Nor did Boyle ask him or Helen or William Payne another reasonable question—after he discovered Donna dead and William Payne had called the police, did John step out in the front yard to see if they were coming?

As it turned out, the boy Oscar Gray himself became doubtful about it. He told the detectives later that it might have been the day before that he saw John out in front. As a result of the unreliability of his testimony, it was not used. But the effect was to make the detectives even more suspicious of John.

The detectives now began to try to fit Mrs. Kentra's evidence into a picture of John's guilt. She was the Branions' neighbor, whose testimony had first been accepted as exonerating John. Mrs. Kentra had been out shopping and then had gone past the Catholic school to give the sisters some cookies. Detective Charles McMullen had questioned her the day of the crime. She said: "I came home from shopping at five after eleven this morning. Before that I came in with seven bags of groceries and then parked my car and came in the house the back way, and at this time it was five after eleven. Then I was putting my groceries away and this took about five or ten minutes. I then sat down at the kitchen table and had something to eat. I don't remember if it was while I was putting the groceries away or while I was eating that I heard the shots. I heard one shot and then I heard two shots."

In other words, it could have been as early as five after eleven, when she began putting her groceries away, that she heard the shots, and the implication is that it was not very much later.

"After I heard the shots I heard a commotion that sounded like something falling or hitting something. About fifteen minutes after I heard the shots I was sitting at my kitchen table looking out my kitchen window at the Branions' kitchen window, and I could see into their kitchen. I saw him, meaning Mr. Branion, running out his kitchen door holding a child by the hand. As soon as he was out he started calling, 'Helen.'"

Over the next months, faced with repeated questioning, Mrs. Kentra would say that it was about fifteen to twenty minutes after she came in that she heard the shots, and about fifteen or twenty minutes after that when she saw Dr. Branion emerge from his back door with Joby. Dr. Branion quite clearly came out the back door with Joby between 11:49 and 11:53. Mrs. Helen Hudson confirms this; Mrs. Kentra seems to confirm this in other testimony; William Payne's evidence of the time he spent talking with John tends to confirm it, and the call to headquarters at 11:57 is consistent. Unfortunately, from 11:05 to, say, 11:52 is forty-seven minutes, and Mrs. Kentra's two periods of fifteen to twenty minutes each from first coming home to hearing the shots and then from hearing the shots to seeing Dr. Branion run out the back door at most add up to forty minutes. It would be possible, to be completely even-handed, to split the difference and conclude that Mrs. Kentra slightly underestimated both periods, and that she heard the shots about 11:25 and saw John run out the door a bit after 11:50.

Certain contextual evidence, however, suggests that she heard the shots earlier than that. She speaks of hearing three shots and then a noise like something falling. The falling sound was most likely the heavy table in the utility room being knocked over. But as to the three sounds of shots, the reason she did not hear all the shots is most probably that she heard them while she was still walking around the apartment putting groceries and presents away. If the shots had been fired while she was sitting at the kitchen table, in a room contiguous to the Branion apartment, she would have heard all of them, or at least all of them equally well. And indeed she would later state at the trial that she believed she heard the shots while she was still unloading the groceries.

In any case, Mrs. Kentra repeatedly insisted that her best estimate of the time she heard the shots was just before 11:20. The investigating officers had been to the hospital and knew that John's last regularly scheduled patient had been logged in at 11:30. And it certainly took at least four or five minutes to drive to the house. So they decided that Mrs. Kentra had underestimated the time. She must have heard the sounds about 11:35.

The filtering process also began to work on bits of information favorable to John Branion, causing them to drop out of the record.

After the report dated December 23, 1967, the mention of Leonard Scott's short conversation with John Branion as John was leaving the hospital—a minute or two of alibi and a confirmation of Branion's account—disappears from the police accounts of the day of the crime and never surfaces again.

That same report contains the last clear statement of Helen Hudson's rush upstairs to call the Paynes, and William Payne's rush down the apartment building stairs, his look at Donna's body, his finding of John Branion in the kitchen, his repeating several times "Do you want me to call the police?" before he got an answer. This series of actions would have consumed several minutes—Boyle thought five minutes—before the police were called at 11:57.

The table tipped over in the utility room, the closet door knocked off its hinges in the bedroom, and Donna's slipper lost in the kitchen—signs that the crime took time to commit—appear only in the photos made the day of the crime. They are never heard of again.

The blood spots in the bedroom in front of the closet and in the kitchen on the wall—more evidence of a time-consuming struggle—surface only once, in a crime lab report on the blood types, and are never heard of again.

Meanwhile, the date of the inquest, for which the *Defender* had been clamoring, had been set.

On January 19, 1968, at 10:30 in the morning, an inquest was held on the body of Donna Branion in the Cook County Morgue. The long period of time, nearly a month, between Donna's death and the inquest was explained by a spokesman from the coroner's office as being caused by a shortage of inquest rooms—there were only four in Cook County—and a very large number of corpses.

Calvin L. Smith, the Deputy Coroner, represented the coroner's office. The only witnesses called were Dr. John Branion and Detective Michael Boyle. The coroner's jury consisted of six citizens, all men. It was at that time a firmly established practice to have all-male coroner's juries. The facts of death, and the possible need to view the body, were considered too raw for females.

Donna's uncle William Brown, brother of Sydney Brown and Oscar Brown, had identified the body on the day of the murder, but he was not present at the inquest. So John confirmed what William Brown had said, that the deceased was Donna Brown Branion.

Detective Michael Boyle was the only other witness.

"This was the first time I had seen Boyle since the evening of the day Donna was killed," John said. "This was a month later. None of the other policemen had come to the house since then, either. They never came back to ask about anything—whether I had found anything missing from the house, whether I'd heard anything—nothing. Boyle and I just nodded at each other. I had no idea what he was thinking."

Boyle was called to describe the conditions of the murder scene and the progress of the investigation. He narrated the events of December 22, casting no suspicion on John Branion or anyone else. He described the thirteen wounds on the body and said, "Underneath the victim's body, we recovered four shell casings and three spent pellets. An additional pellet was recovered from the victim's body here at the Cook County Morgue, by the pathologist. These are .380 shells." This, as it turned out, was incorrect. The shells were actually marked Geco 9 mmk.

"We made a diligent search of the victim's apartment, consisting of seven rooms, found no signs of disarray or forced entry.

"The front door of the apartment entered into the living room and secured by two locks. The rear door of the apartment is located in the kitchen and was also secure."

When Deputy Coroner Smith pinned him down on whether the doors were locked, he said, "Shut and locked."

He said the investigators had found no strange fingerprints, but when Smith pursued him about exactly which surfaces had been printed, he said only, "All the doors."

Detective Boyle did not mention the damage in the apartment, or the blood on the kitchen wall, or other crime lab results, or any pathology data such as the bruises, beyond the number and position of the wounds. It was all over by lunchtime.

John went back to the Ida Mae Scott Hospital.

Detectives Michael Boyle and John Mannion went to a conference in the state's attorney's office. The other men present at that conference were assistant state's attorney Thomas Hett and the chief prosecutor of the Criminal Division, Patrick Tuite.

Meanwhile, the Deputy Coroner had recorded the verdict of the inquest jury: "From the testimony presented we the jury find this occurrence to have been murder by person or persons unknown, and we recommend that the police continue to make a diligent search for the person or persons responsible for this act, and when apprehended that he, she, or they be held to the Grand Jury of Cook County, on the charge of murder, until released by due process of law."

The verdict was murder; the inquest was closed.

· CHAPTER ELEVEN ·

O n the afternoon of January 19, after the inquest, a meeting was held in the office of Assistant State's Attorney Thomas Hett. The meeting was private. Present were Detective Michael Boyle, Detective John Mannion, the chief prosecutor of the Criminal Division Patrick Tuite, and Hett. The question to be decided: whether they had enough evidence to go ahead with the arrest and prosecution of John Branion. There are no available notes of that meeting. The Permanent Retention File on the Donna Branion murder at the Chicago Police Department contains no notes of that meeting. The state's attorney's office will not release notes of the meeting or even say whether they have them. But the course of the discussion can be inferred from the case report that Boyle and Mannion filed on January 22, three days later. It tells a great deal about the way the police and prosecutors had begun to home in on John Branion.

By now, close to one month after Donna Branion died, the time of her death had not been established with any greater accuracy than that given by peripheral witnesses. Donna was presumed to have died some time after her sister, Joyce Tyler, talked with her on the phone at 10:15 and some time before the police received the call at 11:57.

Time of death could have been narrowed down somewhat if the first officers arriving on the scene had noted the condition of the blood spatters in the room. Blood spots dry at a fairly predictable rate, first developing a "skin" over the outside, which slows the drying of the inside of the drop. Observations of the dryness of blood spots can be correlated with the temperature and humidity of the room with a reasonable degree of accuracy. This was not done.

The assumption was that the time of death was the time Mrs. Theresa Kentra next door heard sounds.

In this January 22 report, and by inference at the January 19 meeting, the officers summarized Mrs. Kentra's evidence like this: "She stated that *although she could not place the time exactly that she heard the three shots* she stated that approximately 15 or 20 minutes after she heard the shots she saw Dr. Branion emerge from his kitchen calling for Helen Hudson on the second floor." (Emphasis mine.)

The implication is simply untrue. Mrs. Kentra was somewhat more certain of the fifteen to twenty minutes she allowed between arriving home at 11:05 and hearing the sharp sounds than she was about the fifteen or twenty minutes that elapsed after the shots when she heard Dr. Branion calling for Helen. In fact, she repeatedly said that it might have been as early as the time she was putting the groceries away that she heard the sounds, and she never suggested that it was very much later than that.

The suggestion that the time Theresa Kentra heard the shots was completely up in the air is a clear misreading of her testimony. But the report concludes, "The reporting officers place this occurrence at approximately 1135 hours." This time setting, of course, allowed for John Branion to have left the hospital. It did not allow time for him to get home, or for all the events in the Branion home that preceded the ultimate death of Donna Branion.

Then there was the "Joby lie." The January 22 report says that Joyce Kelly, the nursery school teacher, told them that John had arrived at the school about 11:45 to pick up Joby. John had never been sure what time he got there, though he thought around 11:40. It says, "Mrs. Kelly also contradicts Dr. Branion's statement that the child was waiting for him outside the school."

The report summarizes Boyle and Mannion's interview with Maxine Brown. She told them that John had "a girlfriend, Shirley Hudson."

But the most interesting new information in this report concerns the police investigation of the amount of time John Branion would have used driving from the hospital to the nursery school, from the nursery school to Maxine Brown's office, and from Maxine Brown's office to home.

The prosecutors were developing the following argument: if Dr. Branion could get even a few minutes clear, he could drive home from work by a route running past his house, hurry in, kill Donna, hurry out again, and go on to pick up Joby as if nothing had happened. Therefore they were now trying to find out exactly how fast a person could get from the hospital to the school—going past the house—from the school to Maxine Brown's office, and from the office to the house.

Boyle and Mannion say they test-drove the distances with a stopwatch. According to the report, "On six different occasions the reporting officers drove from the Ida Mae Scott Hospital to the aforementioned nursery school; at no time did this trip take longer than five minutes. On six different occasions the reporting officers drove from the Apartment Homes, Inc., offices to Dr. Branion's home; this trip takes approximately one minute; the trip from the nursery school to the Apartment Homes, Inc., office also takes approximately one minute." As far as it is possible to tell from Boyle's report, they did not discuss the other physical evidence surrounding the killing of Donna Branion.

Donna Branion had fought with her killer. There was blood in three rooms of the apartment: the back bedroom, kitchen, and utility room. She had a split lip and bruises on the neck, elbow, and face. These injuries are in the pathologist's report but are not mentioned by Boyle, either as evidence that the crime took a considerable period of time to commit or in connection with John's physical condition. There is no mention of scratches on John Branion's hands or face, bruises on his knuckles, abrasions on his palms from the electric cord, blood on his clothing or shoes or in his car. To have changed clothes would have cost him time, and if he had, disposing of them would have used more time still. The police officers were in continuous contact with him from noon on December 22 to the time, about 5:00, when they let him go home from the police station. There was ample opportunity to look at him closely.

The prosecutors were under pressure from the press to make an arrest. The *Defender*, particularly, was screaming for an arrest. The *Defender* was suggesting that the police were letting the case drop because the victim was black.

Dr. John Branion was not the sort of person that police officers would generally sympathize with. People, by and large, do not sympathize with professionals who earn large amounts of money. A police officer's salary in 1967 was under $7,000. Branion was making about $50,000 a year at the Ida Mae Scott Hospital. His apartment was huge and beautifully decorated. It is quite possible that few of the police officers realized *any* blacks lived like that except entertainers, and they may not have liked it when they saw it. John's many years of working days and going to school nights wouldn't have been visible to them. Add to the luxurious apartment his horses and his Corvette and his girlfriend, and he would seem a most unsympathetic individual. It is possible, in the climate of those times, that calling him to account for his wife's murder—teaching him a lesson— might have seemed a good idea to them.

There was another cultural difference. Most of the policemen and the men in the state's attorney's office working on the Donna Branion murder were Catholics. John Branion had been accused a couple of years before of performing an abortion. The woman had dropped the charges, saying in the end that it was a different doctor, but the police had the record of the abortion case.

They may have believed that John Branion killed unborn babies. And they may have believed he was allied with the Black Panthers. At the very least, they would have resented his assisting the Panthers medically. And his father, the Public Defender, had fought their arrests for three and a half decades. As two people connected with the senior Branion's career as public defender have said, "The Branion family was on the cops' shit list."

Last, he was the only real suspect they had left. All the other leads had run out.

On the afternoon of January 19, 1968, Tuite, Hett, Boyle, and Mannion must have believed they had enough to make a reasonable showing in court. If they failed to convict through lack of solid proof, at least on the books the case wouldn't go "unsolved." At least the black community would know they had tried.

Late that afternoon the prosecutors told Boyle and Mannion to get a warrant for the arrest of John Branion. The detectives went to Judge Dan Ryan in Branch 44. They got their warrant.

By the time Boyle and Mannion arrived at the Ida Mae Scott Hospital with their arrest warrant, Dr. Branion had gone home for the day.

Their report says they couldn't serve the warrant over the weekend because John was out of town. He didn't remember being out of town; he was staying with the children as much as possible. But he thought later that he might have taken Joby along on Saturday and driven out to Indiana to take care of the horses.

On Monday morning, January 22, one month to the day after Donna's murder, the officers went again to Ida Mae Scott Hospital.

John was not expecting them.

He said later, "It was about 10:00 that morning when I saw them come in. At Scott Hospital I worked between three examining rooms—I used to work between four examining rooms—three rooms down one side of a hallway. And, you know, the nurse puts a patient into the one you've just vacated, and you go from one to the other in rotation. Well, I came out of one of the rooms and they were standing in the hall. I said, 'What can I do for you?' And they said, 'We want to ask you some questions and talk with you.'

"Well, I said, 'Okay, let's go down to the doctors' lounge.'"

"And they said, 'No, we'll wait until you're done.'"

"Well, I knew it was serious, then. But I had over an hour of patients in the waiting room left to see. And they sat at the end of the hall in the door of the doctor's lounge all that time."

Just after eleven, as the clinic started to wind down to the lunch hour, they arrested John. It was a quiet arrest in the doctors' lounge. The officers advised him of his rights. John said he had not killed his wife and he asked to call his attorney. He didn't know what attorney to call, so he called Nelson Brown.

He was taken to the County Jail and put in a cell.

"It was *awful*. It smelled of sweat and urine. There was dirt and urine and blood on the floor. I didn't want to touch anything for fear of being contaminated. I was in my suit. I didn't want to sit down, even.

"There were some men, some Organization men a couple of cells away. Prisoners, you know, but the Mafia must have paid for something, because they had steak and champagne for dinner.

"I kept standing up. Nelson came in after a while. I said 'Get me out of here!', but it was too late to post bail for that day. I'd have to stay overnight.

"That was hard. Finally I lay down, but I couldn't sleep. I couldn't believe it all. I kept thinking they would just suddenly realize I was innocent. I couldn't fall asleep and it smelled and people were yelling. And while I was thinking I could *never* fall asleep in there, I guess I did."

That afternoon while John was in jail, Boyle and Mannion went to his apartment. They found three boxes of ammunition on a shelf in a den closet. They took them. Their report that night read:

"Reporting officers recovered from a den closet three boxes of.380 caliber ammunition of the same type and brand name that was recovered at the scene of this homicide on 22 Dec. 67."

That is the totality of their note about the ammunition. The report sounds as if all three boxes are the same brand, and all are labelled ".380." There is no suggestion that any box is partly empty.

"There was absolutely nothing I could do to help myself. Nelson came and got me out two days later, the day the judge had set bond. It was very low, only five thousand dollars, because the judge said there was no significant evidence against me.

"You actually posted ten percent of the set bond, so it was only five hundred dollars. Sydney Brown put up the five hundred dollars. For a while, I thought it was because he had some sympathy. But it wasn't. In private, he was as hostile as ever. I think publicly he wanted to show the world that the *family* was united. Family and respectability was everything to Sydney.

"Nelson got Maurice Scott to defend me. Maurice argued at the hearing that if they actually had a case they should say so. Or otherwise let me go. The arraignment only took one hour. Only Boyle and Mannion appeared. Because there was so little case, they compromised and set the bond low. Bond was set, I think, the next day after the arraignment."

Judge Dan Ryan, explaining the low bond to the press, said, "The state did not furnish any evidence of provable guilt." And Francis Flanagan, homicide commander, told the press that the case against Dr. Branion was "purely circumstantial."

John was frustrated and confused when he tried to imagine how the prosecution could paint a picture of him murdering Donna. His mind went around in circles. "I'd think—well, okay, they figure I went in and shot her. But then, why did I tell them she was careful who she let into the house? Why didn't I tell them she was careless? Or why didn't I just leave the back door hanging open, if I did it, to look like a robber had run out that way? Or break a window, for that matter?

"Why shoot her so many times? I mean, it seemed as if any one of four or five of the wounds were fatal. It didn't make any *sense*! I could have run in and shot her and pulled out a few drawers and broken a window. And if a person did that he really *could* have been out of there in a couple of minutes. But that wasn't what was done! Besides which, I wouldn't have really had to do that. A doctor—if he wants, a doctor can kill a person in a way that is really difficult to detect.

"Or—they were going to make a point that I, as they put it 'had not gone to Donna's aid.' I should never have tried to explain to them that she was cyanotic. I mean, I got to feel I never should have tried to tell them the truth. It would have made a more convincing picture if I'd made something up.

"It was all that much scarier because it was so confusing and so senseless. It was spooky. I knew they couldn't have any evidence against me because I hadn't done it. But they arrested me, anyway. So I thought they were out to get me in some way.

"I couldn't figure out what I was supposed to do. How should I act?"

The state's attorney's office may not have been trying particularly to make sense of it.

Unfortunately, experience teaches police detectives and prosecutors not to try too hard to make sense out of any defendant's behavior. Most of the defendants a policeman or prosecutor deals with are people of below average intelligence who have poor impulse control. They do bizarre, counter-productive, and foolish things. They will go to a neighbor's house, bash her over the head, take money and credit cards, and then go out and try to use the cards. They will rifle an apartment with a stolen key, then break a window from the inside out, leaving glass lying around outdoors, and expect the police to think someone broke *in*.

This is the reality. A prosecutor comes to expect people will behave in foolish, stupid, inconsistent, and counterproductive ways. But this habitual prosecutorial mindset works heavily against the innocent, rational defendant.

If an intelligent, educated man with good impulse control like John Branion says, "Why would I tell you that Donna used good judgment about who she admitted to the apartment if I wanted you to think she let in a prowler?" the prosecutor will say "They all make mistakes." If he asks, "Why would I kill her with my own gun?" they would say, "Happens all the time." If he asks, "Why would I hit her, strangle her, shoot her repeatedly, and force her from room to room bleeding if I was trying to do the murder in one minute?" the prosecutor says, "They all lose their heads."

John Branion, trying to make sense of what had happened and asking himself how they could possibly even suspect him, felt like a character in *Alice through the Looking Glass*.

"And what was just as bad, it was making me have a hard time dealing with the loss of Donna. I was trying to mourn Donna, and I kept getting snapped back to thinking of how I wouldn't have killed her. It was just like getting whirled around. . . .

"Donna was a good person. She was a homebody, but there's nothing wrong with that. She did her job well. She was a good, gentle person. Loving with the children. Really, really gentle. We should have been able to think about her and kind of say goodbye. And here instead we had the newspapers picturing her as some sort of debutante and me as some sort of playboy, and headlines every other day. Plus thinking about what would happen when it came to trial.

"But I didn't really think it would come to trial. I was convinced they'd drop the charges before that, for lack of evidence. I was *sure* of it."

· CHAPTER TWELVE ·

The year 1968 lay directly on the squall line between the conformity of the 1950's and the acknowledged pluralism of the post-seventies. After the upheaval, the United States was forced to acknowledge what sort of place it had always been—the most ethnically diverse nation the world has ever known.

This awareness came at the cost of unprecedented violence.

The nation was running faster and faster into civil insurrection. The long hot summers of the past three years had led everyone—university administrators, police, city government, the National Guard, even the army—to expect worse this time. Police departments were stockpiling riot weapons. None of the causes of anger had vanished. Black rage was expressed against a background of nationwide resistance to the Vietnam War draft. The first four months of 1968 saw angry mass rallies, draft card burnings, boycotts of ROTC and other war-related campus organizations, and the forcible occupation of university administration buildings by students. By spring of that year, resistance to the Vietnam War was so intense, so broad, and so angry that it had driven President Lyndon Johnson to announce that he would not run for reelection.

It was in this context of escalating hostilities between younger and older Americans, between blacks and whites, and between the police and civilians, that the decision to arrest John Branion had been made. Police and prosecutors at the time were under siege not only from the media and from mobs in the streets, but also from their own rebellious children at home. Like any other group, under attack they became more clannish, more defensive, and more self-righteous. Given the tenor of the times, John Branion could have looked to them like a revolutionary monster—a Communist, or at any rate a socialist, a doctor who performed abortions and treated Black Panthers.

Even in the black community, among those who wanted to keep a low

91

profile, Dr. Branion was sometimes disliked. People who knew him well, such as nurses like Betty Adger; patients he had treated for years; and colleagues like Dr. Quentin Young, who would eventually become director of Cook County Hospital but was at this time considered revolutionary by the police—all liked him and many admired him for being outspoken and willing to take a chance. But he was certainly controversial.

Probably most of the policemen who were so heatedly anti-hippie and anti-black in the early sixties would wonder now what they were so upset about. The decade of the Sixties had begun with a type of psychological segregation now almost forgotten. There had been a national furor when Petula Clark, a white singer, had touched the hand of Harry Belafonte, a black singer, on a television variety show. There had never been a black star in a major dramatic series on prime-time TV until Bill Cosby appeared in "I Spy." In the context of the Nineties, it is difficult even to remember the worldview of the Sixties.

By the spring of 1968, John Branion was awaiting trial in a climate of increasing national and local antagonism.

And then, on April 4, Martin Luther King, Jr. was assassinated.

A hurricane of fury broke over the nation. Burning and rioting flashed across every urban area in the United States. In Chicago, large areas of the city went up in flames.

Friday, April 5, mobs raged through the city. Businesses shut down. Rioters smashed windows, set fires, and looted stores. Streams of black young people, many of them small children, carried radios and soap flakes and packs of Coke out of breached storefronts. By Saturday the sixth, 3,000 National Guard troops had been called in to Chicago to patrol the streets. They had orders to shoot if necessary, but no one knew exactly what "necessary" meant. Mayor Daley, never known for his equable temper, issued a statement that was to become infamous: "Shoot to kill arsonists; shoot to wound looters." Between 4:00 and 10:00 p.m. that evening alone, there were thirty-six major fires in the city. All available firemen had been called in and were working twelve-hour shifts. After 10:00 p.m., fire alarms came in so fast that they could no longer be counted. Entire blocks of Madison Street on the West Side were blazing and the air all over the city smelled of oily smoke. Area hospitals treated hundreds of injured. Medical students were called in to help. Two thousand firemen, with a hundred pieces of firefighting equipment, were on the streets and they could not contain the fires. The Department of Sanitation called up a thousand of its employees to help the firemen.

The night sky was orange with flames and shot with spotlights and the flashing lights of police cars. Sirens wailed all night.

By Sunday, April 7, hundreds of buildings lay in ruins. Huge streams of blackened sooty water poured from gutted buildings. Little groups of homeless people stood about, holding whatever belongings they had been able to save, packed in shopping bags and paper cartons. Fire hoses laced back and forth across the gritty streets. Nine people had been killed, all of them black. A total of 10,500 policemen, 6,900 Illinois National Guard troops, and 5,000 regular army troops patrolled the city. They wore full battle dress and carried rifles, grenade launchers, and machine guns. Some of the troops bivouacked in Jackson Park, not far from John Branion's home.

Chicago was a war zone.

A two-mile stretch of Madison Street was totally destroyed, sullen gray smoke rising from the ashes. Over huge areas of the city were burned pockets of destruction. At gutted supermarkets, blacks sifted through the ashes for food.

Mayor Daley ordered a 7:00 p.m. curfew for everyone under twenty-one. He banned the sale of guns, ammunition, and gasoline in portable containers. He banned the sale of liquor in riot areas.

By Monday, police occupied large sections of the city, keeping all traffic off the streets. Police cars, parked as barricades, blocked intersections. Bullhorns blared, "Stay in your homes. Don't come out."

West Side community leaders asked that the riot-torn blocks be declared a disaster area. Fred Peavey, candidate for 29th Ward committeeman, said, "This area should have been declared a disaster area ten years ago. Maybe with the damage done now, we'll get some action."

A group of young people called the Concerned Young Blacks charged that police brutality was the spark that started the riot. They said that some officers from the Austin police district had attacked and beaten young blacks who were marching down Madison Street mourning the death of Dr. Martin Luther King, Jr.

Mayor Daley's order to shoot to kill arsonists had not been followed by the Chicago Police Department. The order went far beyond police guidelines for the use of deadly force. The guidelines stipulated that deadly force was permitted only in cases where the actual life of a policeman or civilian was at stake, or where the police had good reason to believe that the other person was armed with a deadly weapon. It was not permitted in cases where only property was at stake—such as looting or arson of property alone.

The Chicago police actually did a more professional job during this upheaval than police in several other cities—and more professional than Mayor Daley would have had them do. But they were traumatized by the riots and becoming hardened to riot guns, tear gas, machine guns, and mass advances upon civilians, which would have been unthinkable even a year or two before. The riots of April set the scene for the infamous "police riot" at the Democratic National Convention in Chicago in August.

There, finally, the Chicago police would lose their professionalism. In a week of fury, Chicago police, pushed beyond their limit of endurance, charged into mobs, beat reporters, attacked "hippies" and ordinary bystanders with clubs, and smashed the cameras of news photographers, while some of their commanders screamed at them and begged them to stop. Many of the policemen removed their identification badges before the attacks so that their names would not be known. Word of the Chicago police riots went around the world. On the "Today" show, Hugh Downs asked if there was any way to describe Chicago police other than "pigs." The president of CBS News demanded an immediate investigation of an attack on their cameraman. The Chicago Newspaper Guild demanded that policemen who had attacked newsmen be arrested. The president of ABC News protested personally by wire to Mayor Daley. CBS news correspondent Dan Rather was attacked at the convention by an Amphitheater security man, punched in the stomach, and knocked to the floor—while on the air.

The violence at the Democratic National Convention took place two months after the trial of John Branion. But the tear gas, mace, machine guns, and other riot weapons were already waiting in the arsenals. And the attitudes that led to it were already in the minds of men.

To some extent, the violence did much to seize the national conscience. Whites had largely been able to believe that blacks, like whites, were doing better economically in the years after the Second World War. But the news photographs of black children carrying stacks of soap flake boxes from looted stores and sifting through ashes for cans of food destroyed this comfortable picture. Whites saw graphically that many blacks would rather burn their buildings than live in them. And the fact that policemen could beat white press reporters clearly displaying press identification badges gave a great deal of credibility to claims by blacks that they had been beaten by police for no reason at all. The national conscience began to change.

The Constitution of the United States provides for a speedy trial. Because the founders of the country came from European nations where an accused person could be thrown in jail and left indefinitely, without trial or even arraignment, the guarantee of a speedy trial in criminal cases has been upheld for two hundred years as a cornerstone of the justice system.

In Illinois, a defendant held in jail must be brought to trial within 120 days, or let go, a free man. A defendant out on bond must be brought to trial in 180 days. Only if delays occur through the defendant's own efforts, such as pretrial motions, is the time extended.

After John Branion's arrest at the end of January, he began to urge Nelson and Maurice Scott to try to speed up the process. There was no doubt in his mind that he would be acquitted. Since he had not killed Donna, he argued, there couldn't be any evidence that he had. And he wanted it over so that he could get his life and the children's lives back to near-normal.

With the bond posted, John was free to continue working. He went on treating patients at the clinic at Ida Mae Scott Hospital, and picked Joby up at nursery school for lunch. If the hospital had an especially busy day, Maxine Brown would pick up Joby and take him home. She had a son in the same school. Then John would come home as soon as possible and take over.

John had hired attorney Maurice Scott at Nelson's urging. Scott had been a year ahead of John at Englewood High School, so he was a long-time acquaintance.

Nelson advised Shirley Hudson to leave town before the trial. "I had stopped working at Ida Mae Scott Hospital," Shirley says. "I never went back after the murder. I was too afraid to be around there. I thought somebody was out to get John, maybe somebody who hated the civil rights movement. I moved in with a friend and her children, and then I looked for someplace else to work. The trial frightened me but I felt I ought to stay around. John needed support. He was really devastated. Not like himself.

"But then they told me I'd probably have to testify. That was frightening and what was more important, it seemed to me at the time, it was so *unpleasant*. I couldn't imagine getting up in front of strangers and saying I had had an affair with a married man. Maybe I was sort of Victorian still. There were certainly a lot of other people having affairs they weren't being discreet about. And the way it was, it had not seemed wrong. But to think of talking about it in front of strangers—and you can't ever explain, really, how things were—it just made me feel terrible. Still, I'd have to do it.

"But Nelson told me it would only hurt John if I was around. I think it was a mistake. I think now maybe Nelson and the Sydney Browns wanted me away because they didn't want the publicity. But anyway, I left the country."

John later came to believe that he let Nelson Brown make too many decisions for him. He let Nelson make plans for him, when his own instincts might have been different. Going to Vail was a case in point. During the weeks of preparation leading up to the trial, Nelson told John he was working "night and day" on his case.

Many years later John told me, "I didn't seem to have any energy. If Nelson thought I ought to do something, I just did it. It seemed like it was less trouble than thinking about it. I'm really not that kind of person. I make my own decisions, or I always did before that. But I was just—after Donna died, it was like there was something wrong with me. I didn't have the same gumption."

Maurice Scott was taking on a case that was going to be highly scruti-nized, one that would generate a great deal of publicity, and one which would be emotional for him because it involved a person he knew well. Scott was a smallish, balding, dapper man who liked to dress well. He was forty-two years old and his experience included very few, if any, trials this important or with this amount of media attention.

Scott told the press that John Branion was a gentle man, a man incapa-ble of violence, who was being "crucified" on circumstantial evidence. And as the January 24 *Defender* admitted, he included that paper in his ac-cusations. He said the *Defender* had "pressured the police department to step up its investigation and that consequently a hasty arrest had been made."

Assistant State's Attorney Thomas Hett had intended to prosecute the case. But Hett got stuck on another case—a man who was accused of mur-dering a policeman—that had consumed more time than expected. The Branion case could have been delayed, but the judge who was to try it re-fused. "There's a sword of Damocles hanging over this doctor's head," he said, "and he has a right to have it cleared up."

John Branion himself had been telling Maurice Scott the same thing. He wanted to get it over with. In fact, he pushed Scott to go ahead. Here again, John's optimism and impetuousness may have worked against him. Maurice Scott felt he was being rushed.

Patrick Tuite, chief prosecutor of the Criminal Division, took over the case against Branion. Tuite was a youngish, active man, who was an ex-tremely experienced prosecutor. He had, as he said, "gone to verdict sixty-six times." He was keeping count. His junior assistant would be Daniel Weil. Weil in appearance looked a little like Tuite but was less experi-enced. It would be the first time in a trial that Weil would be permitted to address a jury.

Tuite and Weil had just a week to prepare the case, although Tuite had been in on it generally since the January 19 conference on whether to arrest Branion. "I worked day and night for that week," Tuite said later. "Dan Weil and I took the case over and we went out every night, seeing witnesses, visiting the scene, interviewing policemen, running that route, the whole bit. And we put the case together in a week and tried it."

PART TWO

Trial

· CHAPTER THIRTEEN ·

"**M**ay it please the Court," Tuite began his case. "Ladies and gentlemen of the jury: I have an opportunity of speaking to you now in what is known as the State's opening statement, the purpose of which is to tell you what we expect the evidence to show in this case. What I say to you and what defense counsel says to you is not evidence. The evidence that you will hear will come from that witness stand under oath.

"We expect the evidence to show that on December 22, 1967, three days before Christmas last year, Dr. and Mrs. Donna Branion, his wife, lived in a first-floor apartment at 5054 South Woodlawn Avenue in the City of Chicago. By the evidence we expect to show the doctor left the home about 9:00 that morning to take his four-year-old son, by the name of Joby, to a neighborhood club or school for preschool children, located at about 55th and Kenwood in the City of Chicago.

"We expect the evidence to show that about 11:57 that morning the police department of the City of Chicago received a call of a woman being shot and went to 5054 South Woodlawn. An officer arrived there and found Mrs. Donna Branion lying in a utility room, which is a small room just off the kitchen of that apartment, lying there in a pool of blood.

"The evidence will show that Mrs. Branion talked to her sister, Mrs. Joyce Tyler, as late as 10:15 that morning or thereabouts, that she had been well and in good spirits.

"We expect to show that the Crime Laboratory arrived at the scene and recovered at or about the body four expended cartridges as those that are fired from an automatic weapon; it discharges the cartridge; and that under the body were three pellets."

It was 10:00 on a cool Wednesday morning in May, with a forecast of rain. Patrick Tuite, though a young man, had been prosecuting for several years, mostly serious crimes including murder. He was aggressive, articulate, energetic, good-looking, and alert, and affected scholarly hornrim glasses. A juror might well put his trust in such a man. Even this early in the trial, he had accomplished two things:

The first was psychological. He had subtly and constantly aligned himself with the "People" and with large and presumably unprejudiced institutions. He says that he expects "*the* evidence to show" the facts of the state's case. But the defense, he says, will show "*his* evidence." He does not say, for example, "Sgt. Kersten arrived." Nor even the "Crime Lab." He says "the Crime Laboratory arrived." He implies that the scientific institution marched to the scene in all its majesty, with all of its technical expertise, not just a panel truck with some photographic and fingerprint gear. Over time, these techniques have a subliminal but real effect. He would keep it up throughout the trial.

Tuite continued. He told them about John taking Joby to school, about John going to work and then picking Joby up after work, going to Maxine Brown's office—"with whom *he* was to have a luncheon engagement," Tuite said, ignoring the fact that Joby and Donna were presumed to be there as well—then arriving home and finding Donna's body.

Tuite said: "The doctor said he had gone in and seen the body lying there; turned the light on fast, saw the body, turned the light off, and then ran out yelling for help and never went up to the body, never went up to the body, never touched the body, never did anything with regard to the body at that time. But he said he knew she was dead, and when asked why he knew she was dead he said he could see the condition of the lividity in her legs. And we expect the evidence to show Mrs. Branion was fully clothed when found, that she had dark mesh stockings on, and that twenty minutes later, when a doctor pronounced Mrs. Branion dead, the condition of lividity had not yet set in."

Perhaps he wondered whether Scott had studied the crime scene photographs. They show Donna lying with her legs toward the door of the utility room. Her sweater is pushed up, exposing the skin of the abdomen. Her skirt is rucked up high on her legs, showing the tops of the stockings, the garters, and several inches of thigh. Her skin color was easy to see, both in the abdomen and the upper legs. And the stockings themselves? Medium to light, very sheer, showing skin underneath, and made that way especially to set off a pattern of small dark squares.

And yet, though the "dark mesh stocking" argument was trivially easy for the defense to check on, it was also clever. To refute it, Scott might have to call for the photographs to be shown to the jury, and every defense lawyer fights to keep such pictures out of the jury's hands. A jury that sees photographs of the violence done to a victim is more likely to want to convict.

Tuite went on to say, "We expect the evidence to show that Dr. Branion said that he left the hospital at 11:30 and arrived at the nursery school to pick up his son at 11:35, and it is about a five-minute drive.

"We expect the evidence to show that a lady who worked at that nursery school and was awaiting to go to her next assignment kept watching the clock and waiting for Dr. Branion and he did not show up at that nursery school until after 11:45, at 11:45 at the earliest and after that.

"We expect the evidence to show Dr. Branion was a gun collector and had a number of guns in and about his apartment. The officers asked him if he had a weapon capable of firing the bullets found next to the body and he gave them a Colt Commander, and they took it to the Crime Laboratory and the evidence will show that that was not the weapon.

"They returned later that day and they asked him if he had any other weapon capable of firing that type bullet and he gave them another type gun, a Luger, which the evidence will show was not the weapon. They asked him if he had any other weapon which would be capable of firing the bullets fired into the body of Mrs. Branion and he said no."

Tuite described the gun, a Walther PPK, which the prosecution believed was used. Then he turned to the time factor: "We expect further to show that detectives from the Chicago Police Department Homicide Section drove six different occasions at the time of this incident, which was around 11:30 or 12:00 o'clock, in that area, drove the route that Dr. Branion said he took, from the hospital to the nursery school to Maxine Brown's place of employment; they also drove it to the home first and then around; and it shows that that can be done within the time, and that he could leave the hospital, go home, kill his wife, go pick up his son, go to Maxine's, and be home with the time he had and time to spare; they did it six separate times with a stop-watch, so there is no question of time here. . . .

"We expect, ladies and gentlemen, the evidence to show, the evidence from this witness stand, that Dr. Branion, as charged in this indictment, based on the evidence that you will hear, is guilty of the murder of his wife, Donna, and we so ask you to find, at the close of all the evidence.

"Thank you."

The defense presents the second opening statement. Attorneys differ as to the importance of the opening statement, but very few feel it can be thrown away. Maurice Scott rose and said: "Your honor, ladies and gentlemen of the jury: since the defense is not required to prove anything, we will waive opening at this time pending hearing what the state does actually present on their case."

In the avalanche of ill fortune that had come down on John Branion, the political situation outside the courtroom played a part. The city—indeed the whole country—was jumpy and fearful. The riots following the death of Dr. Martin Luther King, Jr. had ended just thirty-five days before in temporary truce, or perhaps exhaustion, but not solution. Large areas of the city looked as if they had been bombed.

The evening before jury selection began, Robert Kennedy and his staff, in Nebraska on the campaign trail, had to vacate their second-floor suite in the Omaha Sheraton Fontanelle because of a bomb threat. In Chicago, at Northwestern University, Roosevelt University, and the University of Chicago, black and white student rebels had seized possession of university buildings and ejected the administrations. Student mobs in France held the Sorbonne.

By the morning of May 15, the first day of jury selection, Richard Nixon had won the Republican primary in Nebraska. Robert Kennedy had won the Democratic primary. A dark-horse outsider, the California governor Ronald Reagan, had made off with a surprising 22 percent of the G.O.P. vote.

Jury selection alone had consumed four days. During the voir dire, as it's called, both sides question the prospective jurors and try to find men and women they hope will be sympathetic to their side. Maurice Scott may have believed the prosecution had a thin case. Still, he knew they would try to prove that John's relationship with Shirley Hudson was a motive for murder, or at least use it to turn the jury against him. If John testified in his own defense, the relationship would surely come out under prosecution questioning. Scott decided to take the bull by the horns. He asked every prospective juror whether he or she would be biased against a man who had committed adultery, and he rejected any who said yes. That first day of interviews of prospective jurors produced only four people who were acceptable to both prosecution and defense, three women and one man. All were white.

The weather was extremely hot and sultry. By night, fifty-five people had died from tornadoes in eight midwestern states.

On Thursday, the second day of jury selection, sixty black students seized the University of Chicago administration building. This made headlines in the papers. On Thursday also, the newspapers reported that Dr. Edward H. Malters, chief medical officer for the sheriff's office, told the sheriff that Mace was not harmful to human beings.

All day Thursday, the sixteenth, jury selection continued. By the evening recess they had chosen only four more, also three women and one man, also all white. There were getting to be a large number of women on the jury.

Potential jurors are called in groups of twenty, known as venires. In the

Wednesday and Thursday venires, out of a total forty people, only two were black. Maurice Scott complained. The judge told him there was no deliberate exclusion of blacks. "The system of choosing jurors resembles a lottery," he said. "The names are selected from a poll sheet at random for such duty, and we have no way of telling beforehand just what the jury's composition will be. On Wednesday there were no Negroes in the venire that came up. But as you can see, today there are two." One was challenged; one was excused because he had a police record.

Jury selection lasted so late on Thursday that no court meeting was set for Friday. That day, the seventeenth, 320 Chicago poor people on a march—most of them black—reached Washington, D.C., where they settled into shacks near the Lincoln Memorial, joining a growing nationwide protest movement against job discrimination.

Sunday, the *Tribune* headlined "Mob Rips Maryland City." The mob was black. The second head was: "New left, Black Power Guide Campus Revolts." Over 120 rebel students had been arrested at Columbia University. Dr. Benjamin Spock, author and pediatrician, would come to trial on Monday for opposing the draft. It was not a good time to be going to trial for anything. It was an absolutely terrible time to be black and going on trial for murder.

On Monday, May 20, prosecutor Tuite and defense attorney Scott interviewed still more prospective jurors and rejected all of them. Even the judge took a hand in the quizzing of jurors. On Tuesday four more jurors were picked, two women and two men. The very last juror selected was the only black, a retired beautician.

Tuite told Bob Hunter, reporter for the *Defender*, that adultery was a motive in the Branion case. The *Defender* printed the remark as a headline on Wednesday. Hunter quoted Tuite as saying, "There is no doubt about that. Adultery was committed and it has to be a key factor." It is not clear whether the jurors had been cautioned at this point not to read newspapers, though the judge did caution them later. But they were not sequestered, and jurors do not obey every instruction.

Tuesday, also, the defense and the prosecution managed to agree on two alternate jurors who would fill in if one of the regulars was incapacitated. These were two white men. Composing the Branion jury had exhausted four venires and nearly eighty people.

Excluding the alternates, there would be eight women and four men.

Tuite surprised reporters just before the trial opened. "We'll ask the jury to return a guilty decision against the defendant," he said, "but we won't ask for the chair."

Veteran reporters found this unusual. John and his friends interpreted it as a sign of weakness in the prosecution case. Some even suggested that the prosecutors knew the murder had taken place about 11:20, when John was at the hospital, and were therefore squeamish about asking for death.

Cynics thought otherwise. In cases that result in the death penalty, reviewing courts typically scrutinize the trial very carefully because of the finality and irreversibility—perhaps the repugnance—of the sentence. The Illinois Supreme Court reviews the trial court record in all death sentences. Cynics thought that the prosecutors in the Branion case chose not to ask for the death penalty for fear that the higher courts would reverse a guilty verdict with a death penalty attached, given the skimpiness of the circumstantial evidence that they had against John Branion. But they would likely let a prison term go by with less attention.

John's place in the courtroom was at a center table, with Maurice Scott sitting on his right and Scott's partner, Lucas Clarkston, to Scott's right. Still farther to the right was the prosecution table, with Patrick Tuite and his younger assistant, Dan Weil. One newspaper remarked that Dr. Branion looked as calm as if he were going out to dinner.

It was not just that his own personality was optimistic. He was surrounded by friends and well-wishers who told him it would turn out all right. Some were friends who knew, from their observation of John and Donna's relationship, that he *would* not have murdered Donna, and some were people from the hospital like Betty Adger, Leonard Scott, and LaHarry Norman who knew, because they knew where he was at the time, that he *could* not have murdered Donna. Relatives and friends stopped by his house in the evenings. His mother and her friends said there was no problem. Nelson came by almost every evening to talk, though he couldn't be in court with John because he was on the witness list. They all assumed the prosecution's case would simply fall to the ground once it got to details.

John's father might have warned them, if John's father had been alive.

The presiding judge in this case, the Honorable Reginald J. Holzer, looked like a large, dark gnome in his black robes. On the street, he favored dark suits and a small-brimmed black homburg hat. Holzer had been a judge not quite two years, and at age thirty-nine was the youngest judge in the Circuit Court. He was far more hidebound than many older jurists. He ran his courtroom firmly. He was quick to sustain or overrule. He required the women to wear dresses and the men jackets and ties. He was reputed to keep a supply of ties in his chambers for jurors who turned up too casually dressed. Judge Holzer also had a fatal flaw—a taste for money. His reputation was already becoming tarnished. It would be many years, however, before the full story of Holzer's corruption became known.

Judge Holzer said, "The State may call its first witness."

The clerk said, "Step up, place your left hand on the Bible and raise your right hand to God."

The witness was Joyce Tyler, Donna's sister. The prosecution had to call her, since she was the last person to contact Donna before death, but Tuite probably did not expect much from her that would be of use to him. Mrs. Tyler was an attractive woman of about thirty-five. Tuite said:

"Would you state your name, please?"

"Joyce Tyler."

He took her quickly through her relationship with the dead woman. Her answers were short. Then he asked,

"And on that date, December 22, 1967, did you have occasion to speak to or see your sister?"

"I had occasion to talk with her on the telephone."

"And about what time was that?"

"I talked with her about 8:30 in the morning and then again about 10:15."

He had her point out John Branion in the court, identify a picture of her sister, tell whether she noticed anything unusual about her sister's voice that day (she hadn't); and he finished with her quickly.

Maurice Scott rose to cross-examine.

"Joyce—Mrs. Tyler, you have known Dr. Branion for how many years?"

"Oh, about 23 or 24, 25 years."

"Your sister and Dr. Branion were married about twenty years, is that right?"

"Yes."

"Now, on the day that you talked to your sister, that is, Mrs. Branion, did she in any way indicate to you that she was having any difficulties with her husband on that day?"

"No, she did not."

"Did she sound happy when you talked to her?"

"She sounded her usual self."

"Now, over the years, Mrs. Tyler, did you ever know of any time or any occasion wherein Dr. Branion ever struck his wife?"

"No, I don't."

This was an important admission. Joyce Tyler probably knew her sister better than anyone else did, other than John Branion. But the prosecution would have been aware that this was coming. They would have asked

Joyce themselves whether she had known of violence between John and Donna, and presumably would have brought it out in their own questions if she had. It was to their interest to let this witness go as soon as possible. When Scott said, after three more minor points, "I have no further questions," Tuite was quick to echo, "I have no further questions."

The second witness that Wednesday morning was vital to both sides. She could furnish the only direct evidence about the actual time of the shooting. This made her, as far as anyone knew at this time, the most important witness in the case.

"Would you call Theresa Kentra."

Theresa Kentra, the Branion's next-door neighbor, was from Yugoslavia and spoke heavily accented English. She presented Tuite with a problem. Mrs. Kentra had consistently stated or implied that the sounds she heard occurred about 11:20 to 11:25. John had been at work then. But Kentra was Tuite's own witness. It was in the prosecution's interest to make her time estimates sound vague, get her to state that it might have been later, that she could have been mistaken, without seeming to bully her. If he were rude or aggressive with her, he would lose the sympathy of the jury. He apparently decided simply not to ask her to be specific.

Tuite said, "Mrs. Kentra, did you have occasion to be in your home on the morning of December 22, 1967."

"Yes."

"And do you remember where you were in the early morning hours of that day?"

"Well, I left 8:30 in the morning, I went shopping, and I came back at 11:00, five after 11:00."

"When you got home did you have anything with you?"

"Yes, I have grocery bags."

"And how is it that you recall when you got home, the time you got home?"

"First I stopped at the school, was a Catholic school, I brought presents for nuns and one of the nuns told me they going to start a party at 11:00. One of the nuns told me that they are waiting for 11:00 because the party would start and the children are very excited."

Tuite asked:

"When you got home did you have occasion to look at your clock?"

"Yes."

"What time was it at that time?"

"Five after eleven."

"And what did you do when you got home at that time with your groceries?"

"First I went and changed clothes."

"All right. And after you changed your clothes, what did you do?"

"Then I started taking groceries out from bags."

"And you were taking groceries out and what were you doing with the groceries as you were taking them out?"

"Putting them in the proper place."

"And were there—what kind of things were in the bags, food?"

"First I have presents for Christmas and then there was food."

"Did you go to various parts of your home or apartment to put these things away?"

"Yes."

Tuite's next question let slip the fact that he knew Mrs. Kentra heard the noises early. And yet, no one noticed, not even defense attorney Maurice Scott: "During the time that you were putting away these groceries, did you have occasion to hear anything unusual, Mrs. Kentra?"

"Yes, I heard, and I thought it was a truck in the alley.

"What did you hear?"

"Well, I heard three sounds. It was like a board fell down, that is what I thought at this time."

"It sounded like a board falling down?"

"Yes."

"Would you tell us what you heard? Go ahead."

"Once, and then twice; two more times and then I heard like a little commotion."

"Now did you continue to put your groceries away after you heard these sounds?"

"Yes."

"And did you hear anything unusual after that, later on that morning, after you were putting your groceries away or following putting your groceries away?"

"Well, not for quite some time, let's say for about twenty minutes or so."

"What happened about twenty minutes later?"

"Well, I didn't hear anything. I just saw Dr. Branion coming out of his kitchen."

"And what did you see him do as he came out of his kitchen, if anything?"

"He was calling 'Helen'."

Tuite asked her a few questions about Helen's relationship to the

Branions and had her identify Mrs. Branion in a picture. But he carefully never asked her to be more specific about how long it was between her arrival home and the moment she heard the sounds.

When Scott rose to cross-examine, he established that Joby was with John when John came out the back door. Then, oddly, he began to ask Mrs. Kentra how close she was to the Branions, whether she ever went over to their home, how far she stood from the Branions' back door, and whether she had ever heard gunshots before.

Possibly Scott had the idea that he should call into question *all* of Theresa Kentra's testimony. Maybe he wanted to suggest she really had heard a truck in the alley, and that the murder had occurred much earlier, maybe shortly after 10:15. At any rate, after several questions he gave up the attempt and homed in on the time of the noises.

"And the sounds you say you then heard, you heard them how long after your arrival home?"

"Fifteen to twenty minutes."

"So the latest it would have been when you heard the shots or sounds that apparently are going to be called shots, would be 11:25, is that right?"

"Could be."

"Could it have been earlier?"

"It could. I did not look at the clock."

"But it could not have been later, could it?"

"No, no."

Now this was not only consistent with Theresa Kentra's statements up to this time, both at her home and at the police station, but it was precisely the statement the defense most hoped for. If the sounds occurred no later than 11:25 and perhaps even earlier, John Branion could not possibly have been anywhere near. He was demonstrably at the hospital at that time, and even the prosecution agreed to that. But Scott went on to blur the impression.

"And we have established by your time that the latest you heard the sounds was 11:25, is that right?"

"Yes."

"Well, let's make it even 11:30, so that if it were 11:30, let's say, it would be roughly 11:50 when you saw them, that is, Dr. Branion and his little boy, right?"

"Yes."

"But if it were 11:25, then it would have been 11:45 when you saw Dr. Branion and his little boy, right?"

"I didn't look at any of the time on the clock, it could be fifteen, it could be twenty minutes, between one or the other way. I cannot tell you the exact time."

He had now confused the witness, whose best recollection had been entirely favorable to the defense. Scott may have sensed this: "But you are positive it was not 11:30 when you heard these sounds, is that a fact?"

Tuite rose. "Objection. That is not the testimony."

Judge Holzer said, "It is cross examination. Objection overruled."

"I cannot be positive, no," said Mrs. Kentra.

So Scott tried to get back to the first answer:

"Are you positive that it was 11:05 when you came home, at the latest?"

"Yes."

"Are you positive it was not longer than twenty minutes when you heard these sounds?"

"No."

"Could it have been less than twenty minutes?"

"Yes.

"Are you positive that it was not longer than twenty minutes?"

"I'm not positive, I just said it could be. I did not look at the clock."

Scott, knowing that she made a statement to the police on the day of the crime, tried to refresh her memory about it. After several questions, he asked Tuite whether he had a copy of her statement. At that point the judge called both counsel into chambers, out of hearing of the jury. Judge Holzer asked Scott whether he needed an opportunity to read the statement. Scott said he had no need to read it. They went back to the jury.

Scott now asked her nine or ten questions about giving the police officers her statement. Then he said:

"Do you recall telling the officers that you came home at 11:05 and that it took about five or ten minutes to put away your groceries?"

"Yes."

But he made the same mistake again, and Tuite remained very quiet, letting him do it:

"Now, did it take you only five or ten minutes to put away your groceries?"

"Well, sometimes it does, sometimes it does not."

"How long did it take on December 22, Mrs. Kentra?"

"Well, I was putting presents away, thinking later on I'd hide them from the children, so I don't know."

"Do you recall telling the officers that when you finished putting away your groceries that you sat down to have something to eat?"

"Yes."

"Do you recall telling the officers you did not remember whether you heard these sounds while you were putting away the groceries or at the time you sat down to eat?"

"Yes."

"Do you recall that?"

"But— "

"Sorry, I didn't mean to interrupt."

"But later on I was thinking about it and I think I heard them when I was putting the groceries away."

This again was *exactly* the statement the defense most wanted. And it was in line with Mrs. Kentra's testimony all along—she tended to think she heard the shots earlier rather than later, and by this estimate somewhere between 11:05 and perhaps 11:20. But again Scott couldn't let it rest. He tried to nail it down and partly succeeded, partly muddied the waters:

"And that took you about five to ten minutes?"

"Five to ten, maybe even fifteen."

"Even fifteen. But the time you are positive is that you got in that house between 11:00 and 11:05?"

"This is the only thing I'm positive about."

"And you are also positive it didn't take you over fifteen minutes to put away those groceries, isn't that right?"

"Well, it takes me ten to fifteen minutes to put away, I'll say that."

"And it didn't take you any longer on this day to put away the groceries than it did on any other day?"

"Well, I think it did, because I went to put the children's presents away. Maybe it did, I don't know."

"I'm talking about on the day it occurred. On that day you knew, didn't you?"

"When I talked to the police officer I say, I think it took me that long. I wasn't certain."

"You know it didn't take you a half hour?"

"Yes, I do."

"It was less than that, isn't that right?"

"Yes."

"And You know you got in the house at 11:05, isn't that correct?"

"Yes."

"So if it was less than a half hour, then at most, let's say, it took you 25 minutes, isn't that correct?"

"Yes."

"And if you got in at 11:05, when you heard these sounds while you were putting the groceries away, then it had to be sometime before 11:30 that you heard the sounds, correct?"

"Yes."

"And you saw Dr. Branion with Joby about twenty minutes later, after you heard the sounds, right?"

"That's right."

"No further questions."

Tuite said, "Fine. I have nothing further."

· CHAPTER FOURTEEN ·

The first two witnesses that Wednesday morning had been civilians and women at that, requiring both Scott and Tuite to be exceedingly polite. But after 10:00, when Mrs. Kentra was dismissed from the stand, Tuite began to call his roster of policemen. These were men whose job aligned them with the state. Tuite handled them in a respectful, even deferential, manner. Scott viewed them as hostile.

Tuite called Officer William Catizone. After establishing that Catizone had been the patrol officer in the police vehicle first to respond to the call, he asked: "What, if anything, did you observe when you got to the utility room?"

"I saw the body of Mrs. Branion laying on the north side of the wall in the utility room."

"What if anything did you do when you saw this body lying there on the floor?"

"I reached for her pulse to see if there was any pulse."

"And what was the purpose of doing that?"

"Well, if there were pulse—"

Scott said, "Object."

But Catizone went on before Judge Holzer could rule: "—I'd call for a wagon or ambulance and rush her to a hospital and save her life."

Tuite now prepared the ground for his later claim that John shot Donna as she lay on the floor. He asked just two questions about the cartridge casings, making no attempt to develop a reason for asking them.

"Did you observe anything else at or about the body when you got to that utility room?"

"I observed two spent cartridges."

"Where were they in relation to the body?"

"They were about, I'd say, ten to twelve inches away from the body."

This is the same Officer Catizone whose filed report dated the day of the murder, December 22, 1967, stated that four empty cartridge casings had been found under the body. Tuite did not ask where the other two

115

cartridges were, but immediately went on to two questions that were trivial, then quit.

Scott cross-examined, and now he seemed surer of himself than he had been with Theresa Kentra.

"You reached for her pulse, is that correct?"

"Yes, sir."

"Which of her hands did you move?"

"I don't recall which one of them I—"

"You moved one of them, didn't you?"

"Yes, I did."

"Did you put it back where it was before you moved it?"

"I put it in the same place."

"As best you could, right?"

"As best I could."

Scott asked whether Donna was breathing. Then:

"Did you put your ear to her chest to see if her heart was beating?"

"No, sir."

"It wasn't necessary, was it, officer?"

There was no response.

"*Was it?*"

"I don't know, sir. I just grabbed the pulse."

"Did she look dead to you when you saw her."

"She looked dead to me."

"Before you ever took her pulse, right?"

"Right."

Tuite on re-cross tried to repair this damage, asking whether Catizone could have seen from the doorway that she was not breathing. Catizone said no, but the exchange ended with a score for Scott, who sensibly declined any questions on re-cross.

Tuite said, "Call Officer Kersten."

Kersten was sworn and stated his name. Tuite established his credentials:

" And what is your duty—what are your duties with the Crime Laboratory?"

"I'm assigned to the mobile unit. The unit is responsible for searching the scene of an incident, recover any physical evidence found and transport evidence to the Crime Laboratory and submit it to the proper units."

Tuite had Kersten explain that he took the photographs at 12:30 and that he searched the area of the body.

"Did you have occasion to recover anything or see anything there?"

"Yes, sir. I saw three expended bullets and four cartridge casings."

Scott, wanting to establish just what these terms meant, said, "Your honor, I don't know what the bullet is."

Tuite snapped, "Stick around and we'll teach you."

Holzer asked hastily, "Just a moment. Is there an objection?"

"No," said Scott.

Tuite said, "Just a comment."

But he never asked Kersten where the empty cartridge casings had been found.

Kersten established the chain of possession when the pellets and empty casings were taken to the lab. Many questions later, Tuite asked about the pellets alone, not the cartridge casings:

"Do you recall where you found the three pellets that have been marked People's Exhibit Number Four, with relation to the body?"

"Two were found under the body, one was found near the body."

After several more minutes of questions to establish that these were the same pellets that the crime lab tested, Tuite ended his examination. He had asked no questions about the blood spots, though Kersten had taken samples, or about the damaged closet door in the back bedroom or the table tipped over in the utility room, which Kersten had photographed, or the blood smear on the kitchen wall, of which Kersten had taken a sample—no questions that would have suggested the murder took considerable time, even though prosecutors usually emphasize any evidence of struggle, chase, injury, violence, and fear. He had asked no questions about where the cartridge cases were. And he asked no questions about the number of wounds on the body. If any of this was to come out of the Kersten testimony, Scott would have to bring it out.

Scott cross-examined: "How did you decide that the body—that she was dead?"

"The condition of the body indicated that she was dead."

"How close were you to it when you decided that the condition of the body indicated that she was dead?"

"Two feet."

"You determined this without touching her?"

"Yes, sir."

"You have seen a lot of dead bodies, haven't you?"

"Yes, sir."

"When you got within two feet you looked at her and knew that she was dead, didn't you, officer?"

"I would say so, sir."

"And you are not a medical doctor, are you?"

"No, sir."

"I don't think I have any more questions for this officer."

The court recessed for lunch.

John and Maurice Scott went to lunch across the street at a restaurant that was known as The Greek's. Friends of John's came by to wish him well.

"I could hardly believe it was lunchtime. The time had gone so fast. There were periods when I seemed to be paying attention to every single word, and then, the next thing, the witness was being dismissed.

"That court building was so familiar to me. In fact, some of the best times of my life were right there. When I was a boy, my father used to bring me here, and sometimes he would let me watch him try his cases. I was so proud of him up there, and would think, that's my father. My father showed me how to pull down the little cone-shaped paper cups that the drinking fountains used to dispense, and how to fill them with water.

"I thought the case was going well. I mean, it seemed to me that Maurice was right. They didn't have a case. The shots were at 11:20. Or before. Well, what could the prosecution possibly do about that? But to some extent I'd abandoned responsibility for myself, for my own defense. I just left it up to Maurice. And Nelson. Since Donna's death I'd been able to carry on my medical practice and go to work, because I was used to it, I was trained for it. But I couldn't make long-term decisions. Or plan any courtroom strategy, for instance. I guess I had no particular plans for the rest of my life. It was just a matter of getting through this, first."

Court resumed after lunch with the testimony of Officer Charles McMullen.

McMullen had been present at the autopsy, where the pathologist, Dr. Belmonte, removed the pellet from Donna's upper arm. He testified at great length to the chain of evidence for this bullet. Although he had witnessed the autopsy, Tuite asked him no questions whatsoever about the number of wounds in the body or any bruises.

McMullen, of course, had also been one of the officers present at the crime scene all of that first day. He made the investigation sound professional and accurate when Tuite asked him questions. When Maurice Scott began to ask specifically about the gun and other details of their investigation, a certain amount of muddle became apparent. McMullen believed, for instance, that John Mannion had been Detective Boyle's partner the day of the murder, though in fact Mannion had been on furlough until January 4.

Scott asked him, "Did you prepare a written report of your activities on this day?"

"Did I what?"

"Did you prepare a written report of the part you did do while you were handy?"

"Anything we inventoried we did."

"Not the inventory. There is the thing police officers, and detectives in particular, prepare which is sort of like a story of what they did in a case. I think it is referred to as a captain's report?"

"Yes."

"Did you prepare one of those in this case?"

"No."

"You did not?"

"No."

"Officer, did either you or your partner ask Dr. Branion in regard to any guns he may have possessed, any questions about guns?"

"My partner did."

"Where did that conversation take place?"

"That was—it must have been in the hallway. I wasn't with my partner when he questioned Dr. Branion about the gun."

Many questions later:

"Did anyone in your presence ask Dr. Branion for a 9 mm gun?"

"I heard talk of it there."

"Did anyone in your presence ask Dr. Branion for a 9 mm gun?"

"I wasn't in the den when they were talking to him about it."

At this point even Judge Holzer became exasperated. He said, pointedly, "Your answer to that question, sir, would be no?"

"Yes, sir."

Officer McMullen had been twenty-eight years a policeman. But when he was pinned down by Scott about the kind of gun under discussion, he said: "I don't know that the caliber of American weapons, .38, .45, and .22 is measured in inches. I don't know that a 9 mm is not measured in inches."

He was dismissed and his partner, Detective John Norris, called.

Norris said he had asked Branion on the afternoon of the murder for a gun "capable of shooting a 9 mm shell."

Tuite asked, "Did you have occasion then to receive any weapon from the doctor when you asked him for it?"

"Yes, I did."

But tests during the day had showed it not to be the murder weapon and Norris went back to the Branion home that evening with Boyle to ask for another gun. Tuite's hope was to show that John Branion had been evasive or had claimed he had only one nine millimeter gun.

"Who was present at that time?"

"Well, there were quite a few people present, I can't very well name them."

"Were these police officers or citizens?"

"No, they were all friends of Mr. Branion."

"And where were these people?"

"Throughout the apartment, in the living room and the kitchen and so forth."

"And did you have occasion to talk with Dr. Branion at that time when you got back to the apartment?"

"Yes, I did."

"And what, if anything, did you ask him at that time or say to him at that time?"

"I asked him if he had another gun in the house that was capable of firing a 9 mm shell."

"And what, if anything, happened then?"

"He says, 'Yes, I think I have another one', and then he went out to this utility room and there was a cabinet, a little cabinet that was locked and they had to look around for the key and after a couple of minutes they located the key and he opened the cabinet."

Scott said, "Judge, he is saying 'they'."

"I don't know who did," Norris said. "I can't tell you who did, to tell you the truth."

"If it was not Dr. Branion then he should say someone other than Dr. Branion," Scott said.

Norris helpfully added, "It might have been Dr. Branion himself."

Judge Holzer: "As far as you know, sir, you don't really know who found the key, is that right?"

"No, I do not, because everybody was looking for it."

In other words, in a situation of some confusion, Dr. Branion let anybody who wanted to look for any gun he could find. Here again, though he tried, Tuite could not demonstrate that John said he had no other guns that could shoot a 9 mm.

When Scott asked Norris about guns specifically, showing him the one Nelson had given them that night, the confusion became more apparent: "Does this gun shoot 9 mm bullets?"

"I was told it does. I don't know. I am not an expert on guns," said Norris, a twenty-seven year veteran of the force, a detective for eight.

"Did it have a clip in it like this when you got it?"

"I think it did."

"Is it in the same condition now as when you got it?"

"I couldn't say for sure."

"You don't know, is that right?"

"That's right."

"Did this one have a clip in it when you recovered it?"

"I think it did."

"Did you ever have an automatic in your possession, Officer?"

"Only that I had recovered."

"Do you know how to load one, Officer?"

"No, I do not."

"Do you know how to remove shells from the clip of an automatic gun?"

"I do somewhat."

"You know how to make one fire, don't you? You know how to arm the guns?"

"Not too well. I am afraid of automatic weapons."

As Scott cross-examined, the police confusion became even more obvious. Scott said, "Did you ever ask to have a cabinet opened in the den? That is the room where the rifles are."

"Only the closet where that one that we recovered was."

"You mean that was given to you."

"It was given."

"It was recovered by someone and given to you?"

"That's right."

"You didn't search for it?"

"No, no."

"And it was not lost, either, was it?"

"No."

"And you never asked Dr. Branion for a Walther PPK, did you?"

"No, sir."

"Did you or any other officer ask him whether or not any money was missing from his home?"

"I didn't ask him."

"Did you ask him whether or not any weapon was missing from his home?"

"No, I didn't."

"When you gentlemen were inquiring about guns did you ask for any ammunition?"

"I didn't."

"Did anyone else in your presence request that he turn over any ammunition he had in his possession?"

"I didn't. Not that I heard."

"And you were present when he was asked about the gun, weren't you, the gun that was capable of firing 9 mm ammunition?"

"Yes."

"In fact, you received the gun on each occasion, right?"

"Yes."

The last witness to be called that Wednesday was Detective Michael Boyle. Young and ambitious, he had made detective early in his career and had been in charge of the investigation. Now Tuite was determined to prove that John Branion had intentionally concealed from them the fact that his Walther PPK was missing.

Tuite asked, "Did you inquire of the defendant whether anything was missing from the apartment?"

"Yes, I did.

"Who was present at that time when you inquired of him?"

"Dr. Branion, myself, and Detective James McGreal of my unit."

"What, if anything, did the defendant say to you when you asked him was anything missing?"

"He said nothing was missing."

"Approximately what time of the day or night was it?"

"This would be approximately 2:00 p.m."

Two o'clock was just forty-five minutes after Donna's body had been taken out of the house, half an hour after John and Donna's daughter Jan returned home and found that her mother was dead. The officers knew that at this point Branion had not searched the apartment; they testified that they saw him sitting in the parlor, unable even to talk.

No officer would ever claim to have asked John any later than this hour whether anything was missing. And no officer would ever testify that John said he had given them all the guns he owned capable of firing *either* a .380 or 9 mm shell. In fact they had asked for a 9 mm during the afternoon, not mentioning a .380. Then, though Norris had thought otherwise, according to Boyle, they asked him for a .380 in the evening, not mentioning a 9 mm and apparently themselves thinking that these were two entirely different calibers of guns.

But what would the jury have believed? They would likely retain the idea that Dr. John Branion said nothing was missing from his apartment and that he had given the police all the guns he owned that would shoot either shell.

In terms of data, score for the defense. In terms of effect? Score for the prosecution.

Tuite took Boyle, his star witness, through the rest of the prosecution's points. Boyle testified that John had said he picked Joby up "out in front" of the school. He testified that John told him he knew Donna was dead "because he could see lividity in her legs."

Then Tuite asked about the gun that was given to them later that night. Boyle confirmed what Norris had doubted or denied, that it was Nelson Brown, not John Branion, who went to find the second gun: "I asked Dr. Branion if he had any.380 caliber weapons and he replied that he only had one, and he told Mr. Nelson Brown where the weapon was and Mr. Nelson Brown then went into this utility room and removed a.380 caliber automatic pistol from a cabinet that is located in that room."

Tuite laboriously confirmed the identity of the gun Boyle received, making the chain of possession through the police department sound wonderfully accurate, and then moved on to the search of the Branion apartment, which took place the evening of the day John was arrested, January 22, a full month after the murder.

"Did you search the premises located there?"

"Yes, sir."

"And would you tell us what, if anything, you found pursuant to that search?"

"From the cabinet in the utility room we recovered a manufacturer's pistol target, a pistol brochure describing Walther Automatic Pistols, a clip from an automatic pistol, and from a den closet in the apartment we recovered three boxes of .380 caliber ammunition, one box containing 25 rounds, a second box containing 21 rounds and the third box containing six rounds. The boxes with the 21 and 25 were Geco manufacture."

The report filed by Detective Boyle the evening of the day they searched the apartment was different: " . . . reporting officers recovered from a den closet three boxes of .380 caliber ammunition of the same type and brand name that was recovered at the scene of this homicide on 22 Dec. 67. From a wooden cabinet in the utility room of the apartment the reporting officers recovered a .380 magazine and a manufacturer's target with a serial 118274 written on the target." In this report there is no mention of the actual brand name of the ammunition, which must have been readily visible to anyone looking at the box. Nor any mention that any of the boxes was not full. Or that one box was not the same brand as the other two. "Three boxes . . . of the same type and brand name" seems explicitly to say that they were all the same brand. The data given about the target, which is much less important, is much more complete. These discrepancies give rise to questions. Was the box with the missing four rounds ever in John Branion's closet? Was it perhaps among the boxes purchased later by the police to test-fire? Or was it found in the closet, but found full and some of the rounds been used for the test-firing?

Tuite went on to try to show that the ammunition had been hidden: "Will you describe particularly where in the den closet that you found these?"

"The closet is located on the south wall of the den; these shells were found on a shelf on the right hand side of the closet."

"Were they on the shelf or were they in a container?"

"They were in a paper bag."

John, aghast, turned to Maurice Scott.

"Would anybody think I'd just leave them there if I'd used them to kill Donna?"

"No."

"I mean, why wouldn't I take them away and throw them out the window of the car or something?"

"I don't know."

"I could have done it on my way to Indiana to feed the horses. I could have done it any time that whole month!"

"I understand."

"It doesn't make any sense!"

Tuite had followed his past procedure again with Boyle: no questions about the number of wounds, though Boyle had testified to thirteen bullet wounds at the inquest. No questions about where the cartridge casings were, though Boyle had testified at the inquest to all four being under the body. No questions about the evidence of struggle throughout the apartment, though Boyle was there and had examined the premises. Tuite went directly to the matter of driving time:

"Now, Detective Boyle, did you have occasion after December 22, 1967, to drive your automobile or an automobile assigned to you through various stops that Dr. Branion said he had made on the day of December 22, 1967?"

"Yes, sir."

"Who was with you at the time, sir?"

"Detective Mannion."

"Did you or Officer Mannion have anything with you when you were driving besides your clothing and weapons? Did you have anything unusual with you that day?"

"I carried a stopwatch."

"Approximately what rate of speed were you traveling," Tuite asked, "at these times you were driving?"

"The legal speed limit, 30 miles an hour."

There followed an extremely long series of questions about the timing Mannion and Boyle undertook. The questions were specific. The officers had driven the route, they said, six times, always between 11:30 and 12:30, on six separate days.

There were questions about whether the streets were wet or dry, whether there was a parking lot behind Ida Mae Scott, what the speed was, what route was taken between the hospital and the nursery school, between the school and Maxine's office, between Maxine's and the Branion house. Times were honed down to a second-by-second level of apparent accuracy.

And yet these times differed significantly from those in the January 22 report, which presumably summarized their test drives and were the reason the state decided to prosecute John Branion in the first place.

Of the trip from the nursery school to Maxine Brown's office Boyle testified, "I couldn't give the exact time . . . but it was always between one and two minutes." The January 22 report had said "approximately one minute."

Of the trip from Maxine's office to the house, he testified at the trial: "The fastest time it took was slightly over a minute, the slowest time less than two minutes." The January 22 report: "approximately one minute."

Of the drive from the hospital to the nursery school, he testified at the trial: "The fastest time it took us to drive directly from the Hospital to the Hyde Park Neighborhood Club was between four and five and a half minutes. The longest time was five and a half minutes." The January 22 report: "at no time did this trip take longer than five minutes."

Why did he allow more driving time at the trial? Perhaps at the trial the prosecution had to allow for the fact that somebody might actually try driving the route. Occasionally judges or juries are taken out of the courtroom to see some setting that they wouldn't properly understand otherwise. Or the defense might have called in an independent traffic expert to drive the route and testify. But even these times were improbable, and their given minimum total time of six minutes was impossible. But no independent analysis of the distance would be made until years later.

There was, in all, a total of sixty-seven questions from Tuite on the matter of the time it might have taken John to drive these routes. The effect on the jury must have been one of extreme care and accuracy.

And never once did any question reveal that they had done it all without starting and stopping the car, getting into or out of the car, parking, or handling a child. Had the defense not asked later about these matters, the jury might have believed that it really took, for instance, "slightly over a minute" for John Branion to go from Maxine's office to his home, with Joby in tow. Similarly with the other times.

In our judicial system this form of deception is perfectly legal. Appellate courts do not reverse verdicts just because the prosecution was clever. And it is almost impossible to have a case overturned later on the ground that the defense failed to bring out important evidence. Nevertheless, if the defense counsel fails to ask just the right questions, the effect of this kind of prosecutorial cleverness is fundamentally to mislead the jury on essential facts.

Scott caught the deception when he cross-examined:

"When you got ready to leave the hospital, were you in the squad car when you started the stopwatch?"

"Yes."

"Was your motor running?"

"Yes."

"Then you started the watch, right?"

"Yes."

"Then when you arrived at Dr. Branion's home did you stop the stopwatch?"

"After we had pulled to the curb we would stop the watch."

"Did you shut the motor off?"

"No."

"Did you get out of the car?"

"No, sir, we didn't."

"Did you go in the house?"

"No."

"You didn't leave the car at all. It was cold every time you did it, is that right?"

"We didn't leave the car."

"It was cold?"

"Yes, it was cold."

"Then you put that time down, then you took off to the next stop on the route, is that right?"

"Right."

"When you got there you stopped the watch again, right?"

"That's correct."

"When did you stop the watch, as soon as you got there or as soon as you pulled in to the curb?"

"On all occasions we would pull to the curb and stop and then we would stop the watch."

Scott said, "By the way, when you got to the nursery school, whose little boy did you use?"

Twenty years later, Tuite would still remember a wave of reaction in the court as Scott said this. Boyle either didn't understand or pretended not to.

"I don't understand your question."

"Well, I assume when you went to the nursery school you went there to cover some time about checking a kid, right?"

"No, sir. I performed these tests in order to ascertain how long it would take to drive from one location to another."

"The purpose of the test was to determine how long it would take Dr. Branion to do the things he told you he did. Isn't that what you did that for?"

"Yes."

"Now you are telling us you stopped the car at the nursery school and as soon as you got to the curb you stopped the watch. You parked the car and stopped the watch, is that right?"

"That's right."

"Then you took off to the—from there you started the watch again and you went over to where Miss Maxine Brown worked, right?"

"That's right, sir."

"What time did you allow for him to pick up his son at the nursery school?"

"I allowed no time for that."

Scott made the same point for Boyle's arrival at Maxine Brown's office. Boyle responded by trying to lecture the defense attorney.

"As I have already said, Mr. Scott, we were interested in finding how long—"

Judge Holzer corrected him, "Just please answer the question, sir."

"We allowed no time."

"You allowed no time is the answer, right?"

"Yes, sir."

"Did Dr. Branion tell you his son was with him when he arrived there at Maxine Brown's office?"

"Yes, he said he took the boy into the office with him."

"You anticipated my question. Now sir, am I going to understand, without belaboring this, that at each stop you made no allowance for parking and leaving the car?"

"On each stop we parked our car. However, we did not allow for leaving the car."

"Cutting off the motor, getting out and returning. Nor the handling of the child in a couple of instances, is that right?"

"That's right, sir."

"So your minimum time of six to twelve minutes, we have to add to that the time it would take to park the car, get out, go into some place and come back to your car, start it over again and leave, right?"

"Yes, sir."

"But one other thing. What month did you make these runs in?"

"January of 1968."

"I know, officer, you are aware that December 22 was three days before Christmas?"

"Yes, sir."

"And this first street you used, 51st Street is a business street, isn't that correct, sir?"

Boyle tried to play it down:

"Between Prairie and South Park there are business establishments, yes, sir."

"And there are stores that sell clothing, there are stores which sell toys, there are stores that sell liquor and, in other words, it is a street of nothing but businesses, isn't that right, sir?"

"That's right, sir."

At this point Boyle began to cough so badly that Scott asked for someone to get him some water and Judge Holzer asked him whether he was all right.

By the end of that day Scott had scored four more points: That even Boyle himself did not know on December 22 that a 9 mm short was more or less interchangeable with a .380 shell, so he could scarcely have asked John for either in a way that would have necessarily included the other; that John Branion had left Boyle free to search the whole Branion apartment if he wished on the day of the murder, because John never objected to any search; that Boyle had never informed John that he was in charge of the investigation, so John could hardly have known he should tell Boyle if he later found anything missing from the apartment; and that his report containing the word "lividity" had been written and filed *after* John's arrest, a month after the day, December 22, when the word had presumably been uttered.

John was very optimistic. Billy Hooks, LaHarry Norman, Maurice, and others crowded around. "Everybody told me at the end of the day that it was going well. I thought they were right. I didn't like the way that Boyle said things. It seemed to me he was trying to twist things and sound a little too sure of what he said and did.

"But I couldn't see what difference it made. The point was, I hadn't been in the house when Donna was killed.

"All my friends said it was going okay."

Judge Holzer said to the jurors: "We are about to close up shop for the day. You have appeared to be a very attentive and indulgent group thus far. I am confident you will retain this composure and attitude. . . .

"I instruct you not to attempt to learn any facts about this case from any source outside this courtroom. Don't get in a car and start driving around the South Side."

· CHAPTER FIFTEEN ·

Thursday morning Tuite opened with Joyce Kelly, the teacher at the Hyde Park Neighborhood Club where Joby went to nursery school. Joyce Kelly usually worked at the school from 11:15 to 3:15, so she ordinarily did not see Joby Branion in the morning. That particular day, however, the head teacher was sick and she was filling in. She worked from 8:30 to 3:30.

"Mrs. Kelly, do you recall the time you saw the defendant, John Branion, Jr., pick up his son at the Hyde Park Neighborhood Club on that day?" Tuite began.

"It was between a quarter to 12:00 and ten to 12:00."

"And how were you able to ascertain the time?" Tuite asked.

"My break began, which was 11:35. I went to the lounge about ten minutes and walked out beyond the lounge into the office to notice the time. It was about ten to 12:00 and I saw a man pass."

"Was John Branion, the boy, out in front waiting for his father to pick him up on that day?"

"No."

Now Tuite had laid the groundwork for the "Joby lie," the idea that John Branion had intentionally lied, telling the police he had picked his son up in front of the school, instead of going in.

Scott cross-examined:

"Now, what room," he asked, "was Dr. Branion in, if any, when you saw him helping his son with his coat?"

"I was in the office and he was outside standing. I mean, as he walked from the all-purpose room there is some chairs there and there was a table and he laid his coat on the table and held Joby."

"His coat?" Scott asked.

"His coat."

"Who is "his'?'

Joyce Kelly said, "Dr. Branion's coat, his own coat."

"Dr. Branion took his coat off and put it on the table, right?"

131

"Yes."

"And then he helped his little boy on with his coat, right?"

"Yes."

"Now, from the time you saw him arrive to the time you saw him leave, about how much time would you say elapsed?"

"I don't know."

"Five minutes?"

"About five minutes I would say."

Scott could not know that Tuite was going to develop the "Joby lie." There was no way at this stage for him even to know it was being considered. From the defense point of view, he had got it into the record that John had spent several minutes inside the school.

"Now you say when you saw Dr. Branion arrive you noted the time, is that correct?"

"Yes, it was about quarter to 12:00 or ten to 12:00."

Scott asked a long series of questions about the accuracy of the clock, trying to cast her entire estimate of the time into doubt, but the primary effect was to annoy Mrs. Kelly.

When Scott said, "No further questions," Tuite wisely did not ask for re-cross, but let the impression of Mrs. Kelly's certainty remain in the minds of the jurors.

What followed turned out to be the most bizarre testimony of the case. Maxine Brown, friend of both John and Donna, who had been at the party at Nelson Brown's the night before the murder, was about to make John look like a heartless monster.

Maxine Brown caused as much debate in the judge's chambers as she did in the courtroom. Before Maxine was even called to the stand, Tuite asked for a conference in chambers. He wanted her treated as a hostile witness. If Holzer granted it, Tuite could examine Maxine Brown as if she were under cross examination.

But Scott objected. He knew Tuite wanted Maxine to testify to John's affair with Shirley Hudson. Scott wanted to keep it away from the jury. Tuite wanted the jury to hear it, but for his purposes it would be almost as good if he asked the questions, if Scott then objected, and the jury was left to use its imagination. Tuite had a second point he wanted Maxine Brown to prove—that John called her up out of the blue the night before the murder to ask her to lunch. Tuite wanted later to claim that John needed Maxine to witness his finding Donna's body.

There is a theoretical problem with a witness who is not reliable. Who knows what is a lie and what is the truth? The attorney, in this case the state, wants some of her testimony to be disbelieved and other statements to be believed, an inconsistent and difficult position to take. But answers that are dragged out of a witness seem more convincing. Tuite may have been hoping for that.

Holzer denied the state's motion to call Maxine as a hostile witness. If they called her, he ruled, it would be as a state witness.

But before any further testimony was heard that day, Judge Holzer sternly addressed the jury: "It has been brought to my attention that one or two of you may have been taking notes. I don't know whether this is the case or not. I will instruct you that you are informed not to take notes. You are to observe carefully and use all of your mental resources, including your memory, but you are not to take notes. If any of you have taken notes up until this point, I request you tear them up and throw them away."

The courtroom ban on jurors taking notes is an anachronism in the law. In the days when many jurors were illiterate or semiliterate, such a prohibition may have made some sense. It was believed that the jurors who could write would use that skill to overawe the others and force their opinions on the jury as a whole.

In the case of the Branion jury, all of whom could read and write, it made no sense at all. And in the case of John Branion's defense, which was going to depend heavily on a specific sequence of times, juror notes were a necessity. It would be of the utmost importance to John Branion for the jury to keep track of what time certain events happened and how long they took.

All federal courts now permit jurors to take notes. Most state courts have now also reformed their rules on note-taking.

Maxine Brown, a pretty, usually vivacious, and cheerful woman, walked to the witness stand. John thought she looked confused and very frightened, but he knew her well. The newspapers described her as poised. "She wasn't a smart person," John said. "She had other good characteristics. A sweetness. Warmth. But she wasn't smart. And I thought she looked on the stand like she'd had a few drinks." She perched on the witness chair, to John's eye as if she wished to be anyplace else.

Tuite had Maxine testify to where she lived, in the same apartment complex as the Branions. Then he brought up the subject of the lunch invitation. He asked: "About what time of the day or night did you talk with Dr. John Branion, Jr.?"

"Well, I would say probably after 10:00 or 11:00."

"At night or in the morning?"

"It was at night."

"And where were you when you talked to him?"

"Sitting on the side of my bed getting ready to go to bed."

"Was this a personal conversation or a telephonic conversation?" Tuite asked.

"Telephonic."

"Did you call him or did he call you?"

"He called me."

"Did you have occasion at that time during that telephone conversation to make arrangements to see John Branion, Jr. the next day?"

"I was invited to lunch from that conversation."

In fact, Maxine had been at the party at Sonja and Nelson's condo the night before the murder. Both Sonja and Bill Hooks remember Donna and John together inviting Maxine to lunch during that party.

A few minutes later, she gave a wildly wrong answer to Tuite's question about John and Joby coming to pick her up for lunch the day of the murder.

"Where did you see Dr. Branion?"

"He came into my office, he and Joby, to pick me up."

"And about what time of the day or night was this?"

"I think it was a little after eleven—"

"And—"

"Or very close to eleven."

Not only did the prosecution know it had to be close to twelve, not eleven, they *wanted* it to be closer to twelve. It is inexplicable that she was so far off, when she would have been expecting John and glancing at the clock. Tuite moved quickly on to other questions.

Maxine testified that John and Joby had spent a couple of minutes in her office.

Tuite asked about the route to the nursery school from the office. Then, without warning, he said:

"Now, Mrs. Brown, do you know a woman by the name of Shirley Hudson?"

"Yes."

"Who is Shirley Hudson?"

Scott said, "Object."

Judge Holzer said, "Sustained."

Tuite went ahead anyway. "Do you know what Dr. Branion's relations were with Shirley Hudson?"

Scott said, "Objection."

Judge Holzer said, "Gentlemen, let me see you in chambers."

And they were out of the court again. When they returned, the judge asked the jury to disregard the last question. Unfortunately, neither jurors nor other people can erase their own minds at will. The jurors probably remembered at this point Scott's questions in voir dire, when he asked them whether they would be prejudiced against an adulterer.

Prosecutor Tuite went right back to asking questions about Shirley Hudson, and after several more such questions, and more objections from Scott, he asked:

"Did you know whether Dr. Branion had any girlfriends?"

The defense objected. This time Judge Holzer overruled the objection, and Maxine Brown said she did not. Tuite asked a similar question, the defense objected again, the judge overruled it again, and Maxine ducked it again. And again. And again. Finally, Tuite said:

"Mrs. Brown, did I have—did you have occasion to talk to me yesterday, which would have been the twenty-second day of May, 1968, in my office on the second floor of this building? . . . Did I ask you the same question I just asked you as to whether you were at that apartment with Dr. Branion?"

The defense rose to object.

The judge said, "Let me see you in chambers, gentlemen."

And the jury sat there, more suspicious than ever.

When the prosecution, defense, and judge returned, Holzer had overruled the objection, and Tuite went on questioning Maxine Brown about what she had told him the day before. But she was still vague.

"At that time did I again ask you if you had been in Shirley Hudson's apartment with the defendant on the day after the death of his wife?"

More objections.

The court ruled she could answer, Tuite asked:

"Do you understand the question?"

"No."

He repeated it.

"And what was your answer then?"

"I said no."

In a skeptical tone, Tuite said, "You said no."

Scott said, "Your honor, I object. He is echoing the witness' answer and putting his own inflections on it."

Judge Holzer overruled.

Tuite asked question after question after question and Maxine Brown still said she didn't know. The jury must have been growing more and more suspicious. Then Tuite sprang a new one: "Following the death of Mrs. Branion on the twenty-second day of December, 1967, did you accompany the defendant on a trip to Colorado—"

Thus, Tuite subtly suggested to the jury that John had gone to Colorado shortly after the death of his wife. Maxine had not gone to Colorado, of course, but because the question was inserted into a series of questions about Shirley Hudson, it left the impression that John went off with his girlfriend two days after the murder.

Tuite went back to the lunch invitation after dropping this bomb. Again he developed the theme that the luncheon invitation was the first time John had ever called and invited Maxine to lunch since Maxine had started work in September. Maxine apparently was having misgivings about what she had said in Tuite's office and kept trying to duck these questions:

"I don't rightly remember."

Later she said, "I really can't be positive that that was the first time he called me—"

Finally, Tuite gave her the typed statement she had made the day before and asked her to read it to herself. He asked solicitously, "Would you like some time to read that through, Mrs. Brown? It is a single-spaced document and the typing looks pretty small."

But Judge Holzer mercifully called recess for lunch. It was now a quarter to one. He said sternly to Maxine Brown, "I will instruct you, ma'am, you are not to talk to anyone—" But Maxine must have seemed distracted, so he said, "Are you listening, ma'am?"

"Oh, yes."

"I will instruct you that you are not to talk to anyone. You are on the witness stand. You are under oath. You will return to this stand at a quarter to two. . . . When we return in one hour you are to be exactly the same person you are now except you will have read that document. It is as though we are taking a two-minute break for you to read that document, do you understand?"

After lunch, Tuite asked Maxine: "Now, calling your attention again to the twenty-third day of December, 1967, did you have occasion to go to the apartment of one Shirley Hudson?"

"Yes."

"And were you with the defendant in this case, Dr. John Branion, Jr.?"

"Yes."

"Then did the defendant in this case have occasion to speak with Shirley Hudson?"

"Yes."

"All right, and were you present during that conversation?"

"No."

"Where were you?"

"I was in the bathroom crying."

"And when you testified earlier this morning that you had not been there, that was not true, is that correct?"

"Correct."

Prosecutor Tuite demanded, "And you are telling the ladies and gentlemen of this jury under oath that you were not there, was that to protect the defendant?"

Scott objected.

Judge Holzer sustained the objection. Now Tuite mounted a long series of questions about John and Donna, which he must have known would be objected to—and must have guessed the objections would be sustained.

Tuite said, "Would you consider it to be a happy, normal marriage or normal relationship?"

"Object."

"Sustained."

"Did you notice anything unusual about their marital relationship?"

"Object."

"Sustained."

"Did you know of any difficulty between Dr. Branion and his wife prior to her death?"

"Object."

"Sustained."

"Did you know of any plans for divorce by Mrs. Branion prior to her death?"

"Object."

"Sustained."

Tuite had caught Scott again in a double bind. Though there was no evidence of trouble or plans for divorce between John and Donna Branion, the jury received the impression, first from the questions and second from the objection, that there was something to hide. But Scott could not comfortably have let Maxine Brown answer. She was so unpredictable that she might have said almost anything.

The jury must have believed John could hardly wait to see Shirley after Donna's death, and most jurors may also have believed that John and Donna were on the verge of divorce.

What was Maxine Brown trying to do?

She may have been trying, misguidedly, to help John. He said later he thought that was her intent. Or she may have been simply confused. But if she had carefully worked out a plan to make him look bad, she could hardly have thought of one more successful.

The rest of Thursday was bad for John, too.

Tuite devoted the remainder of the day to showing that one of John Branion's guns might have been used in the murder.

Bill Hooks, who had been at Nelson's party the night before the murder, testified that he had bought a Walther PPK for John as a belated birthday present many months before. Hooks was exceedingly uncomfortable testifying against a man who was his close friend. When the attorneys finished with him, he hurried from the stand.

A bullet fired from a Walther PPK has ballistics characteristics like the bullets that had killed Donna. A Walther PPK is not necessarily the only gun that does this, though the prosecution would try to show that it was.

In fact, the defense could perfectly well have stipulated that, as far as anyone knew, the gun that shot Donna might have been John's, since he had a large collection of guns and it could have been stolen by an intruder that day.

Maurice Scott chose not to stipulate any such thing. If he had, he would probably have been able to avoid the jury hearing a lot of the technical testimony that followed. Strictly speaking, the prosecution can bring in evidence even if the defense stipulates to it. But if the prosecution tries to bring in too much of it, the defense can properly ask the judge to cut it short, since it does not prove anything that is at issue. The problem with this expert gun testimony was that, while it only showed—after hours of questions—that John Branion's gun might have been used, it *sounded* so official, so scientific, that a juror could hardly help but believe it was important. Why would the state go to all this trouble if it weren't?

Tuite first called John Mannion, the detective who had been Michael Boyle's partner. Mannion had been on furlough at the time of Donna's death. And now the only new piece of testimony he had was that he had gone out and purchased a Walther PPK at the Oak Lawn Gun Shop for the lab to test fire. Tuite, however, also had him testify to going to the Branion apartment with Boyle on January 22 and finding the target and the boxes of ammunition. Boyle had already testified about this. Thus Tuite re-emphasized the discovery of the ammunition for the jury.

Tuite then had Mannion testify to buying the test gun.

Scott cross-examined but succeeded only in emphasizing the ammunition and target a third time in the jurors' minds.

Mannion was followed by Burt Nielsen, firearms identification technician at the Chicago Police Department Crime Laboratory. Nielsen would be the last witness that day. Prosecutor Tuite asked a dozen questions, some ludicrously intricate, to set up Nielsen's qualifications and knowledge.

Tuite said, "And approximately how many weapons have come into your hands since you have been working at the Crime Laboratory firearms identification section for the last seven years for your comparison and for your identification?"

"That would be in excess of 15,000."

Tuite asked Nielsen exhaustive questions about guns. He had Nielsen describe what lands [the raised ridges inside gun barrels] and grooves [the depressions between the lands] were, and how they impart spin motion to the bullet when it is fired, and also mark the bullet. He had him describe how a comparison microscope is used to compare these barrel markings on spent pellets. He had Nielsen elaborate the chain of possession through which the pellets, cartridges, and guns passed as they were tested. He asked seventy-one questions in all, designed to show that Nielsen was an expert and that Nielsen believed only a Walther PPK could have fired the bullets that struck Donna:

"Do you know in your experience in the crime laboratory and in your experience prior to that with weapons, of a weapon that fires .380 automatic ammunition that gives a characteristic of six lands and grooves with a right twist that has a loading indicator other than the Walther PPK?"

"No, that's unique to the Walther PPK."

The most Tuite could prove was that a Walther PPK had probably fired those shots. The best he could hope for was for Maurice Scott to be drawn into an unconvincing fight about it.

Maurice Scott rose to cross-examine.

"Have you ever, sir, examined an Ortgie, manufactured in Germany?"

Scott named several unusual guns whose barrel left ballistics marks on the pellet similar to the Walther PPK. But these guns were all very rare in the United States. In addition, Nielsen had never said that the markings on the pellets by themselves were unique, but that taken together with the loading indicator markings on the empty cartridge casings found at the scene of the crime, they indicated a Walther. Hoping to cast doubt on this, Scott said:

"Now, is there anything about these pellets that makes you know they had to come out of these casings?

"No."

Technically, the implied argument was correct. But with both the pellets and the casings found at the scene of the crime and both of the same caliber, this suggestion must have seemed utterly far-fetched to the jury. It implied that Donna had been struck by pellets from one gun and the empty casings of another gun had been left at the scene of the crime. Had Scott been able to support this notion with any other evidence, it would have been helpful. By itself, it gives an impression of desperation.

Scott did better in casting doubt on the care Nielsen took in identifying the guns themselves.

"You probably examined a thousand guns in January and February?"

"Last year we got in 10,000 alone," Nielsen said.

"I'd like to know how you remember examining this one."

"Our laboratory case number is inscribed."

"What is inscribed?" Scott asked.

Nielsen took the gun to point out the case number. "Our laboratory case number. Each gun that comes in, we have a laboratory case number, and that is marked on all the weapons." He was turning the weapon in his hands, in increasing confusion. Puzzled, he said, "We have a laboratory case number here some place."

Nielsen kept looking for the number and not finding it.

"Take your time," Scott said. "That's the first time I noticed you doing that, now. I didn't notice you doing that before. I want the record to show that this witness is now somewhat dismantling this weapon in an attempt to find the laboratory case number to ascertain whether or not he examined it."

"I don't seem to be able to locate it, but possibly it might, be—"

"It might be somewhere, right?" Scott said sarcastically.

Scott did the same with the Colt Commander, and again Nielsen couldn't find the case number. Scott said, "So when you sat up there a few moments ago and looked at this gun and said that you fired it, tested it, and the shells didn't come out, you were guessing, weren't you?"

But while the impression may have been that Nielsen was a little too proud of his knowledge of firearms, a little too proud of the number of guns he had tested, and a little too ready to identify any weapon handed him by the prosecutor, this questioning did no more than that. It did not really undermine his basic expertise. No juror was likely to decide on this evidence, for example, that a Walther PPK was not used to shoot Donna Branion.

When Scott had finished with Nielsen, Tuite wisely had no cross-examination. It had been a very good day for the prosecution, and Tuite must have been thoroughly satisfied.

The court adjourned until Friday morning at 10:30.

CHAPTER SIXTEEN

On Friday, Tuite planned to present his last witness and close his case. But his final witness, the pathologist Dr. Belmonte, was about to blow the case out of the water.

The Friday session did not begin until 2:00 in the afternoon.

"Just after the jury was seated," John said, "and just before the entrance of the judge, I noticed the jurors looking at something on the table or bench in front of them. They would look down at it and then glance up at me. Since the judge had not yet come in and the court was not in session, I just got up and walked over to the jury bench to see what it was. I guess it was bold of me, but after all it was my whole future, whatever happened here. What they were looking at turned out to be a photograph of Donna, dead and bloody. I hurried over to Maurice and asked him if this was proper. He said it wasn't, and he spoke to the prosecutors about it."

Then the attorneys went into the judge's chambers.

Tuite told Judge Holzer, "For the record, People's Exhibit Number One was a photograph of the deceased, just for identification purposes. We would not seek to introduce that." He asked, though, to introduce another photograph of Donna lying dead on the floor of the utility room.

Scott objected. And then, apparently referring to the first photograph, Scott said, "There is no dispute that this woman is dead and that she is Donna Branion, so I couldn't see the purpose for it, nor did it contradict the police officers as to what position she was laying or what they saw."

In chambers, Scott and Tuite argued at great length about admitting other evidence as exhibits—the guns the police had purchased that had *not* been involved in the crime, the casings found at the scene, the pellets, the target, the clips, the box of ammunition with the four missing rounds, and so on. This ate up the early afternoon. By the time Tuite, Scott, and Holzer went back to court, there was not much afternoon left.

The only witness the jury would have time to hear that Friday was Dr. John Belmonte, coroner's physician with the Cook County Coroner's Office. He described Donna's wounds in an abbreviated way: "There were

141

multiple bruises and abrasions about the head and neck of the decedent. There was a bullet wound in the right upper eyelid, two bullet wounds about the right clavicle in the area we refer to as the supraclavicular area; one in the left supraclavicular area." In fact, the autopsy protocol describes two in the left supraclavicular area.

"There was also a bullet wound, several bullet wounds, of the right shoulder and there was another bullet wound of the back." The autopsy protocol lists three wounds in the back.

"About the neck, there was an indentation about the neck which would be similar to one which would be inflicted by a rope or cord, and this was three-eighths of an inch deep about the neck and there was a discoloration in this indentation about the neck, and that was about the extent of the findings on the external examination."

Tuite asked no questions about any of the bruises, or the indentation around the neck. Instead, he asked about the internal examination. Dr. Belmonte, not surprisingly, described massive bleeding. There was damage to both carotid arteries, both jugular veins, and the arch of the aorta, which is the largest artery of the body, leading from the heart. Rupture of the aorta ordinarily produces death within seconds, though Tuite did not ask about that.

Belmonte said, "We also found that the larynx, which is the voice box, and the small bone about the larynx were undamaged."

Tuite left that remark alone.

"Doctor, you mentioned the bullet wounds. Could you tell whether these wounds were of entrance or exit?"

"I was able to determine that the bullet wound of the right upper eyelid, and of the right base of the neck, the two on the right base of the neck, and the one at the left base of the neck were bullet wounds of entrance. The remainder of the bullet wounds I could not in truth say whether they were entrance or not."

The autopsy protocol states that the wounds of the back were believed to be wounds of exit.

Tuite asked forty more questions about the autopsy. But not once did he ask how many bullet wounds there were altogether, nor did he ask how many shots Dr. Belmonte believed would be necessary to inflict the wounds on Donna Branion's body.

John was whispering furiously in Maurice Scott's ear.

"Ask him about the bruise on her neck!"

"Why?"

"It must have been from pressure, a depression like that—I mean, pressure over quite a long time."

"What makes you think so?"

"If the hyoid and cricoid weren't broken, it can't have been very *hard* pressure. So to get that deep a bruise, it must have been a long time!"

"Hyoid and what?"

"Just say voice box. Ask him!"

A bruise does not develop on a dead body, because bruises are produced by blood under pressure from the pumping heart being forced out of damaged capillaries. And bruises do not develop instantly. Generally, the more severe the blow, the quicker the bruise will form. Bruises that develop not from sharp blows but from continual pressure take quite a while to form. Scott asked:

"How long would it take a bruise, say, ordinarily, to form?"

"It depends upon the severity of the blow and the location of the hemorrhage," Belmonte said.

"Can a bruise form in ten minutes?"

"It could."

"Now, you saw a bruise on her neck which was three-eighths of an inch in depression. There was a discoloration of the skin which would be like a mark left by a rope, which was seven inches long, approximately. How long would you say that it would take that bruise to form?"

"That particular type of a bruise, sir, would be considered as one which would be formed under pressure, and could be formed within the length of time it would take to apply significant pressure to make a depression three-eighths of an inch to form within that length of time."

Belmonte said that with a great deal of hard pressure, such a bruise might be formed in thirty seconds. But in this case, as Scott rightly pointed out, there was evidence that the pressure was not great:

"Well, you made a statement a moment ago that the voice box wasn't damaged."

"That's correct, sir."

"What else did you tell us wasn't damaged under there?"

"A small bone above the voice box called the hyoid bone, sir."

"Now, if a person put enough pressure on to do what you say you could do in thirty seconds, they then have to apply pressure to those bones, a terrific pressure, wouldn't they?"

"The amount of pressure that would have to be applied would, in most likelihood, result in a fracture of a portion of either one of those structures."

"But none of those structures were fractured, were they, sir?"

"That's correct, sir."

"So as a consequence, we can now assume that this discoloration about her neck was not caused by a tremendous pressure, but by a pressure over a long period of time, can't we?"

"You may likely assume that."

"Wouldn't you assume it?"

"Excuse me, so I may more accurately answer the question. When you say a long period of time, what length of time did you have in mind?" Belmonte asked.

"Would you tell me how long would be a long period of time to make a bruise like that if the pressure weren't great?"

"I would say fifteen minutes to a half hour."

Sensation at the defense table! John Branion's friends in the gallery sat up. John held his breath.

The crime took fifteen to thirty minutes, just for the bruise on the neck alone, leaving out everything else! This made it impossible for John Branion to have murdered Donna, even if the shots had been fired as late as 11:35, because the strangling would have had to start by 11:20 at the latest.

Scott, anticipating that Tuite would try to find ways around this answer, pinned the point down even further:

"In other words, like you put a rope around a person's neck, say, and you drug them about with this rope and kept it on their neck, right, but not enough to strangle them?"

"That's correct, sir."

"If you put a great pressure on, you would cut their air off, wouldn't you?"

"In the location of this, well, if I may clarify that statement...you would fracture either one of the two structures, I would say."

"Which would cut off the air?"

"Yes, most likely."

"Without air you die, is that right?"

"Correct, sir."

"Now, doctor, there is something that I want to ask you that I am curious about. If I placed a rope about the neck of a woman who was dead, could I turn it pinkish-blue by choking her?"

"No, you would not."

"I have no further questions."

Tuite had no questions, either. Skilled prosecutors have a rule—when testimony has gone against you, do not ask extra questions that will only emphasize the answers in the jurors' minds. He would cast doubt on Belmonte when he couldn't be contradicted—in closing argument.

Dr. Belmonte was the last prosecution witness. At the end of the Friday session, the prosecution rested its case.

The court adjourned until Monday.

CHAPTER SEVENTEEN

J ohn Branion was suffused with relief.
"I figured now I could put it all behind me. I'd be out of the shadow of the crime—not just that I was found innocent because there wasn't enough evidence, but *proved* to be innocent because I wasn't even there when the crime took place. I couldn't feel like celebrating. Some of my friends wanted to. But there was still Donna's death. And there was still whatever was left of the trial.

"I had gotten way past the stage of wanting to find out who had really killed Donna. I had been under just too much of a threat myself. I figured we'd never know. You hardly needed convincing that there was random violence in the city. I figured Donna had opened the door that morning without being sure it who it was. She let somebody in. The wrong somebody. Maurice had told me all along—and he'd said it to the newspapers too—that it was not up to the defense to prove me innocent, it was up to the prosecution to prove me guilty. And they hadn't. I mean, here was the state's own witness, Dr. Belmonte, showing I couldn't possibly have killed Donna. Maurice told me that on Monday morning he was going to ask Judge Holzer for a directed verdict."

A directed verdict is one in which the judge instructs the jury to find the defendant innocent. It is granted in the rare cases where insufficient evidence has been presented, or where evidence exculpating the defendant has come out, and the judge therefore feels it would be improper even to let the jury consider guilt. Defense attorneys frequently ask for a directed verdict at the end of the prosecution's case, sometimes just for effect, when there is not much hope of the judge granting it. But in this case Maurice Scott believed he had an excellent chance.

On Monday morning at 10:00, Scott introduced his motion for a directed verdict. He argued to Judge Holzer, in chambers, "The state, I'm sure, is well aware, and I know the court is, that basically, what we have had up to this point is a circumstantial evidence case, that the burden, of course, is on the State to proceed and to prove the defendant guilty or at least to establish at this point that the deceased met death in this instance as a result of a criminal agency, this, of course, is undisputed. We are not going to tell the court she committed suicide. The burden is on the State to show that the defendant, Dr. John M. Branion, was present at the time that the offense occurred. And finally, the State must eliminate, if nothing else, the possibility that some other person may have committed this offense."

Scott argued that the State had never proved that the shots could have come only from a Walther PPK. This was a losing argument. He might better have argued that there were thirty guns in the Branion home and there was no evidence whatever that John Branion was anything more than their owner. He went on to the more telling points: that John did not have time to commit the crime and that Theresa Kentra's testimony tended to place the shooting before 11:30.

Then he hit the most important evidence, that Dr. Belmonte said the bruise alone would take fifteen to thirty minutes to produce. This was far more time than John Branion had to spare.

He concluded, "I think because the State has failed to place Dr. Branion at the scene when these events began—if I assume they got him there before they ended—I do not think the State has shown that Dr. Branion did anything to his wife other than to have the tragic experience of walking into his home and seeing his wife lying dead. I think the State has failed utterly to establish a prima facie case. I think they have, in effect, shown that it is impossible through their own witnesses for Dr. Branion to have been present when this crime was committed."

Patrick Tuite countered by making the times as vague and fluid as possible: "We have the evidence that the police were called at 11:57, we take fifteen or twenty minutes from that and we've got it (Mrs. Kentra's noises) at about 11:37 or 11:42, plenty of time for Dr. Branion, whose testimony— we've got testimony he left the hospital about 11:30, we also heard testimony he is only two to three or two to four minutes away from the hospital to his home, which would give him sufficient time, making the time about 11:35 or 11:37, 11:42, for him to be home."

Tuite repeated that the gun was John's.

For the first time Tuite argued the "Joby lie." "We further showed that the defendant said, when he went to pick up his child, the child was out in front; we showed the child was not out in front."

And he repeated the "lividity lie." "The defendant in effect lied to the police when he said he didn't go to the body because he saw lividity. . . ."

Tuite made the sociological claim "that fabrication or falsification of evidence is an admission of guilt and that innocent people do not lie to the authorities about their whereabouts or what they did on a particular day and we have had the defendant doing it on more than one occasion." In fact, one of the favorite sayings of police detectives who talk with a lot of witnesses is "everybody lies."

Tuite then summed up Dr. Belmonte's testimony this way: "He said at one time, he said, the pressure is thirty seconds and he said—how long would it take for the bruise to form? He said, about fifteen minutes. The bruise was there when the police got there. . . . You can put something around somebody's neck and apply pressure and leave."

Was Tuite trying to plant the idea that John stopped home, put a cord around Donna's neck, for some inexplicable reason, left her there alive (and doing what?) while he went to get Joby and call on Maxine, and then came home to shoot her? But this notion would make hash of the idea that John intended to bring Maxine home so that she could witness him finding the body. Or did Tuite want the judge to think that John put the cord around Donna's neck, shot her, left her dead—since those gunshot wounds would kill her in seconds— and that while he was out the bruise would continue to develop, even though she was dead? This scenario was inconsistent with the facts, too. Donna's neck bruise is described as seven inches long. Just about the length to go around the front half or two-thirds of her neck. This is precisely the characteristic physical picture of a bruise inflicted while a person is being restrained by a cord held in an assailant's hands. Had the cord been tied around her neck, there would have been dents in the back of the neck from the knot, and the bruise would have extended all the way around the neck to the knot.

Or did he simply want to confuse the issue sufficiently so that Judge Holzer would think *something* could have been arranged by John Branion to produce those effects?

Maurice Scott indignantly reread the relevant eight questions and answers between him and Belmonte. Then he summarized, "I don't think, Your Honor, there is any doubt Dr. Belmonte meant this pressure had to be kept up continuously, you could not apply it and stop, it had to be a continual pressure and the person had to be alive."

Judge Holzer then read his own notes on the testimony:

"The Court's note with regard to the neck are as follows: Marks on neck, like rope, as left here would be applied slowly as to not break bones, as though a person was roped and dragged around for fifteen minutes or thirty minutes, neck discoloration was pinkish bluish." So far, this sounded good for the defense. Then in an apparent nonsequitur, he said:

"Motion for a directed verdict will be denied."

John, when Scott told him, was thunderstruck. But Scott reminded him that the jury had heard Dr. Belmonte's testimony, so there shouldn't be anything to worry about. Judges don't often grant a directed verdict, anyway.

It was the defense's turn to mount a case. Judge Holzer asked Scott, "Are you ready to proceed with your defense, sir?"

"I would like about a ten-minute recess," Scott said.

There was research that could have been done in John Branion's defense, and was not done. The defense could have hired an expert to drive the route that John would have driven the day Donna was killed. An expert could have impeached the police claim that the whole route could have been driven in six minutes. The defense could have hired a criminologist to study the crime scene photographs. Such a study would have revealed evidence around the apartment showing that other events surrounding the murder took quite a long time to take place. The defense could have given the pathology report to an independent pathologist, to try to determine how many wounds there were, how quickly Donna died after she was shot, and how many shots were fired to produce those wounds.

There were also several witnesses who could have been called. Weeks before, when the defense and prosecution exchanged their lists of witnesses, Scott had included the nurse, Betty Adger, the pharmacist, LaHarry Norman, and the lab technician, Robert Wadley, all of whom had seen John as he left work that day. They could have testified that Dr. John Branion was at the hospital past 11:30. So could the hospital administrator, Leonard Scott, who was not on the defense list, presumably because John Branion did not remember running into him on his way out of the hospital. The police knew about Leonard Scott's evidence, but of course the prosecution would not call him. Cottrell Meadors, a friend who had seen John and Joby stopping at a stop sign at 54th Street and Dorchester, was on the list, because, as he says, "I called Maurice Scott and notified him of the time and the conditions under which I had seen John."

But Scott had not interviewed them. The pharmacist, LaHarry Norman, was not even subpoenaed.

Betty Adger had been subpoenaed and was waiting to testify in the witness room. But she says Scott had not interviewed her as to what her testimony would be.

Cottrell Meadors was there, too. Many years later he said in an affidavit, "During the trial, I was subpoenaed to testify by John's attorney. I went to court and was interviewed by two members of the State's Attorney's staff, who informed me that they had a right to ask what the nature of my testimony would be. I never met John's attorney and was never called to testify. I have not met John since prior to Donna's death. Though almost eighteen years have elapsed, I can still picture John talking to his son."

In view of all the disasters that later rained down upon John Branion, it seems strange that a stronger defense wasn't mounted at the trial. But that is hindsight. At the time, it must have seemed that the jury verdict was a foregone conclusion.

The prosecution in its opening statement had claimed that Branion left the hospital at 11:30 and the murder took place after that. The next-door neighbor heard shots most probably around 11:20. John Branion had visited the two stops, the nursery school and Maxine Brown's place of work, and spent some time inside both places. The pathologist for the prosecution testified that the strangulation alone, without all the other activities that must have surrounded the murder, took fifteen to thirty minutes. No testimony had ever placed the weapon in Dr. Branion's hand. No testimony had suggested that he was scratched or showed any sign of having been in a struggle.

Each time an attorney places a witness on the stand, he risks the possibility that the other lawyer will make the witness look bad—confuse him, suggest some ulterior motive, question his eyesight, discredit him or his testimony some way. Therefore, it is often better not to use witnesses you don't absolutely need. Scott had for ample reason argued to Judge Holzer that the prosecution's own evidence had proved John Branion couldn't have killed Donna Branion. He may have felt it best to leave well enough alone.

Tuite must have expected Betty Adger to be Scott's first witness. Instead Scott called Nelson Brown, Donna's brother. Nelson had not been at the house the morning of the murder, nor had he been at the hospital. He had been in court that day. But he had gone to the police station with John on the afternoon of December 22, when the police were questioning John. Scott wanted to use Nelson to refute the Joby lie and the lividity lie. But he probably also wanted Nelson's presence on the stand to show that the family of the murdered woman was willing to testify on Dr. Branion's behalf. He probably wanted to show what kind of person John Branion was.

Scott attacked the "lividity lie." He asked Nelson to tell the jury what John had said when the detectives asked him how he knew his wife was dead.

"He said that when he came into the utility room he flicked on a light and he immediately could tell that she was dead," Nelson said. "And the question was 'How?' And he said, 'From her coloring.' And he went on to—he sort of felt his skin and said, 'You could see that cyanosis had set in.'"

Scott asked, "At any time did you hear Dr. Branion tell officer Boyle or any other officer that he knew that his wife was dead because he had observed lividity in her legs?"

"No."

Scott turned to the "Joby lie."

"Do you recall a statement by Dr. Branion relative to where or what he said concerning his picking up of Joby?"

Nelson said, "Yes."

"Would you relate what he said as best you can recall it in relation to Joby?"

"That he left the hospital, went by Hyde Park Neighborhood Club, and that his son was ready."

Nelson also had an interesting piece of information about the gun. He said that about 10:00 or 11:00 the night of the murder, John told him there were two guns missing from his collection. As this was after they got back from the police station and after John had finally got the children to bed, it was a reasonable time for John to have started to search the house. Nelson testified also that, at the police station that afternoon, no one asked John whether any weapons were missing from the apartment.

And he testified that, after a long period of waiting at the police station the afternoon of Donna's death, Sgt. Anderson came and told him that they had talked to Theresa Kentra and as a result of her statement they knew John was not guilty.

Tuite's best strategy was to discredit Nelson. It was too much to ask the jury to believe that Nelson, if he were a good man, would defend a person he thought had killed his sister.

His cross-examination started off mildly enough. He asked Nelson's profession. Nelson said he was an attorney. Then he had Nelson describe the locks on the Branion apartment doors. Next, he asked Nelson what had happened at the police station that afternoon and whether Nelson was there as John's lawyer or as a family member. And then he attacked:

"You were at the apartment, except for the time you were at the police station, you were at the apartment from 2:30 into the late evening hours?"

"Early morning hours."

"Or early morning hours. And did other people go over to the house—"

"Yes."

"—besides yourself?"

"Yes."

"Other members of the family or other friends?"

"Yes."

"Scotch and bourbon flowing pretty good?"

"No."

"A lot of people drinking?"

"No."

"No?"

With considerable restraint, Nelson said, "It was not a happy occasion."

Insinuation. Tuite did it again later:

"Mr. Brown, do you know a girl, a person, by the name of Shirley Hudson?"

"Yes."

Scott objected; Holzer sustained.

"On the Sunday following the killing, were you still in Chicago, sir?"

And again:

"Were you aware, Mr. Brown, of the marital relationship, that they were married, the marital relationship between your sister and the defendant?"

Tuite also asked about Nelson's testimony that Sgt. Anderson told him John had been exonerated, trying to cast doubt on it. When Tuite finished, Scott took over on redirect examination and asked Nelson to elaborate.

Nelson Brown said, "We were walking toward the front of the police station to go out the door, Dr. Branion, Sgt. Anderson, and myself, and Sgt. Anderson said, 'Everything is okay, we've talked to Mrs. Kentra and what we first heard—she has been to the station, she has talked to us and there now seems to be about a twenty minute or half hour time lapse between what she heard as shots and what she—'"

Tuite quickly rose and objected.

Tuite then asked questions on recross examination, making Nelson Brown the most cross-examined witness in the trial. He had Nelson admit that he had never mentioned to the prosecutors that John had told him guns were missing from the apartment. The implication was that Nelson did not really know the guns had been stolen, John had merely told him so. Or that Nelson was the kind of person who was not eager to help the police.

After Nelson was excused, Scott asked to speak to the State's Attorney and Judge Holzer outside the presence of the jury.

Scott was worrying about whether he should put John on the stand. The guarantee in the Constitution of the United States is that "no person shall be compelled in any criminal case to be a witness against himself." No defendant has to testify. But Scott knew that jurors wonder why a defendant won't testify—as they see it, he is afraid to testify. The prosecution is not allowed to comment negatively on the fact that the defendant doesn't take the stand. But the prosecution hardly needs to comment; the jurors notice it.

"I wanted to testify," John said. "It seemed to me I had to testify. The jurors naturally wanted to know what sort of person I was. Of course they would. So would I, if I were a juror. It just makes sense."

Scott had spent long hours the night before at the home of Eugene Pincham, an attorney and black community leader who would later become an appellate court judge. Pincham argued that Scott *must* put John on the stand, that the effect of not doing so would be suicidal.

But Scott was afraid the prosecution would ask about Shirley Hudson.

Pincham argued that nothing the state's attorney could ask about would be so destructive as not putting John on the stand. He argued that adultery was not proof of murder and that John simply had to say to the jury, "I did not kill the mother of my children."

Pincham said that the case might well be lost if John did not testify. He talked with Scott until 2:00 a.m., at which time he believed Scott was convinced and would put John on the stand.

Pincham came to court that Monday, May 27, to see John Branion testify.

In chambers, Scott's partner Lucas Clarkston told Judge Holzer that they had been thinking of putting the defendant on the stand "to testify what took place December 22, 1967, only, and we feel that the law is that cross examination can only go to what is raised on direct examination and would be limited to what is raised on direct examination, that is what we feel the law is."

This meant: we don't want him asked about his relationship with Shirley Hudson.

Tuite said, "There is no question, except if he gets up and says he didn't do it, we can go into everything, into his background, that would indicate he did do it."

Meaning we'll ask about Shirley Hudson.

Scott said, "And this leads us to this adultery."

"I don't know where it leads to," Tuite said. "I wasn't the first to bring up the adultery in the first place. It wasn't in the record, the whole voir dire was conducted by the defense on the question of whether adultery and a man having affairs with a woman for six years would affect them."

As of that moment, Scott knew he could not keep Tuite from asking John about Shirley Hudson. He decided not to let John testify.

The defense rested its case.

· CHAPTER EIGHTEEN ·

With the defense case at an end, the prosecution was entitled to call rebuttal witnesses. Prosecutor Tuite intended to drive home the "lividity lie" and the "Joby lie," which Nelson Brown had claimed John never uttered. Tuite wanted to discredit Nelson Brown and other parts of his testimony, particularly his claim that Sgt. Anderson had told them on the afternoon of the murder that Theresa Kentra's testimony cleared John. If the jury believed Anderson had said this, they might believe that the charges against John had been trumped up later. Tuite hoped to show that Anderson had never even met Mrs. Kentra.

He called Detective McGreal first, who restated all three points, very much as Tuite wanted.

"During that conversation did you have occasion to hear the word lividity?" Tuite asked.

"Yes, sir."

"Tell the ladies and gentlemen of the jury what the circumstances were under which you heard that word."

"I asked Dr. Branion how did he know his wife was dead and he stated he saw lividity in her legs and blood," McGreal said.

"At any time during the course of this conversation with the defendant did you hear the word cyanosis?"

"No, sir."

"At any time during that day did you hear the word 'cyanosis?'"

"No, sir," McGreal said.

"And will you tell us what if anything was said with regard to the picking up of his son at the Neighborhood Club?"

"The doctor stated that he went to the Neighborhood Club and he was in a hurry and as he pulled up to the Neighborhood Club his child was standing on the sidewalk and he put him in the car and left."

When Scott cross-examined McGreal, some interesting facts emerged about the way the police had kept records of what John said:

"Did Dr. Branion answer all the questions you asked him?"

155

"Yes, sir."

"Was anybody writing while he was answering?"

"Yes, sir."

"Who was writing?"

"I was, sir."

McGreal showed Scott the paper on which he had written John's answers.

"You didn't double up or write very tiny to squeeze in the answers, did you?"

"No."

"And the only answer you squeezed in and wrote real tiny was the one about lividity?"

"That is the only one, as you call it, squeezed in, yes, sir."

"What do you call it? Is it written smaller than the other writing on the paper?"

"Some of it is."

Later, after McGreal had claimed that Nelson Brown told John not to give a written statement, Scott asked, "Now, just what is a written statement to you, sir?"

"A question and answer type statement."

"What is this, sir?"

"Those were notes that I had made of questions that I would—that I wanted to ask the doctor and I jotted those notes down and then as I received the answers I would write the answers in, that is the reason why you call it crowded, because that question was already written before the answer was given."

A few questions later, Scott said, "Now, sir, I'll ask you if those questions were all pre-written, without a double space between them? If you will look at that question and the question that follows it, how did you know to leave a large space of almost an inch between that question and your final question, before you knew the answer?"

"The only reason I can give to that is because I hadn't thought of that question at that time."

Scott said, "May I suggest a better reason, sir?"

Tuite said, "Objection, judge."

"Sustained."

Scott said, "Now, sir, if that be true, when you told this jury a moment ago that all these questions were pre-written, that wasn't true, was it?"

Tuite objected, but Judge Holzer decided to let McGreal answer. McGreal wanted the question repeated. The reporter repeated the question.

"Now, sir, if that be true, when you told this jury a moment ago that all these questions were pre-written, that wasn't true, was it?"

McGreal said, "No."

Scott also made the point that John Branion was cooperative about the questioning, as he had been about letting the police search the house.

"Now, officer," Scott asked, "did Dr. Branion at any time tell you, don't write down my answers?"

"No, sir."

Scott let the jury know that the police did not need to keep such casual notes. He asked McGreal to tell the jury about Area One homicide, whether they had a stenographer employed there.

"There are several in the building, sir," McGreal said.

"Were there any employed on that day?"

"I suppose they were around there, sir."

"Did you bring a stenographer into that room where Dr. Branion was?"

"No, sir."

Tuite re-called Detective Michael Boyle.

"Officer Boyle, on that date, on December 22, 1967, in the police station or anywhere, did you have occasion to hear the word 'cyanosis'?"

"No, sir."

Then Scott cross-examined. Boyle admitted that John never asked anybody to stop making notes on what he said. Boyle claimed Anderson never talked with Nelson at the station outside of Boyle's presence. But Boyle was busy with many different matters that afternoon, and Nelson was left alone for long periods of time. There really was no way that Boyle could have known for certain of his own knowledge that Sgt. Anderson never spoke with Nelson alone.

Scott also hit the bad note-taking again:

"Do you have any stenographers employed there?"

"Yes, sir, there are stenographers employed."

"Did you bring one in?"

"No, we did not."

"Did Dr. Branion refuse to answer any of your questions?"

"No, he didn't."

"And Detective McGreal was busily writing, right?"

"Detective McGreal took notes."

"You would rather say most anything than to say Detective McGreal took a written statement, wouldn't you?"

Tuite objected. Boyle was excused as a witness. Judge Holzer called a short recess.

The prosecutors were frantically hunting Sgt. Anderson, who was not in the witness room, but was just coming on duty at Area One about this time. The recess was called in order to give him time to get to court.

Sgt. Harry Anderson was a light-skinned black man, about six feet in height and balding, wearing plainclothes, who was assigned to Area One homicide. Once he arrived, Tuite took him through the lividity question and then to the Joby lie, but what Anderson said about Joby was: "The nearest I can recall he said he picked up his son at the nursery school."

It was important to Tuite to get more, and he asked the question again and again, with different phrasings. "Do you recall if he said where his son was when he was picked up?"

Scott objected. "It has been answered."

Judge Holzer said, "Sustained."

"Do you recall what the words the defendant used were at that time?"

Scott objected.

Holzer overruled.

"As near as I can remember," Anderson said, "he stated, 'I left my office and went to the nursery school and picked up my son."

Tuite said, "And did he say where—"

"Object," Scott said.

Judge Holzer sustained and Tuite dropped the subject.

When Tuite gave way to Scott to cross-examine, Scott immediately asked, "Did you at any time state to Nelson Brown that we have talked to Mrs. Kentra and we have cleared up the crime and Dr. Branion is now absolved or words to that effect?"

"No, sir."

"Did you talk to Theresa Kentra that day?"

"No, I did not."

"You have never talked to Mrs. Kentra in your life?"

"No, I haven't."

"Never heard of her before?"

"Only in the reports."

But he also did not remember seeing Detective McGreal taking notes, even though he had been into and out of the room where they were questioning John.

"Was Detective McGreal taking notes?"

"I don't recall, sir."

"You didn't notice that?"

"No, sir."

"Was anyone else taking notes?"

"I don't recall anyone taking notes, sir."

Sgt. Anderson was released. Tuite had no further questions. But Scott wanted to call Nelson Brown for rebuttal of his own about Sgt. Anderson.

Nelson Brown was adamant. He testified in greater detail about the conversations with the police at the station. "They asked him to recount his time again that day, at which time Detective Boyle took down only the times, no answers, just the times, and I could see him, he was sitting right across from me."

After they had been at the station for a long period of time, Nelson said, and the policemen had talked with John in Nelson's presence and out of his presence several times, he and John became concerned about what was happening to Jan and Joby at home, so he went and found Sgt. Anderson.

"I told Sgt. Anderson this, 'What are you going to do?' He said, 'Just a few more minutes.' A few minutes passed and he came in and said, 'You can go,' and as we left the room where we were sitting, where they had talked to Dr. Branion, we walked down the hall to the front of the police station to leave, at which time Sgt. Anderson then said, 'We've talked to Mrs. Kentra,' who was the back door neighbor, 'she has been here, we talked to her and we are satisfied that there was twenty minutes or a half hour after she heard whatever noise she heard that she saw Dr. Branion around the back and therefore you can go.'"

It appeared that the trial was at an end. Judge Holzer asked the jury to be in place at nine on Tuesday morning, and then adjourned.

· CHAPTER NINETEEN ·

The jurors, however nervous they may have been about deciding a man's fate, expected to get the case Tuesday morning. But Maurice Scott surprised the courtroom Tuesday morning by asking that Theresa Kentra be called back to the witness stand. He said, "I feel that Sgt. Harry Anderson took us by surprise in regard to the fact that he had never seen or met Mrs. Theresa Kentra nor did he see her at police headquarters or at the Area One detective headquarters on December 22."

Tuite fought it. He claimed that Mrs. Kentra couldn't testify to what Sgt. Anderson recalled. "She can't say that he recalls meeting her."

But Judge Holzer said, "I cannot see how justice would be thwarted by allowing this lady to testify. I'll allow the defense to open their sur-rebuttal for this purpose."

Scott asked Mrs. Kentra to recall who was present when she was giving her statement at Area One.

"There were three officers with me."

"Do you know their names?"

"No."

"Do you recall the race of these officers?"

"Yes, they were white."

"Did you at any time, while you were in that room, see any Negro police officers?"

"He came in later on."

"And would you describe that man to the ladies and gentlemen of the jury?"

"He was tall, a good six feet, and he was bald, partially bald."

"Well, was he—when you say partially bald, was he as bald as I am?"

"Yes."

"And his skin coloring, would you say he was lighter or darker than I?"

"Lighter."

"Was he as light as Dr. Branion?"

"Yes."

She said she had been introduced to him, "When he came in they said, 'This is Mrs. Kentra.'" But she thought his name was Sgt. Nelson. She wasn't certain of the name. She saw no other black officers, and she remembered he was not in uniform, but civilian clothes. It sounded very, very much like tall, light-skinned, balding Sgt. Anderson, who wore plainclothes.

"Was this man present when you signed the statement?" Scott asked.

"Yes."

Tuite immediately moved to cut down the importance of Mrs. Kentra's words.

He asked her whether there were a lot of people in the police station. She said there were. He asked whether the sergeant himself asked Kentra any questions. She said no. He established that "this Sgt. Nelson" was present only about five minutes. The impression in the jurors' minds he was aiming for was that, even if "Nelson" was really Anderson, he saw Mrs. Kentra so briefly that he might have forgotten.

It would seem to a layman that anything so momentous as the closing arguments in a murder case should be preceded by some sort of pause, as if for respect that the fate of a human being hangs in the balance. But that isn't the case. The exhibits were carried in from the judges's chambers—the photographs, the boxes of bullets, the guns, and so on—and the arguments started immediately.

Because the State is viewed as having the harder job, proving its case beyond any reasonable doubt, and the defense, presumably, does not have to prove the defendant innocent, the State is given two closing arguments. The State speaks first and last, and the defense has the middle.

This first argument by the State is called the opening argument. In the trial of John Branion the opening argument was taken by the junior member of the State's team, Daniel Weil. It was one of his first cases, and the very first case in which he was allowed to speak to the jury.

After praising the jury, Weil summarized the testimony of Donna's sister Joyce Tyler, and Theresa Kentra. He spoke of Officer Catizone, finding the body and taking Donna's pulse: "She didn't have a pulse and that was the way he knew she was dead." (Catizone's actual testimony was: A: She looked dead to me. Q: Before you ever took her pulse, right? A: Right.)

Weil continued, "Officer Catizone also told you of seeing next to the body four spent cartridges." (Catizone testified to two spent cartridges next to the body. In his report written and filed the day of the murder, he said all four were found under the body.) "These cartridges occurred, in terms of testimony, many times, and that was the first time you heard of these cartridges. He also testified he noticed, when he went into the room and turned on the light, there was no excessive bleeding that would make anyone wonder as to life and death, that just wasn't there." (Catizone never testified that there was no excessive bleeding, and Tuite, in his opening statement described Donna lying "in a pool of blood.")

"The next officer that testified was an Officer Kersten, and he is in the crime laboratory mobile unit, he arrived that morning and he testified that he picked up from next to the body four spent cartridges." (Kersten never testified as to the location of the spent cartridges, only the pellets.)

Weil spent many minutes repeating the testimony about the gun, the ballistics tests, the meaning of the lands and grooves, and the fact that, while Dr. Branion had given the officers the guns they asked for, he had not volunteered a Walther PPK. This was Branion's "gun lie." But Weil rightly did not claim that any police officer had ever asked John for any gun after 8:00 in the evening of December 22.

He spoke of the ammunition found in the paper bag in the den closet: "Then there was a third box recovered, it was this box of bullets, Geco brand with the die on it, with the name on it, and this is exactly how it was found, with four bullets missing. I submit to you, ladies and gentlemen, these four cartridges that were found next to the body, Geco brand, are the four cartridges that belong in these four slots of this box which was found in Dr. Branion's apartment on the twenty-second day of January, 1968."

Weil reminded them again of the lividity lie and the Joby lie. He talked about Maxine Brown and her lies on the witness stand. He talked about Nelson Brown. And he suggested that the whole Brown family was suspect: "The Browns I really can't comment on. Nelson Brown is a brother of the deceased and you heard him testify. You heard the cooperation he gave the police and the information. You heard Maxine Brown say she perjured herself on that stand. I don't know what more to say."

He was not much happier with the state's own witness Dr. Belmonte. Weil reduced his testimony to idle assumptions: "You also heard Dr. Belmonte testify and he generally told how the deceased died and there was some question as to a rope burn around the neck of the deceased. I simply say to you all that came out of that, Dr. Belmonte was asked whether you could assume certain things happened to cause this rope burn, something about dragging the deceased for fifteen to thirty minutes in order to cause it, and he said, yes, you can assume that. You can assume a lot of things, ladies and gentlemen, but we are not here for idle assumptions, we are here for the facts, and the facts as they are logically and reasonably presented to you, and all Dr. Belmonte said was that there are assumptions that could be made but when he originally spoke he said a great deal of pressure could have been applied to cause this rope burn, and when he said that he knew that that was the condition of the deceased's throat, we didn't get any testimony as to each of our throats being different, as to what would happen to one person's throat with a rope around it, people have different types of skin pigment and different types of muscles in their throats, so there is not much more to be said.

"Where does motive fit into this, where does motive fit in? Why would Dr. Branion have killed his wife? I can only speculate, I don't know. I can't tell you what happened in these twenty years of marriage. I do know this, that was a particularly cruel type of killing, that there was a vengeance to it and a passion, and I can tell you there was a hatred evidenced here, a deep abiding and cold hatred, yes, in order to shoot your wife and then go pick up Joby and then go to Maxine Brown's and then go back and find the body; there is a hatred that he couldn't bend down to see if she was dead. Aside from that there was a different kind of hatred here, a hatred that is almost inexplicable. Different things through a person's lifetime can build up and become big things, they are not really big things but to that person it kind of balloons in their mind, pushes out the thought of humanity and reasonableness. I submit to you that that is what happened here. We all know that love can be a magnificent force, can enable a man to do deeds beyond which anybody ever thought capable. We also know that hate is just as strong a force and it too can cause someone to do things that are almost unbelievable that any man can do; but we cannot get rid of the body of Donna Branion lying there with four bullet wounds, we can't do it. This was planned, but it wasn't well enough planned, the man wasn't a machine and hatred is an emotion, when you get emotion into something it is not as cold and calculated as you would like to think, this plan up through the time of the murder, the immediate time of it. You can't plan for all those little threads that afterward start coming down. . . .

"Somewhere, someplace something became twisted, something became demented. Just because the man has the right training and ability to save lives, given the tools to do that, that doesn't mean he has the right to take a life. I say to you, you must find the defendant guilty, you must find the defendant, Dr. John Branion, is guilty of murder of his wife, Donna Branion. You must find him guilty, not because I ask it of you, but because the evidence demands it. Thank you."

CHAPTER TWENTY

Betty Adger sat outside in the witness room, still waiting to be called to testify, not knowing the defense had rested its case and the trial was into closing arguments.

This was Maurice Scott's final chance to affect the outcome and win the jury to John Branion. In a legal sense, he had all the proof necessary, and virtually all of it from the witnesses for the prosecution. He could prove, if he was sufficiently precise, that Dr. Branion did not have time to commit the crime. As if that weren't enough, Mrs. Kentra, independent of how long the murder took to commit, tended to put the time of the murder before Dr. Branion left the hospital.

But the jury had not heard John Branion speak. The trial had not roused any great sympathy for John Branion, a man who was carrying on an extramarital affair. And the primary goal of the prosecution had been to convince the jury John Branion lied.

Maurice Scott would have to answer every single doubt in the jury's minds.

At this point in the trial, the defense case was essentially logical, the prosecution's emotional. Where the prosecution was vague, the defense had to be detailed. Where the prosecution resorted to emotion, the defense had to be logical, organized, and compelling. Where the prosecution moved times around like a shell game, the defense had to show John's irreducible minimum times in precise order.

Maurice Scott asked for a blackboard to write a time schedule on. He said to the jury, "I have prepared a sort of resume of the time involved in this case.

"You know, many years ago I was defending a case and a State's Attorney, I can remember him saying to the jury after I had finished my argument, he said, you know, when the defense doesn't have any case at all they talk about everything but what was really involved, and, you know, as I listened to Mr. Weil talk to you today those words came echoing back into my ear, they came right back because Mr. Weil really talked to you about everything but what is really important here. The important thing here is that Dr. Branion is charged with killing his wife and he is charged—not just charged, you were told by the State's Attorney Tuite in his opening statement that the State was going to prove to you that Dr. Branion committed this crime between the hour of 11:30 and 11:45 a.m. All of the evidence that you have heard about what went on on that date, December 22, was presented to you by the State. Every person they put on the witness stand was their witness."

About Maxine Brown, he said that all Tuite could hope to accomplish with her was "to clutter your minds." Then he started to talk about times. About Theresa Kentra, he said, "She said it was twenty minutes after she arrived home, and I said are you sure it couldn't have been longer, and she said, no, no. Twice. She told this to the police the very first time she was questioned and she told you that twenty to thirty minutes later she saw Dr. Branion run out the back door of his home. I don't think it takes much to realize that if you add thirty minutes to that time it comes out 11:55, which means she is a pretty accurate lady since the police call was received at 11:57. That is from the State's witness. And, at 11:25, if the State is to be believed, Dr. John Branion was at the hospital.

"Now, keep something else in your mind, if Dr. Branion saw the patient at 11:30, no matter how swift Dr. Branion may have been, he had to spend some time with the patient, so obviously Dr. Branion didn't leave the hospital at 11:30. Dr. Branion left some time after 11:30. Now, at 11:45 Dr. Branion was at the nursery. This is all their evidence, remember that, these are their witnesses, they are telling you you must accept these times, this is the evidence you have.

"All that is involved here is whether Dr. Branion could possibly have killed his wife between 11:30 and 11:45, and don't let Mr. Tuite or anybody else tell you that isn't the whole case.

"Lividity? If they are going to make a case out of lividity: if you think they're not going to make a case on it think of how many times you have heard it so far. And I have a piece of paper here that Officer McGreal would like to eat, and this piece of paper will show that Officer McGreal is an uncontroverted liar and I'll show you why.

"Now, going back to these minimum and maximum times Officer Boyle, God, was he diligent. . . . Wasn't it something when he admitted he never stopped the car and got out? As soon as he got in front of the house, click, the stop watch is stopped and off we rush to the next stop. Isn't it strange he allowed no time for Dr. Branion—if he is really trying to be fair as to how long it takes to do these things, if he is really trying to prove the guilt or innocence of the man or not trying to guess him guilty somehow isn't it strange that an intelligent, trained police officer like Officer Boyle, or Detective Boyle, never, never once, never once told you ladies and gentlemen of the jury that . . . how shall I put this, I don't want to be insulting to one of Chicago's—I won't say finest—Chicago's police officers, but for that officer to get on that stand and tell you he was establishing, and this is when Mr. Tuite was questioning him, not me, tell you, in effect, this doctor could make it around that route he described in four minutes and never once tell you he parked, that he allowed time for going in and going out, you know if he killed her, he had to hit her, choke her, hit her on the chin, and nobody yet has told you that Dr. Branion looked anything but unruffled up until the time he found his wife, I don't know what kind of ogre they think this man is, and I don't know what kind of actor they think this man could be, but I certainly want you to remember that somebody was trying to kid you about the time when they didn't allow any times for any of the events that were supposed to have transpired, all they allowed for was the driving; unless they were able to say Dr. Branion was able to wing her from the car as he went by the house and then we don't have to allow time to park."

Scott reminded them of the strange appearance of Detective McGreal's notes, which McGreal had first said were prewritten, then admitted they weren't. "You will see these questions could not have been prewritten, he has a question where the answer is three lines long, the answer is three lines long, he is either psychic and left enough space because he knew that was going to be a long, long answer."

He repeated Dr. Belmonte's testimony about the time it takes a bruise to develop.

"The other thing to remember here from Dr. Belmonte, and these are the state's witnesses, and I don't know what Mr. Tuite wants to say about him now, I don't think they love him too much, because somehow he didn't say what they wanted him to say and they didn't go back and ask him any more about it, Dr. Belmonte said this bruise couldn't form on a dead body."

He continued. Tuite had asked the policemen whether the apartment showed any signs of forcible entry. Scott said, "What is he talking about? Is he talking about broad daylight, somebody went with a sledge hammer and broke in the house? This is December 22, three days before Christmas. What is the easiest way to get in the house? Ding, ding, who is it? Marshall Field. Buzz the door, you open it."

" . . . And we know in this wonderful and cruel city of ours, and it is both things all at one time, and many other things, some I love, some I hate, but it is all these things, we know these things happen particularly at

Christmas time, for some warped reason of the criminal, I guess they have Christmas for their family, their idea how to do it is discouraging for all of us. And there are those bruises. And do you realize when Mr. Tuite talked to Dr. Belmonte he wasn't interested in talking about the bruises because he knows full well there is not enough time for Dr. Branion to be in there and inflict bruises and fight and struggle and do all these things and not get mussed up, not get a speck of blood, nothing. Did you hear Mr. Tuite ask Mrs. Kelly to tell him what state of mind or how did Dr. Branion appear to her? You didn't hear him ask any of those people that. He knew the answer, but after the body was found, after the body was found you have a distraught, upset man."

And back to the time schedule. "... gee whiz, if we accept Dr. Belmonte's testimony as being true, and that is the witness they offered and they are bound by their witnesses, they took fifteen minutes to get the bruise together, if that is true and Mrs. Kentra is right [about the sounds she heard], that makes the strangling begin at 11:10."

He moved away from the time schedule again.

"Do you know these men in effect want you to think Attorney Nelson Brown got on that witness stand and told some lie that might possibly help a man that murdered his sister? . . .

"Here we are at the lividity again, he [Tuite] is going to sing it a long time and he has been sitting there a long time to get another spot to run to because he had lividity picked out because he had every police officer get up and testify to it and he is going to try to get home on it. . . .

"You know, if a man could be convicted of murdering his wife because four hours after he just looked at her body he made a statement that had an error to it or two or three, it would be a pretty tragic situation . . . "

And he hit the gun and ammunition. "A thug coming in might have picked up any gun around, the house was full of guns, but do you think if John Branion murdered his wife that thirty days later the police could come in his house, find the box of bullets to go with the gun, the target, the bill of sale, the box it was in? Now, a murderer or any other person might be upset for a day or a week, but thirty days later and it's still sitting around, well, maybe they want you to think John Branion is cheap, he is saving a four dollar box of ammunition."

The police were throughout the house the day of the murder and could certainly have seen the ammunition on the den closet shelf. Scott wanted to know why they didn't take it then or ask about it: "And do you know what I'm left with? And it's a frightening thing, because I'm not a gun expert, and it really bothers me. It may be the markings on these bullets and on the pellets don't conform to the markings on a PPK."

Scott ended by telling the jury that they did not have to be emotionally involved, "and you don't have to explain away mysteries, all you have to do is sit there and add them up and say that those times came from the State's witnesses, and if you do this there is only one possible verdict you can return and that is not guilty."

There had always been a fundamental problem with the prosecution's case. If John Branion had planned this—had decided that he could kill his wife very cleverly by leaving the hospital, driving to the house and shooting her quickly, then getting to Joby's nursery school and Maxine's office and home again so fast that everyone would think he had an alibi, then why not just shoot her in the back of the head and leave? Why hold a cord around her neck for a considerable period of time first?

The physical evidence of the crime, both the pathology findings on the body and the physical evidence all around the apartment, had always suggested a time-consuming, hot-headed, gratuitously vicious murder.

To fit John Branion into the time available, the state had to posit extreme efficiency in his use of the time available and considerable planning. In other words, the evidence at the murder scene was inconsistent with the way John Branion would have had to commit it.

The prosecution's solution was to formulate essentially two pictures: John Branion acting out of hot-blooded passion and hatred, and John Branion planning coolly and executing efficiently.

They split the two descriptions of the crime between the two prosecutors. Dan Weil had just described a crime of passion and inexplicable hatred formed over "twenty years of marriage." Patrick Tuite would now call it cold-blooded and ruthless. Since the two prosecutors' closing arguments were separated by the defense closing argument, jurors could have it either way, and might not notice the fundamental inconsistencies.

Now Tuite could present *his* picture of the crime. Four shots. Donna had to be lying on the floor, both because she had been half strangled first and because otherwise unless someone was holding her, why wouldn't she run or at least turn away? The time for presenting evidence was over. There was no chance now that anybody would bring up Catizone's first report about the four empty cartridges being under the body, which, ejected from the gun after the bullet is fired, would not get under a body that was already lying down. And no one had ever asked why there were thirteen bullet wounds if there were only four shots, so the idea of four shots, four rounds missing from the box found on the closet shelf, should be very convincing.

No one could challenge this picture now. Tuite would have the last word.

CHAPTER TWENTY-ONE

Tuite's closing argument converted the prosecution advantage of going first and last into a burden.

"May it please the court, ladies and gentlemen of the jury: The State has the burden in every criminal case . . . to prove the defendant guilty beyond all reasonable doubt, and because of that, the State has an opportunity in its jury trials to speak to you last as I am doing now. And we submit, ladies and gentlemen, that this is a proper burden, that there should be no less burden put on any prosecutor in this country than to prove a defendant guilty beyond a reasonable doubt. I would not want it any other way, I would not want us guessing guilty verdicts. . . . We want proof from that witness stand from witnesses under oath who raise their hand to God and subject themselves to cross examination."

He talked about Maurice Scott's board diagrams, saying that Scott had done a great job at misstating the evidence. He played about with times for a while, never becoming very specific. Of John's arrival at the nursery school he said, "When does he get there? 11:45 or 11:50." He talked about the route John might have driven, very specific about the streets, much less so about the time consumed. "Was he in the area? Of course he was in the area."

Then he got to Dr. Belmonte's testimony. "And counsel makes a thing about Dr. Belmonte's testimony and again I thought I was at a different trial, I thought I could have been across the hall, maybe that is where the Branion trial was going on. He never asked Dr. Belmonte and Dr. Belmonte never testified that you can't make a mark on a dead person like that . . . but the fact is, he (Scott) never asked him would it still form after she is dead because that question was never asked. . . . So you see how you can expand and play with the evidence if it fits your picture. Sure, it fits his picture that it took fifteen minutes to form, that it had to form before she died. There is no evidence in the record like that. You have seen bruises, you have knocked yourself around and a few minutes later it forms and sometimes it doesn't form, and sometimes the next day it forms, and we don't know the strength of her neck, we don't know if she had strong bones, brittle bones, weak bones, if she had a good voice box, if she had strong muscles, it depends on all different variables, but we know she was shot through the eye and she was shot through the neck, and she was shot through the shoulder.

"Another interesting aspect about it, she was shot like a dog because she is laying down when she catches the bullets, because the bullets are found under her, not through her and into a wall, not through her and into a chair, under her. You stand over her like a dog and put the bullet through her eyeball. Terrific man, the doctor, wonderful man. . . .

"Counsel says we have based our case on lividity, we have not. It strikes you, I'm sure, as funny, as it strikes us, that a doctor walks into a home, sees his wife lying there, and does not go to her aid. He is trained in aiding people who are injured, he does not go to her aid, he does not go and feel the pulse. Officer Catizone testified he felt the pulse because if she is still alive he would call an ambulance and try to save her life. Did the doctor even do that decent little thing? . . . We can show he didn't go to the body because he knew she was dead because she was at the receiving end and he was at the sending end of those bullets, he is standing over her and putting them in her eyeball and that is how he knows she is dead."

Maxine, Tuite said, tried to lie about the luncheon appointment. "And she admitted lying about other things, about where they were the next day, some apartment of some girl named Shirley, she said it was the first time, the first time since I have been working there since September that he called me? And when does he call? 11:00 the night before. How is this significant? Because he wants a witness with him when he finds the body, he wants somebody with him as he walks in that front door to pick up his wife to go to lunch, she is with him. Oh, my God, there is my wife."

Tuite talked at some length about the gun and the gun lie, and about the bullets. "Way up on a shelf in his den, in his closet, is a paper bag, and in that paper bag what do we find? The same brand, the same color, the same markings as the four found next to the body, one, two, three, four."

Later: "We can look at it cold and hard because this was a cold and hard killing, we can't be sympathetic, we can't say, the doctor, if we have one standard for doctors and one standard for everyone else we might as well close this building. . . . "

And finally, Tuite appealed to the jurors' fears. Amid assassination, ghetto riots, student rebellion, looting, and burning such as the United States had never seen, he said: "The verdict that you return in this case will be known publicly, there are people on the street now with guns in their pocket, as Mr. Scott said, sometimes it's a cruel city and they make their living sometimes with guns and you have got to let every punk on that street out there who is menacing the people in the community know that a doctor couldn't get away with it and you are not going to get away with it, and if they know, gee, a doctor couldn't pull the wool over the eyes of the jury and they were able to convict him, what are they going to do with me, I'm just a poor punk out with a gun, you may save an innocent life here or there. You may help clear up crime on the streets. . . .

"When I sit down here I will be finished with my job, presenting the evidence to you in a logical, we hope, in a forthright fashion, then the job will be up to you, and you have within your power to destroy everything that has been done up to now or to reward everything that has been done up to now and say, yes, the defendant has been proved guilty beyond a reasonable doubt. You may say to yourself, well, there was no eyewitness. Nobody saw him coming or going out of the building. Well, if you just think of human nature, if you are going to kill someone, are you going to gather a crowd, are you going to call the neighbors over as you would at a party and say, come on over, I'm going to put one in my wife's eyeball. . . . He never told the police his PPK was missing when they asked about it [No policeman ever asked John Branion about a Walther PPK, not even several days later, after the ballistics lab suggested to them that such a gun might fit the cartridge and pellets.]; but now he has got to say it so he gets Nelson to testify to hearsay." Tuite claimed that if Nelson had actually been told he would immediately "have been scurrying down to the police department."

"Ladies and gentlemen, it has been a fairly long trial, you have heard a lot of evidence. . . . You told us during your examination as jurors that you would sign a guilty verdict, we believed you then and we believe you now and I submit, based on all the evidence in this record, the defendant has been proved guilty beyond all reasonable doubt of the murder of his wife, Donna Branion.

"I thank you."

It was 2:05 when Tuite finished. Judge Holzer instructed the jury and sent them out, where they would have lunch and then begin their deliberations.

Maurice Scott did not expect to lose. He felt the state had mounted no case. There was nothing to show John had been on the premises at the time of the murder, nothing to show he held the gun, everything to show he had been elsewhere. He had communicated his confidence to John all through the trial. John was optimistic.

Bill Hooks, taking the cue from Maurice Scott's optimism, had even brought a bottle of champagne and paper cups to the last day of the trial. John's friends wanted to celebrate when the long ordeal was over. John thought he could get on with his life, go back to work without this terrible cloud over his head, and raise his children.

They expected a quick acquittal. John paced around in the back of the courtroom, and then outside for a drink of water, then back. After a little while, Scott told John that a rumor had come from the jury room that a first straw poll had been eleven to one for acquittal.

But at 4:00, and 5:00, and 6:00, the jury was still out. Hooks, Scott, and others took John across the street to the Greek's to eat dinner, but he couldn't stand food; he was too tense. He had built a wall between himself and the courtroom full of staring eyes during the whole of the trial, but now that the stress of the actual trial was over, and he felt hopeful of freedom, the wall didn't work so well. He wanted to go home, to hide for a while and rest.

It had been clear and sunny earlier in the day, a wonderful day, just under seventy degrees, a day to make a person optimistic. But while the jury was out it had clouded up and as John and Maurice and John's friends walked back from the Greek's, it started to drizzle.

At seven, when the jury still had not come back, John began to be truly fearful. Who would raise his children if he was gone? What would happen to them? What would happen to him?

At eight they heard that the jury was coming back. John took his seat, sick with dread. The jury filed in.

They avoided his eyes.

They found John Branion guilty of murder.

He wept.

· CHAPTER TWENTY-TWO ·

Out in the witness room, Betty Adger heard that it was all over, and that John had been convicted. She was still waiting to give evidence. She couldn't believe what had happened.

John went directly from the courtroom to jail that night, May 28, 1968. Maurice Scott immediately filed a motion for a new trial and a motion for a judgment notwithstanding the verdict. A "judgment notwithstanding" is a judicial decision to throw out the conclusion of the jury. It is used in cases when the judge believes the evidence is clearly insufficient to support the conviction. It is a decision that cannot be appealed by the state, and therefore is final.

After the filing of the two motions, Patrick Tuite heard a rumor that Judge Holzer was going to grant the motion for a judgment notwithstanding the verdict. In fact, he heard that Holzer had already dictated his opinion to the head court reporter at the Criminal Courts Building at 26th and California.

Tuite asked the court reporter directly whether the rumor was true. The reporter was evasive, but said, "It doesn't look good for the prosecution." Tuite went to Judge Holzer, without Maurice Scott present. Such communication between a prosecutor and a judge, without the defense attorney present, is called an ex parte communication and is considered impermissible in the law because it deprives the defense of its right to respond to the arguments. Tuite asked Holzer straight out whether he intended to set aside the verdict of guilty. Holzer said yes. Tuite then argued that Holzer should let the appellate court decide. Judge Holzer told Tuite that he didn't want John Branion in custody, waiting for an appellate court decision. Such decisions may take many months.

At 9:45 one night, just before the rulings were due, Judge Holzer called Tuite at home.

He said, "Pat, this is Reggie."

Holzer told Tuite that he wanted him to ask for a one-week postpone-

175

ment before ruling on Branion's request for a new trial, but Holzer didn't say why he wanted this.

Tuite said, "But I'm ready to proceed."

Holzer insisted that Tuite ask for a postponement.

So when Tuite appeared on the motion, he did ask for the postponement. Judge Holzer then became angry, or pretended to become angry, and gave Tuite two days to prepare the response. Tuite did not need the two days, or any time at all.

Twenty years later Pat Tuite said, "Looking back on it, I believe that Judge Holzer, by asking that I request a postponement of the ruling on John Branion's motion for a new trial, may have been trying to put pressure on the defendant for corrupt reasons."

In 1986, John's friend Bill Hooks, described what he remembered: "After Dr. Branion was convicted, and while Judge Holzer was deciding what to do about the defense motion for a judgment notwithstanding the verdict, Nelson Brown came to me and said that Judge Holzer was looking for a bribe, and Nelson asked me if I had any money. I said I did not have any money.

"A couple of days later, Nelson Brown told me that he was able to get $20,000 from other friends of John Branion's, but they had imposed a condition that $10,000 be paid to Judge Holzer in advance and the remaining $10,000 would be paid to him as soon as John Branion was freed. I asked Nelson who put up the money and Nelson replied that the less I knew the better.

"A day or two later I inquired of Nelson Brown what was going on, and he informed me of a meeting that was held at the Holiday Inn on Lake Shore Drive, at which Holzer and his bailiff, and Nelson Brown, were present. At that meeting, $10,000 in cash was passed to Judge Holzer.

"A day or two later (I cannot remember the exact number of days), Nelson Brown informed me that Judge Holzer said that he could not accept the remaining $10,000 in addition to the $10,000 he had already received, because the state's attorney had somehow gotten wind of the meeting in the Holiday Inn and threatened to arrest everyone concerned and to lock up the judge too if the judge reversed the jury's verdict. Nelson Brown added that Judge Holzer said he would, however, release John Branion on bail in return for the $10,000 that was paid.

"Judge Holzer in fact released Dr. John Branion on the same $5,000 bail that John was on prior to his trial.

"I believed then, as I believe now, that Nelson Brown acted out of his own conviction that Dr. John Branion was innocent of the murder of Nelson's sister, and that Nelson was responding to a situation where a judge asked for a bribe, and was fearful that if it were not paid John Branion would be sent to prison."

On June 10, 1968, Judge Reginald J. Holzer pronounced sentence: "Dr. Branion, I hereby sentence you to the Illinois State Penitentiary for a term of years not less than 20 nor more than 30."

PART THREE

Flight

March for fair housing in Marquette Park, Chicago, August 5, 1967. Jesse Jackson is at center, in dark shirt and dark hat. Martin Luther King, Jr. is directly behind Jackson. Dr. John Branion is to the right and behind Jackson, in dark glasses and cowboy hat. Shirley Hudson is next to Branion.

Donna Brown Branion, 1965.

The murder site: 5054 S. Woodlawn, where the Branions had a ten-room apartment on the first floor

51st Street, the major thoroughfare Dr. Branion traveled on the morning of December 22, 1967, as pictured in 1991. Then, as now, the street was lined with businesses, there was snow on the ground, and more snow was falling.

Branion in Africa. Pictured at left, among friends, in Uganda's Rowenzori National Park. Late 1970s.

John and Shirley Branion, Uganda, early 1980s.

Branion in the state penitentiary at Dixon, Illinois, 1987. Photo by Loren Santow.

CHAPTER TWENTY-THREE

From the moment of his conviction, John Branion lost everything. He didn't realize it at first; there seemed to be steps he could take, efforts he could make. But from that day in May, his life in Chicago ran out like sand in a sieve.

"Maurice Scott immediately said we would appeal, of course. People were telling me—and these were friends of my father's, lawyers, criminal lawyers, who should know—that they'd never heard of a case where a man was convicted on such thin circumstantial evidence. Circumstantial evidence, yes, but where the defendant had at least been placed at the scene of the crime, or seen with a weapon, or fingerprints, something. They were convinced the case would be reversed on review.

"Maurice started the appeal process.

"So, after thirteen days in jail between May 28 and the sentencing, June 10, I was granted bail and went home."

But it was not the same. "The first thing, I found out that I had lost my license to practice medicine. As a convicted felon.

"Medicine was what I *did*. I mean, I would get up in the morning and put on my suit and go to work and see patients. And there would be emergencies and babies to deliver. In normal life, in the old days, that was how my day had been formed. I wasn't suited to sitting at home. And anyway, I was a doctor. I practiced medicine. That was what I wanted to be doing.

"But that wasn't even the worst. I started running into people who believed I had killed Donna, because of the verdict. Not my closest friends and not the people who worked at the hospital. They knew I hadn't. But other people. People I'd considered friends.

"There's an instinct in the black community to steer away from trouble. And steer away from the police. And a lot of people, people I had considered friends, people I liked, were avoiding me. There were other people, real friends, who were telling them, 'Listen, he didn't do it. He's going to

be vindicated on appeal.' That sort of thing. But you know how people figure. They think, 'Oh, sure. You think he's a nice guy because he's your
friend.'

"People would point me out in the street. And they did the same with
the kids. School was out the first or second week of June, but Jan had to go
through having her friends—friends!—pointing at her and other kids asking her humiliating questions for those last couple of weeks.

"Joby, thank God, was too little really to know about it.

"Everything was in a mess. Nelson was chagrined. He didn't know how
it had happened, how it had all gone wrong. Maxine knew she had messed
up. All that waffling and changing testimony. If she had just told about
Shirley in the first place, straightforwardly, and everything—oh, well.

"And then the money problems started to hit. Donna and I had spent
what I earned. I had a good income, and we spent it. We were never in
debt. We didn't spend beyond what I made, but I didn't save much. I figured if I dropped dead or got run over by a bus, the Browns wouldn't
abandon Donna and the kids. And anyway, I'd been in practice less than
ten years. You don't think as much about saving at forty as you do, maybe,
at fifty.

"I had nothing to fall back on. Having lost my license to practice, my income stopped. It was like cutting off a water faucet. In an instant there was
just nothing. I had enormous attorney fees, and more bills coming in for
the appeal. Even if I dug ditches, I couldn't keep up with them. And there
were other bills coming in all the time. Food, clothing for the children,
nursery school, insurance on the cars, insurance on the house, heat, electric bills, they never stopped!

"First I sold the horses. It hurt, but what was I going to do? Then I sold
my car. But it was all never going to be enough. You could sell your clothes
or your record collection, but it doesn't add up to the kind of money you
need for attorney's fees. It would never be enough, no matter what I did.

"And on top of that, the lawyers told me the appeal could take months,
and maybe even years. And a lot of money."

Shirley recollected, "John couldn't live in Chicago, either financially or
emotionally. Between the hostility of the Browns and reminders of Donna
and reminders of the trial and the time he had spent in jail and the lack of
money . . .

"He went before Judge Holzer and requested permission to move to
Wyoming, while he was still under bond. Judge Holzer granted it. And he
asked me to go with him. I was feeling as much of a leper in Chicago as

John was, I guess. Everybody stared at me. Even though I had changed jobs, people immediately found out. I was the other woman in the case.

"And people who didn't know any of us just assumed John was guilty. Well, they would, of course. They didn't know what went into a trial, and they didn't know the facts. I suppose if the higher court overturned the conviction, then they'd decide he was innocent. But I thought, right then, I wouldn't mind getting out of Chicago."

John picked Wyoming because his old friend from medical school days, C. Rogers Wise, now lived and worked in Cheyenne. And also because it was the real West. He could ride horses there. Maybe he could work with horses.

"I invited him to come out," Roger Wise says. "He was really catching it in Chicago."

"I sold the furniture. It didn't bring much. And packed up Jan and Joby's clothes. I had sold the Corvette, but kept Donna's Buick, and we packed everything in there and just left.

"We drove to Cheyenne. And it was beautiful! Cheyenne is on this high plain, and the air is so clear in the mornings you can see a hundred miles. In the late afternoon the air gets to be a pale blue in the distance and everything turns purple around sunset."

Maurice Scott had finished a brief for the appeal, and John and Scott had decided to bypass the lower appeals court and go directly to the Illinois Supreme Court. But John decided to switch attorneys. John felt that Scott should have let him take the stand; Scott felt that John had rushed him into trying the case hastily. John fired Scott and hired Howard Savage. Savage began writing additions to the brief. There was no telling how long that might take. Some of John's friends, Bill Hooks and LaHarry Norman and others, took up a collection to help John pay for the appeals.

Shirley got a nursing job in Cheyenne. They lived in separate apartments. She and John had decided to marry, but thought they should wait a year, out of respect to Donna's memory. Despite all his education, John couldn't get work that paid more than a pittance. He tried, but Cheyenne had a large number of out-of-work blacks and Indians. Shirley supported both her apartment and John's family—John, Joby, and Jan—with her nurse's salary, about $600 a month.

It wasn't enough. The money ran out constantly. Shirley could not support two households on a nurse's income. They married on the first of October, 1968.

• CHAPTER TWENTY-FOUR •

John was forty-two years old. Middle aged, though he didn't think of it that way. He was adrift without a job at an age when most men were established in their careers and reaping the rewards of earlier efforts. Even though John and Maurice Scott had decided to appeal directly to the Illinois Supreme Court, there was still a lot of dead time ahead. Scott wrote the appeal brief. Then, when John changed attorneys, Savage added to the brief. It was filed. Months passed. John worked with horses and talked with cowboys. A year came and went without any change. John exercised horses for friends; he had met a great many people in Cheyenne. He spent hours at the shop of an elderly saddlemaker, watching him make saddles, chatting with him, hearing stories about the Old West, handing him tools.

On April 15, 1969, Shirley and John's son Jeff was born. Shirley went on working as a nurse, but John could not get steady work. He liked working with horses, but he couldn't make any money at it. Desperate, feeling emasculated by having to live on Shirley's income, he sent for an application to veterinary school. He started filling it out, and partway down the form, he found the question: "Have you ever been arrested?" He threw the form away.

A year and a half went by just waiting for the Supreme Court of Illinois to give them a date when they would hear arguments in the case.

In September of 1969, twenty-one months after Donna died, the Supreme Court of the state of Illinois at last called Howard Savage to argue John's appeal. Because of the death of one of the justices and the resignation of two others following a scandal, Savage argued before only four of the usual seven judges. Now the case might be in limbo many, many months, while the court reached its decision.

In the meantime, John was marooned, economically, professionally, and emotionally. His psychological condition was growing worse, and Shirley knew it. He would go out for long rides on horseback twenty miles into the wilderness. He would talk to the horse.

"He'd come home at night and tell me that he'd been telling the horse how much he loved me. And he did love me. I knew that. But at the same time, it wasn't enough. He couldn't go on this way. If his conviction had been overturned and he got back his license to practice medicine, everything would have been different. But he was becoming desperate and hopeless."

John's mental state became a kaleidoscope of fears and unrealistic solutions. He felt he was dragging Shirley down. She was on a treadmill of work and child care, and she was supporting not only their son, Jeff, but Joby and Jan as well.

He felt he was losing stature in his children's eyes. He had nothing he could give them. He had earned $50,000 a year in practice. He had been able to provide everything they needed. He himself had had a profession, self-respect, a job he loved and the buoyancy and happiness that had come from it. Now he was a beggar on the fringes of his family.

"You'd be better off without me."

"I wouldn't," Shirley said. "And the children wouldn't, either."

"I'm a . . . a thing they have to explain. What happens if I have to go to prison? I can imagine Jan when she starts college. 'What does your father do?' 'Oh, he's in prison for murdering my mother.'"

"They know you didn't do it."

"That's not the point. *Other* people don't know it."

"*We* know it."

"And we saw how much good that did, too."

John was always a good cook, so he shopped and cooked while Shirley was at work. And he loved children. He didn't even mind changing diapers. He played with the two boys, Jeff and Joby, and took Joby to ride the horses. But all that would be gone too, if he went to prison. He began to think about fleeing the country in the event his appeal failed. He felt there was no justice for him in the United States. He and Shirley discussed the idea, which she resisted; the prospect of trying to take care of three children—especially baby Jeff—while taking flight half a world away seemed unrealistic to her.

A few months after Jeff was born John and Shirley made a decision.

"Joanna Phillips (not her real name) had always been interested in John," Shirley says, "even way back. And she had lots of money. She was willing to help him. Pay for the appeal, help Joby and Jan financially, whatever. I think John convinced himself that I would be better off with just Jeff to support, on my income. I told him he had to do what would work best for him. He had to make up his own mind. You can't force a person, and especially not under circumstances like that."

"We decided to get a divorce," John said. "It was a stupid, *stupid* decision." Back in Chicago, Sydney and Vivian Brown remained hostile to John. Sydney was keeping a file of all the press stories on Donna's murder. But other friends kept in touch. John talked with other people in Chicago frequently—Billy Hooks, several hospital friends, his family. He had known all along that Joanna was there in the background and had been indirectly hearing of her from time to time. But John was ambivalent about almost everything, including Joanna. He was susceptible to beautiful women, and Joanna seemed to have everything to offer.

John was not able to plan. His sense of control of his own life had been seriously damaged when he found Donna dead. Now the feeling that his life could be cut in two at any minute by prison left him without direction. "It's one thing to work hard—I always had worked hard—or overcome an obstacle, or come back after a tragedy. But when you think somebody's going to come along and pick you up and put you in prison for decades, you just can't make plans for tomorrow. You can't structure your life. I mean, how do you plan with a twenty- to thirty-year hole looming up ahead?"

Life looked like a road with a washed-out bridge.

John and Shirley divorced and John married Joanna. Shirley moved away. She says, "You have to play fair. We had decided to call it quits." Shirley and Jeff moved to California. Joby and Jan stayed with John and Joanna in Cheyenne, in a house Joanna bought. Jan finished high school.

But Joanna and John did not get along. "We fought. I'd never had that kind of a relationship, where I fought with my wife. But we were not suited to each other and I should have known it before getting married."

John's friends were still trying to help him where they could. In 1970, Oscar Brown, Jr. hired John to act as his business manager in New York, where Brown was mounting a musical. John received permission from the court in Chicago to move to New York.

Then, on October 13, 1970, thirty-four months after Donna's death, the ruling came down from the Illinois Supreme Court. John's conviction was upheld. With Judge Kluszinski dissenting, they affirmed the lower court decision. Some of their reasons were "facts" no one had testified to at the trial. And, utterly crushing to John, they did not even mention Dr. Belmonte's testimony that the bruise on Donna's neck would have taken fifteen to thirty minutes to form.

John said to Howard Savage, "Can they do that? Can they really do that?"

Savage just shook his head. Not in negation, in amazement.

"I think we should ask for a rehearing," he said.

They did. It was denied.

The only recourse was the Supreme Court of the United States. Now nine men in Washington would decide whether John would spend perhaps the rest of his life in prison.

He went to find Shirley. He told her marrying Joanna had been a mistake. He told her he was thinking more than ever of going to Africa. Donna's parents would take care of Jan, who would be going to college in a year, anyway. But they would not take care of Joby, who was adopted. For some reason they never accepted Joby, even though Donna had loved him as her own. John wanted Shirley to come with him to Africa and bring Joby and Jeff. Shirley didn't want to go. But to John, the alternative—prison— was unbearable.

In April of 1971, more than three years after Donna's death, the Supreme Court of the United States denied certiorari. They would not review the case.

John was to surrender himself to the authorities.

· CHAPTER TWENTY-FIVE ·

April, 1971

The big DC-10 lumbered down the runway, gathering speed but roaring with the effort. Dr. John Branion looked out the window and then felt tears behind his eyelids. Quickly, he closed his eyes and tried not to think. He must not draw attention to himself.

The plane was airborne. Suddenly it was light and graceful; he felt only the gentle drag of its rise. When he was certain his face was calm, Dr. Branion looked out the window again.

Below him Denver revolved in a stately arc, and as the aircraft turned toward the east, he saw the Rocky Mountains in the distance slide away from his sight for the last time.

Dr. John Branion was taking a giant step into the unknown.

He had virtually no assets, almost no money, no way of proving his innocence. Most important, he was a middle-aged, professional American. He simply did not know *how* to be a fugitive.

On the credit side, he had four things going for him: some connections with black leaders in Africa through having met some of them in Chicago; an ability to learn languages quickly; his marketable medical skill; and a rare capacity for making friends.

He had made arrangements with Joanna. First, he would go to Africa and find a place that was safe. Then she would follow, bringing Joby. Meanwhile, she was caring for Joby.

John's passport had been confiscated when he was sentenced. In his muddled state, when he began to think about fleeing to Africa, he had considered buying a forgery, but he didn't know where to start to look for forgers. He fretted and worried and then an idea struck him. He could apply for one in somebody else's name.

John had had a long-time friend named Arthur Lord McCoo III who

189

had died several years before. Art McCoo had done some travelling and had a passport.

The answer was simple. John sent to the Bureau of Vital Statistics in Chicago for a copy of Art McCoo's birth certificate. With the birth certificate, he applied for a Colorado driver's license. Then, with the driver's license and a Colorado address, John simply went to a passport office in Denver and applied for a copy of McCoo's passport. In fourteen days it arrived. The picture on the passport was no problem. He looked quite a bit like McCoo anyway, and he thought that, to the white airport authorities, one black man would look much like another.

He got a plane in Denver and flew to Boston. From there he intended to go on to Paris. Since the Supreme Court decision had only just come down, it was unlikely that any warrant had yet been issued for his arrest. But by the time he reached Boston he was in a lather of fear. Passengers who were boarding international flights were being searched, and John was sure the search was a ruse—the officials were looking specifically for him. In fact, he got so paranoid that he thought they were only pretending to search the other people, while really looking for him.

As he passed through the metal detector, it buzzed. He jumped. He thought they had buzzed it intentionally, for a chance to detain him, because he knew he wasn't carrying any metal contraband such as knives or guns.

The guard said, "Where is it, sir?"

John stammered, "I don't know" and started patting his pockets. His hand hit his coat pocket. He pulled out a small metal box of Band-Aids he'd forgotten about. He handed it to the guard and went back through the metal detector. It was silent. They let him pass.

When the Boston-to-Paris plane was airborne, he felt only a little easier. He had picked Paris because it was a familiar city to him. He spoke French and knew he could get along there. It was also the gateway to Africa.

But in Paris his terror increased. He believed that by now the United States authorities would know he was gone. Everybody in the airport looked like an agent, watching for him, poised to seize him and take him back. He bought a ticket on the first flight leaving for Algeria. He had five hours to wait until it boarded. He spent them huddled in an abandoned restaurant at one end of the building.

In Algiers, he immediately felt freer. Algiers had become a haven for hundreds of people, both black and white, who had fled the United States for political reasons in the 1960s. Many of them were antiwar demonstrators and draft protesters who had gotten into trouble during the years of resistance to the Vietnam War. Others were blacks who had given up on the United States. The Black Panthers had a house and a sort of "embassy" in Algiers. John believed they owed him assistance. After all, he had been willing to put himself on the line, treating injured Panthers in Chicago.

The small amount of money John had brought with him was a fortune in Algiers, although the city was more expensive than he had expected. He moved to a cheap hotel. For two whole weeks he toured the city, looked at the architecture, walked through the marketplaces, and got used to the feeling of being free. But he wanted a job and an income. He wanted to practice medicine again.

At the end of the second week, he went to Black Panther headquarters, thinking they would help him. Their compound was situated in the Arab sector, about ten minutes' drive from the United States Embassy. Panther headquarters was a large, two-story structure. Like most Arab buildings, it was completely surrounded by a wall. On the first floor were classrooms, a kitchen, two suites used as apartments, and some storerooms. Upstairs was a large conference room, as well as a communications room and newsrooms. At first he was welcomed. Everybody was friendly to him except Eldridge Cleaver, a Panther leader and the celebrated author of *Soul On Ice*. Cleaver was suspicious and behaved as if he didn't want John around, and his attitude both puzzled John and worried him. It may have been a simple difference of personality and background. Cleaver might well have seen John as a black person who had nevertheless been born with all the advantages—an educated father who had a respected job, a childhood with adequate income, and educational advantages all along the line. Certainly compared to most of the people in the compound, John had been born with a silver spoon in his mouth. Or again, it might not have been personal antipathy on Cleaver's part. The Panthers were on constant alert for infiltration by United States agents posing as outcasts. They might have believed John was a spy. The Panthers were planning the overthrow of the United States and were making plans for an invasion.

"This was a silly idea," John said. "And obviously, they gave it up later. But they wanted me to teach them first aid, because they assumed that when they invaded the United States there would be injuries. Well, I'll teach first aid to anybody. Everybody ought to know how to handle basic medical emergencies."

The second week, disaster struck. John lost his passport while riding in a taxi. He was wearing a light poplin jacket and the fabric was getting old. The passport, he thought, must have slipped out of the limp cloth while he was sitting down.

The passport was a necessity. He decided he had to go to the American Embassy—he couldn't think what else to do. He told them it was an emergency, hoping they would issue him a three-month temporary passport, if nothing else. They asked him for the information that his old passport contained. He answered all the questions until they asked the birth dates of Arthur McCoo's parents. John couldn't remember. He made something up.

After hours of haggling, they gave him a three-month passport. Meanwhile, the information was on its way to Washington that the new passport had been applied for in Algiers.

John knew that within days, if not hours, Washington would be aware of where he was. He needed asylum. When John told Cleaver about the lost passport, Cleaver was even more suspicious of John. When Cleaver heard that John had gone to the U.S. Embassy for a new one, he was furious. John did not know whether Cleaver thought he was a spy for the United States or simply jealous that John had gone on his own without asking Cleaver to act as ambassador.

A day later, a taxi driver arrived at the embassy with John's old passport, which he had found on the floor of his car.

Eldridge Cleaver's wife took John to a government bureau that dealt with people seeking asylum in Algeria. He was hoping not only for asylum but also work. His money was running out, and though there was supposed to be some coming from the States, and Joanna would bring some if she arrived with Joby, he didn't know when either would get there or even if they would ever find be able to him, if he had to run.

At the government bureau he felt welcome. He had a real skill he could offer—Swiss-trained gynecologists were rare among people seeking asylum—and he spoke the language. They said they would accept him. They wanted just one thing—a letter from Eldridge Cleaver endorsing him as a person needing refuge. Cleaver refused.

John was adrift again. He had seen Algeria as a haven for so many months and now it was snatched away. He had no idea where else to go. He had no plan, no money, and now, it seemed, no friends.

In great desperation, he buttonholed acquaintances, people he met in restaurants or bars, traders, everybody anywhere, and told them about his plight. One man, himself "just passing through," suggested Tanzania. And more, he was willing to give John air fare to fly to Tanzania via Cairo. John took the chance.

Tanzania had always been at the back of John's mind, because there were a great many African-Americans living there, as well as the great champion of the Pan-African movement, Julius Nyerere, whom he had met at the Browns'. They didn't in any sense "owe" him asylum, as he had felt the Panthers did. But at least they should be sympathetic.

While Algeria is 80 percent arid land, nearly empty of life and unable to support even nomadic herding, Tanzania is much more hospitable to man.

Located just south of Kenya on the Indian Ocean, Tanzania is bordered by Lake Victoria on the north, Lake Tanganyika on the west, and Zambia, Niassa, and Lake Nyasa on the south. Tanzania harvests pearls from the Indian Ocean, grows cotton in the north near Lake Victoria, and farms cattle and tea farther south. Zanzibar, the "isle of cloves," lies twenty-three miles off the coast. Mount Kilimanjaro, the highest mountain in Africa, is in Tanzania. The nation is about twice the size of California. The official languages are Swahili and English.

John's flight took him to the capital, Dar es Salaam, which means "haven of peace." He hoped at last he had found just that. "When I got off the plane, I found that the airport for Dar was eight miles from the city. I had met a man on the plane and I told my friend that I was going to walk. He said 'You're crazy, but go ahead. See you in town.' Well, the reason I was so eager to walk—there was something about it—the look, the smells. I started to walk along the road, and it was dusty with a sort of red dust.

"Then I knew what it was! Mississippi when I was a child! Here was the same red earth, the same wooden houses raised off the ground, like in the southern United States. Large wooden porches. Outhouses. Storefronts, small markets. The same slow style of movement you find in any hot climate.

"And in the background, in the villages as I passed through, there was singing and drums! It was Mississippi in 1935! I could almost feel my father there.

"And when I got to Dar, it was wonderful. I was not a minority person any more. Almost everybody was black. I didn't know the language, and I didn't have any money or work, but I was really optimistic. Dar was all contrasts. Twelve-story hotels and grass huts. Electrical appliances and kerosene lamps."

He stayed in a small place with three other men, and told Joanna where he was. After several weeks, Joby and Joanna joined him. He had a family again.

December, 1971

"By now it was eight months since I had left the United States. I felt like I had been running forever. In Dar es Salaam, I went immediately to the

Attorney General, seeking asylum. I still believed that, if anyone read the history of the case dispassionately, my innocence would be obvious. I totally believed Tanzania would give me asylum because I had been unjustly convicted of a crime I never committed.

"The Attorney General, Mark Bomani, listened attentively while I told the story of Donna's death. He seemed completely sympathetic, you know, interested in details. When I had finished talking, he said that he would send to the United States for a transcript of the trial. I should come back in six weeks for his answer."

John still had the problem of physical survival. He could not get work without a permit. Fortunately, Joanna had money and food and shelter in Tanzania were cheap. Even today, per capita yearly income in Tanzania is about $250. In this economy, Joanna's money would last a long, long time. They moved into a modern apartment in a community called Oyster Bay.

For six weeks he and Joby and Joanna lived in Dar es Salaam. Joby, now eight, entered the international school there. But John still had not received his work permit. He worried constantly about what was happening to the children at home. He knew Shirley would take care of Jeff and visit Jan in college, and he knew that Sydney and Vivian Brown were putting Jan through school.

When he went back to the Attorney General, he got the first good news in months. Bomani said he could stay in Tanzania and sent him directly to the Minister of Health, a Dr. Akim. Akim seemed uncomfortable with John, and did not offer him a job. John became worried during the interview that Akim did not like him. Later, in talking with Tanzanians, John heard that Akim did not like African-Americans. John waited, then went back to see Akim. Akim flatly refused to give him a job.

John searched for work. Wherever he asked, people would say, "Yes, yes, come back soon." John would return and they would say, "Yes. We are working on it." Attorney General Bomani never stepped in to help.

Very, very slowly, John came to realize that in Arab cultures, people do not like to say no. They agree to requests, but the results do not take place. John was angry. He felt lied to and betrayed. He was wasting his life going from bureau to bureau. "The realization that these yeses are really nos was really devastating. Eventually, very slowly, I came to realize I had to accept it as a cultural difference. But I still didn't like it."

John got a job with the Group Occupational Health Service, a project sponsored by the Netherlands. He was appointed gynecological consultant. He had just settled in, when he was called to Immigration. He was sure this was going to be his work permit, issued at last. Instead, they stamped his passport persona non grata.

John's high hopes of African asylum were falling into ruins. Where could he go now? "I started to think of South America. Brazil had a long, liberal history of extending asylum to fugitives. And no extradition treaty with the United States. Also—Joanna did not like Africa. She didn't like the weather, the insects, the food, the lack of conveniences that were easily available in the United States. She didn't even like the people." She argued that it was no place to bring up a child. They continued to fight.

John and Joanna decided that she would fly to the United States with Joby and he would fly to Rio. Then, when he was settled, he would send for her. He saw them off at the airport in Dakar, Senegal, on a hot February day. Joby was nine years old.

March, 1972

Rio was far more expensive than Tanzania—and John did not know the language. He enrolled immediately in a class in Portuguese and there he met an ex-CIA man he called "Felix." Felix took John under his wing. He began to educate him in the proper, safe way to be a fugitive.

Meanwhile, John was consulting attorneys about how to gain asylum and become a citizen of Brazil. The attorneys invariably asked him first how much money he could spend. John had under two thousand dollars left now, with Joanna gone, and no chance of a job to earn money until he could gain some sort of official status—resident alien, extended visa, a work permit, something, anything.

And apparently he could not get official status without money.

Felix was frightening him more than he was helping. All his cautions, his advice about how to recognize policemen, his talk about people being kidnapped by police, were beginning to terrify John. Brazil seemed so close to the United States. There were U.S. products everywhere. Travel bureaus advertised U.S. tours. Classes in English were very popular among Brazilians—in American-accented English.

Time went by and still Joanna and Joby did not come. He telephoned her, but she was evasive. She said the FBI was watching her house. When he asked to speak to Joby, she said he was out playing.

May, 1972

In despair John gave up on Brazil and returned to Algiers. He went directly to Panther headquarters.

In the six months since he had last been there, the Panthers had deteriorated. Many of the women and children had left, going back to the United States. There were only three families and several single people left in the compound. The whole building looked in poor condition. There was less revolutionary zeal and more sullen desperation. Where before there had been plenty of money coming in, from donations sent by well-wishers in the U.S. and from Eldridge Cleaver's writing, now funds were short and likely to dry up further.

The Algerian government had become impatient with the Panthers. Some had been accused of drug-running and some had been involved in violent arguments with each other or the local population. Politically, they were beginning to look like a liability. There was a rumor in Algiers that they were going to be expelled.

John walked in not knowing this. But as soon as he was inside the building he sensed the hostility. He had been there a matter of minutes when three men carrying guns entered the room and placed him under house arrest. They found the last of his money on his body and took two-thirds of it, a thousand dollars. Then they locked him up.

In the next few hours he heard his captors talking about him. Their plan was to ransom him back to the United States for money.

Over the next days, John made friends with his house guards, two Algerian men named Elim and Habib. He tried to find out from them what was happening, but they were low in the hierarchy and were not told much about what Cleaver was planning.

But one night at 2:00 a.m. Elim and Habib slipped silently into John's room. They had heard rumors that he was going to be killed. They were going to let him escape. They left the door unlocked 'accidentally'.

John ran down the deserted stairs, slipped out of the compound, and ran until he found a cab to take him directly to the airport. He still had two hundred dollars. He wanted an immediate flight to Cairo but there was none leaving for several hours. He knew Cleaver would follow him and he begged the airport personnel to let him wait in the international waiting room. If he had not been able to speak French, he probably would not have succeeded. He convinced them that his life was in danger.

Meanwhile, the Panthers had discovered that he was missing. They knew he must have run for the airport. Minutes after John entered the international waiting room, Cleaver and a group of Panthers arrived. They shouted for the authorities to let them in to arrest John, or to throw John out of the airport so that they could seize him. Airport management refused. John had escaped again.

Late that morning, in a hot, dusty, elderly aircraft, John arrived in Cairo.

He sought out the home of a family friend, Dr. W. E. B. DuBois, who had lived in Cairo with his wife and son. W. E. B. DuBois had been a well-known African-American writer and thinker, civil rights activist, and founder and editor of the periodical *Crisis*. The DuBois family had left the United States some years before. DuBois himself had lived to be ninety-five and died in 1963. John had met DuBois' widow, Shirley Graham, years earlier in Chicago at the home of Oscar Brown, Sr. The DuBois family put John in touch with physicians in Cairo who, they hoped, could help him get asylum.

Cairo is a cosmopolitan city of five million, but skilled doctors are in short supply. "Egyptian-trained doctors are the worst I've seen anywhere," John said. "They graduate them too fast, with too little classroom time and too little experience. Infant mortality runs over a hundred deaths per thousand live births. Sweden, for contrast, has six per thousand. There was always a need for trained gynecologists."

John had no work permit, but he consulted on an informal basis with two gynecologists over the next three months, and constantly called on politicians and government officials, hoping to get some sort of regular status. "I'd go back and beg for a permit, then wait, then go back, then wait some more. Everyone kept putting me off. I never got a yes, but I never got a no, either. It was utterly frustrating."

Egypt occupied an in-between position both geographically and politically at this time. It was neither quite east or west, neither pro-American nor pro-Soviet. It had been fighting sporadically with Israel for years, but in 1970 had agreed to a cease-fire and to negotiations, proposed by the United States. Sadat had been accepting economic and military aid from the U.S.S.R. But in July of 1972, shortly after John arrived in Cairo, Sadat ordered the 20,000 Soviet military advisers and other personnel out of the country. In this ambiguous and fluid political situation, the government probably did not want to accept a fleeing felon from the United States.

John could not stand living on tenterhooks much longer. "I was existing on bajia, a kind of deep-fried meat patty, heavily spiced, that you can buy cheap at stands, and moving from one native rooming house to another." He was not yet really aware of the damage the constant tension and fatty food were doing to his health, even though he had already had a mild heart attack years before, but he knew that—psychologically—he needed to find peace somewhere.

"I knew, really, that Egypt was never going to give me a work permit. One day in the Sherdan Hotel I happened to meet an Asian I had known in Tanzania. He was on his way to Tanzania, but was going to stop over in the Sudan. He suggested that I try the Sudan. The political climate was favorable, he said, and there were contacts, names he could give me there, who might help get me a place. The very next day we flew together to Khartoum."

Sudan is the largest country in Africa, a quarter the size of the United States. Through it flows the upper Nile. In the north is the Nubian Desert and on the northeast Sudan touches the Red Sea. Khartoum is on the river Nile, in the north central part of the country. It has a medical school, and John's friend introduced him to the dean. With John's Swiss diplomas and United States internship and residency plus years of experience, the dean was ready to offer John a teaching job.

But there was a snag. The name on all of John's diplomas, John Marshall Branion, was different from the name on John's passport, Arthur Lord McCoo. After several weeks of bureaucratic consultation, someone decided to issue him a work permit in one name and a resident permit in another. Unfortunately, because he had moved around so much, and crossed so many borders, his passport pages were filled. There was no more room to stamp his passport.

John went to the American Embassy to have additional pages inserted. What else, he thought, could he do? This is an automatic procedure that ordinarily takes ten minutes. He waited an hour, while his passport was taken into a back room. Then he was told to come back the next day.

He knew he was in serious trouble. Just minutes after he got back to his room, a friend indirectly connected with the embassy called him. Word was out that he was going to be arrested when he went back to pick up his passport the next morning.

He spent the evening with friends, distraught and weary. The friends held a wake for him, with him present. They talked about trying to get him out south, by road, but it was the middle of the rainy season and all the roads were flooded. He had no money, no way to leave, and no place to hide.

At 9:30 the next morning, before he had decided what to do, three men in turbans and jalabias burst into his room and arrested him at gunpoint. "They held a printed sheet, with my picture on it under my nose and demanded 'Is this you?' I was going to say it didn't look like me, but one of them said, 'Get your things.' I did, slowly, watching the guy with the gun. Then I said, 'Point that thing in a different direction.' To my surprise, he did, and I collected my things.

"I was taken to my first African jail. It was old and dirty—no toilets, no running water. The floor was swarming with vermin and the whole place reeked. There were twenty people wedged into a tiny room. The only place to sit was on the slimy, urine-drenched floor. In fact, it was the only place to sleep! I stayed there three days. They served us smelly soup I couldn't eat.

"On the third day I was transferred to Khobar Prison, on the outskirts of Khartoum. Infamous Khobar. Its outer walls are three feet thick. Inside, there are several smaller brick structures of one room and some larger multi-story brick buildings which house local criminals. The political prisoners were housed in the smaller buildings. There were two kinds of political prisoners, separately housed. Communists were one, Sudanese and international were the other. The communists had less freedom; they were kept locked up all the time. Around the buildings lay a courtyard of sand. No trees.

"When I first entered, they asked me 'Do you have a cooker?' I didn't know what they meant. It turned out that the guards gave each prisoner a ration of meat and vegetables once each day and the prisoner cooks his own food on his own hot plate.

"I was alone in my cell, although most of the cells housed two or three men. I was considered dangerous. After all, I was an escaped murderer! The cell had tiled walls, in an oriental design of black and white. It had a fold-up cot, a chair, and an electrical outlet. During the day, it was 110 to 120 degrees. For the first ten days the door was always locked.

"After ten days, my cell door was opened, and now I could use the hole-toilet, which emptied into a bucket. All Sudanese toilets, except in European or upper middle class Arab homes, are just holes in expensive tile floors.

"In keeping with the Arab caste system, the common criminals cleaned our area and emptied our latrine buckets and so on. Every day when the guard came by with the food, I asked 'Why am I here?' He'd smile and say the commander would answer my questions. The next day I'd ask, 'What's the charge?' or 'When will I be charged?' and he'd smile and say the commander would answer my questions. I never saw the commander.

"The prison was next to the Nile River. In the old days I think they just tipped the dead bodies into the Nile. Because of the abundance of water we were allowed to shower as much as we wanted. Sometimes I showered four times a day. It passed the time.

"In the morning when the temperature was just 100, I jogged around the sand space, twenty times. The other prisoners thought I was crazy, but I thought I needed to stay strong.

"I always cooked my one meal in the evening and ate it just before I lay down. That way, I slept better.

"I wrote letters to Shirley, twice every day. I didn't know until years later that the prison authorities were destroying them."

Back in Chicago, the *Tribune* ran a story on August 16, 1972, titled, "Murder Fugitive Caught in Sudan." The article said John Branion, "is in custody of police in Sudan and may be returned to Chicago.... Chicago police and Federal Bureau of Investigation agents have been looking for Branion since December, 1970, when he disappeared." It added, "the U.S. has no extradition treaty with the Sudan."

Whether the American Embassy precipitated this arrest or whether the Sudanese did it on their own, John never knew. Over the next weeks, United States Embassy officials visited him in prison. They offered him cigarettes, copies of *Time* magazine—and sanctuary in a United States prison. He refused, and kept on refusing.

Before he left the United States, John had weighed two hundred and ten pounds. During his flight, he had started to lose weight, which seemed almost a benefit at first. Losing weight might help his heart problem. In Khobar prison, however, with its heat, insects and inadequate food, he started to waste away. He was forty-five years old, in a situation that would be difficult for the health of a twenty-year-old. In the first two months he lost fifty pounds.

More months passed. Meanwhile, the United States Embassy kept pressing the Sudanese to release John into U.S. custody. "One morning they came and told me to get ready. I was going to court next day, and they said I had to wash my clothes. Well, I had been washing them every day for months. The next day there was a large metal enclosed van in the courtyard. The guards bundled me and seven other men into it. I didn't really know—I mean, they could have taken us some place and shot us, although I didn't think they would.

"And then I was in court. An imposing building, and when I entered there were African judges wearing white British-style judges' wigs! The attorney my friends had arranged for was there. I was to be tried for passport fraud. He asked for continuance and bail—and got it! I walked out. I had been in Khobar six months."

He weighed a hundred and sixty-two pounds.

That night John's friends held a party for him at the house of the attorney who had got him freed. In the end the attorney convinced the Sudanese court to refuse to release John to the United States Embassy. The court considered the case and decided to fine John ten dollars for entering the country with a false passport and released him, but ordered him to find some other country to go to. Unable to stay in the Sudan, he wandered from embassy to embassy in Khartoum for several weeks, looking unsuccessfully for a country that would take him.

A friend from Dar es Salaam stepped in. He interceded with the Minister of Health in Uganda, telling him John's medical qualifications. The Ugandan minister contacted the Ministry of the Interior in the Sudan and convinced him to send John to Uganda.

John was put onto a plane, then given a one-way visa to Uganda.

April, 1973

In the spring of 1973, John entered Uganda and found sanctuary at last.

Uganda desperately needed physicians. At the time John Branion entered the country, Uganda had twenty physicians per 100,000 people. The United States runs around 176 physicians per 100,000 people. The infant mortality rate in Uganda is 120 per 1,000 live births—12 percent. Incubators are virtually unknown.

John was immediately appointed Consultant Gynecologist for the Ministry of Health and assigned to Mbarara.

Uganda is about the size of Oregon and totally landlocked between Kenya, Tanzania, Zaire, and Sudan, but its southern border lies against beautiful Lake Victoria. The capital city, Kampala, overlooks the lake. Some of the best coffee in the world is grown in Uganda, though it is sent for packaging to Kenya and from there it is exported as Kenyan coffee. Ugandans speak English, Luganda, and Swahili. John set about learning Swahili. He applied for Ugandan citizenship.

Uganda had become independent of Great Britain in 1962. However, the ancient traditional kingdoms within Uganda remained highly independent. Indeed, the kingdoms had never been in any sense welded into a nation, but had simply been lumped together as a country for convenience by the colonizers. In 1967 the kingdoms were officially abolished and the central government consolidated power.

It was one thing to abolish the tribal kingdoms on paper. It was another thing to try to wipe out centuries of tribal allegiances. In 1971, two years before John Branion arrived, General Idi Amin seized power from President Milton Obote. When John Branion arrived in Uganda, Idi Amin's greatest excesses lay in the future. Amin knew himself to be an uneducated man, and he had surrounded himself with educated advisers.

"I believed, from what I actually saw when I got there, that Amin was making a real effort at that time to establish peace. But in the barracks, at least, the tribal wars went on. That's where you heard the trouble was. Not among the citizens in general. In the barracks, men were murdering each other.

"The two most warlike tribes are the Langi and the Acholi, both from the north. They were the tribes the colonizers used in their police and armies, and they were the two responsible for most of the bloodshed during the Amin regime."

As an educated man and a new citizen, John was the sort of person Amin would want to meet. John's new friends arranged an audience soon after John's arrival. Amin appeared reasonable.

"The first time I saw Idi Amin Dada," John said, "was at the dedication of a new water source in the western province of Uganda, about forty miles from Rowenzori National Park. Clean water was a major need and a real medical concern. The president had been engaged in building hospitals and drilling water taps throughout the country. This was genuinely necessary and the people believed he was doing them good.

"Senior civil servants from throughout the province had been invited to witness this much-waited event, and since I was the gynecologist at Mbarara Hospital, I was among those invited.

"I had been in the country only two months. This was my first state occasion. The air was festive, with dozens of automobiles and hundreds of people covering several acres of grass in this remote village. To one side of the designated area a large rectangular tent shadowed two groups of straight-backed chairs, placed facing an ornate upholstered seat for the president.

"As I watched the seats fill, I felt proud to be a part of this black country. It was exciting. The weather was hot and breezy (as usual) and the president was on his way.

"Shortly after all the seats were filled, I heard familiar voices. I was surprised to see Roy Innis—an old friend I had met frequently in New York with Oscar Brown, Jr. Innis was chairman of C.O.R.E., the Congress of Racial Equality. He was here with several other African-Americans visiting the president. Roy stopped and greeted me, then introduced me to the president. I can still feel Amin's strong handshake as I watched a warm smile fill his immense, oval face. There was an ease and confidence about his six-foot, three-inch, 200-pound frame. 'So this is our doctor in Mbarara? Welcome, brother, welcome,' he said. I felt self-conscious. I took his hand once again but this time I held my left hand on my right forearm, a Ugandan sign of respect.

"Later that day, during an open-air lunch, I spoke with the president again, and he urged Innis to bring me to Kampala for the Organization of

African Unity Conference. Idi Amin was to be chairman of the O.A.U. Conference."

In much of Africa, Asians are regarded as interlopers. A large number of Asians live and own businesses in Africa, but do not take on citizenship. The Africans see them as refusing to take on the burdens and responsibilities of the African countries, but simply living there, engaging in commerce, and draining the economies of the countries that house them.

In 1972, Amin had given the Ugandan Asians an ultimatum: either become citizens or leave. Most chose to leave. The few who remained tended to be the poorest Asians, who had nowhere else to go.

The world at large viewed this as an expulsion of Asians from Uganda. The event marked the beginning of more negative pictures of Amin in the United States media. The United States, Norway, and Canada called a halt to their economic aid programs to Uganda, and the United States withdrew all diplomatic personnel. It had been this last move that had led John's friends to suggest he go to Uganda in the first place. The United States could no longer reach him there.

"I did *not* perceive Amin at that time as being insane or out-of-control. True, he had not mastered the intertribal fighting. We knew there were tribal rivals killing each other, but we believed Amin was doing good things as well.

"One morning my phone rang at 7:30 and it was the president himself on the phone. He wanted me to come to Kampala, 180 kilometers away, that very afternoon, to attend a reception for a group of African-Americans given by Elisebeth Bagaya, a Toro princess, who was the first female government minister in Uganda's history. He said he thought my presence would be a positive image. He seemed to be honest, direct, and straightforward. I went, of course.

"I saw him again in September, I think, 1973. They were going to celebrate the foiling of an invasion attempt from Ugandan exiles in Tanzania. There was going to be a whole week of dances, sports events, and shooting competitions, culminating in a formal dance at the local army barracks of the Simba Mechanized Brigade.

"The evening of the finale, the president was in a cheerful mood. His personal troops had won the shooting competition. Food and drink were plentiful and I partook of both to an excess. My table was well placed on the edge of the dance floor and I could see the president seated at the center of the high table.

"I don't know if it was the happy, relaxed atmosphere or a drink too many, but I suddenly found myself at the high table, making my way to the president. He turned, turned his chair half to the side, and extended his hand.

"'Well, my dear doctor, how are you tonight? I hope you are having a good time.'

"I said, 'Oh, yes, sir. Everything is wonderful.'

"Turning to the general on his left, the commander of the Simba Mechanized forces, he said, 'This is our very good doctor here in Mbarara, who is doing a fine job for the community.' Then he turned to me and said, 'What can I do for you?'

"'Mr. President, I would like to become a Ugandan citizen. Will you make me one?'

"He turned to the General as if he himself had written this whole scenario and said, 'General, you bring the doctor to meet the military council so we can make him a citizen.'

"'You mean you'll make me a citizen, Mr. President?'

"'Why, of course, my brother.'

"There wasn't a word written anywhere that could have expressed my joy. Freedom and security at last. Shirley flashed through my mind.

"A few weeks later I was ushered into the famous—later to become infamous—Makindi Barracks in Kampala and told to wait in a lavish sitting room where drinks of all kinds sat on the table. In those days imported alcoholic beverages were only found in government establishments. I was nervous and anxious, but fortunately I didn't have to wait long. After a few minutes the president himself burst into the room smiling and escorted me to a large council chamber. The room was the size of a small ballroom with an enormous oval table in the center. Men in uniform were sitting around it.

"'Dr. Branion, this is our Military Council,' the president said. 'We have just voted to give you citizenship.' Before I could respond, he introduced me to the council. I shook each man's hand in turn and thanked him. They had TV cameras rolling and press people taking pictures. I wondered if pictures of this would find their way to the United States."

John was given a Ugandan passport. And he changed his last name to Busingye, which means "peace" in Kiswahili.

He had found a haven at last.

By this time Shirley was living back in Chicago with Jeff. She worked as a nurse at an emergency child care center run by the State of Illinois for battered or abandoned children. After a time, though, the inherent sadness of the job was too much for her; she applied for a job as a nursing home inspector and was accepted.

"Then Jeff developed asthma. He was just five years old, and I'd have been out all day on the job—you go to nursing homes to check their procedures, and sometimes they'd try to fool you or convince you what a good job they were doing, or they'd resent the fact that you were there. I'd get home tired and Jeff would wake up in the night wheezing and trying to get his breath.

"I thought about going west. Chicago was sooty and damp and cold. I thought about Denver. In Denver, even when it was cold, it was dry and clear. I started to tell Jeff we might move to Denver, and that if we did, his asthma would clear right up."

"My Ugandan immigration file was not complete," John said, "although I had received my naturalization certificate, because I hadn't obtained a certificate of renunciation of my U.S. citizenship. I renounced my citizenship before a magistrate in Mbarara and forwarded it to the U.S. Embassy in Nairobi, but they said I had to come there and renounce it in person. This I obviously could not do.

"One day in the fall of 1974, I went to a meeting with Roy Innis and President Amin at the Nile Hotel. I told the president the problem I was having and he dictated a decree on the spot exempting me from having to fulfill the renouncement requirement.

"But they still did not issue me a passport.

"Several months later, the president made a call for all doctors in Uganda to report to Mulago Hospital in Kampala. By this time, many professional Ugandans had begun to leave the country, and there were complaints that health care quality was falling. Amin in the past had had success with direct personal appeals for help in raising living standards.

"I arrived at Mulago auditorium and sat in the back, which was also the top, since the slope of the seats was two stories high. Anticipating the president's exit route, I left the meeting as he finished his speech and proceeded along the upper walkway, which intersected with the walkway he used leaving.

"I had planned it perfectly. We met in the walkway surrounded by TV camera and hordes of people. He said, 'Good afternoon, Doctor. Why do you look so disturbed?'

"I said, 'Well, sir, you made me a citizen but it seems others don't agree.'

"He frowned and ordered the TV cameras to stop and led me away from the crowd. He was angry. I knew I was taking a risk. He said, 'What do you mean, Dr. Branion?'

"'I've been trying to get my passport for six months, but the bureaucrats—'

"He raised his hand and cut me off. 'Take this brother to the passport office,' he said to his secretary. He looked at his watch. 'You have thirty minutes before it closes and I want him to have his passport today.' Thirty minutes later, I had a valid passport in the name of Dr. John Busingye.

"During that same conversation, before I left for the passport office, the president asked me to see a patient for him—one of his wives—who was at Mulago Hospital, and report to him the next day. I did, and I reported to his office in downtown Kampala. After I explained his wife's condition, he asked if there was any special project in medicine I was interested in. I told him I wanted to update the country's cancer registry for carcinoma of the cervix. He said I could have everything I needed to do it. I began testing patients and collecting data from all over Uganda.

"Over the months, I went to the president's office to discuss medical projects, and the president would ask me to examine one of his wives or girl friends. Although he was always polite and considerate, I was never completely at ease in his presence. His absolute power generated a sense of fear.

"A couple of times he started to ask me about some medical problem of his own, but I always passed it off, saying I was a gynecologist. There was a story in the United States that I had become personal physician to Idi Amin. It just wasn't true.

"By 1975 his popularity had really begun to wane and I became more self-conscious with him in public. Sides were being drawn up for and against Amin, and those seen with him were perceived as the enemy by the other side.

"I tried to distance myself from him."

November, 1975

John lived in Uganda, working as a physician, for two years. But while the United States authorities could not reach him there, another enemy could. Stress, bad food, and his history of heart disease were stalking him. He had chest pains and shortness of breath. As a doctor, he knew perfectly well what this meant.

He tried not to think about it. With the end of economic aid, medical supplies in Uganda had started to dry up and equipment was deteriorating.

He could not possibly get adequate care in Uganda if he was going to be a coronary patient.

In November of 1975, while visiting Rowenzori National Park, he had a heart attack. Now it was really a life and death matter to get treatment, even if he risked putting himself where United States authorities might find him. Nairobi was the nearest city with good health facilities. By December he thought he was well enough to travel. He packed up everything he could and in a jam-packed vintage Mercedes-Benz arrived in Kenya.

Drugs were available. He medicated himself with antihypertension drugs and nitroglycerine when his angina was severe. In spite of persistent shortness of breath, he applied to the Kenyan Ministry of Health and began working as a consultant gynecologist in the Central Province in Nyeri. Meanwhile, back in Uganda, Amin, fearful of overthrow, was increasing reprisals against dissenters and had himself proclaimed President for Life.

By February of 1976 John's chest pains and shortness of breath were much worse. By March he could not walk across a large room without stopping to gasp for breath. By April, he knew that he would not live long. The choice was to die in Kenya or go somewhere and have his constricted coronary arteries replaced. He telephoned an old friend who had been in medical school with him in Switzerland, who was now professor of cardiovascular surgery at the University of Geneva. He was told to come there—at once. He telephoned a message to Shirley that he was going, then got on a plane to Switzerland.

His old friend, Dr. Charles Hahn, met him at the airport. John could not walk faster than a shuffle and had to stop to breathe every few steps. Dr. Hahn got an ambulance for him and took him to the clinic, located between Lausanne and Geneva. John had managed to save five hundred dollars from his practice—a princely sum in Uganda—and believed he could pay for his hospitalization with it. He learned it would not even cover one day.

The first day Hahn did a cardiac catheterization to look at the coronary arteries and see which were clogged. As the dye was injected, John went into cardiac arrest. The doctors restarted his heart and prepared him for immediate surgery.

Dr. Hahn performed bilateral coronary bypass surgery and charged John nothing. John stayed in Switzerland recuperating for four weeks. Then, free of chest pains and breathlessness, he flew back to Kenya. Uganda was not possible; it was sinking into civil war.

He moved to the beautiful town of Kisumu on Lake Victoria, and opened a private practice. He had been there several months and was building the practice, when a man he did not recognize accosted him. The man claimed he was a Kenyan Interpol policeman, and he wanted $50,000 not to tell Interpol where John was.

Meanwhile, Shirley and Jeff had moved to Denver. Both of them loved the city. The air was clear. Jeff's asthma had gone away, just as Shirley had told him it would. Jan was in Denver also, and graduated from college there in 1975. She spent summers with the Browns in Chicago, usually.

John sometimes telephoned Jan at the Brown's house. If he happened to get Sydney, Sydney would speak with him. But later John discovered that Sydney did not necessarily pass on all his messages to Jan.

June, 1977

John did not have $50,000 to pay off the Interpol man. He did not have $5,000. The only solution, now that he had been recognized, was to flee again—to go some place where he could not be extradited. He left his practice and clinic and home and flew to Juba, Sudan, in a small private plane owned by a friend.

Juba is a town of 10,000 people in southern Sudan on the very upper reaches of the Nile. John had friends there and now he had so little money left that he needed their help badly. They were warm and welcoming and gave him housing and a job at the local hospital.

During the previous year, increasing tales of random murder in Uganda had been reaching the international news media. It was said that 200,000 of Amin's opponents had been killed since 1971. In June, just as John was reaching Juba, the Commonwealth Conference condemned the Amin government for "disregard for the sanctity of human life."

John, of course, had been ordered years before to leave Sudan. Now he hoped the government would not realize he was living in a small town in the south. But word that John was back seeped slowly northward from Juba toward the capital and after three months he was arrested by the Sudanese government and thrown in prison. The same friends who had helped him when he was arrested in Khartoum five years before came to his rescue again. They negotiated his release, helped him to a private plane, and sent him to Nairobi.

But here he was back in Kenya, where the Interpol policeman might recognize him. John met an old friend from Dar es Salaam, who offered to help John get to Dar if John would help him close out his business in Kenya first. John spent four weeks, filled with constant tension and nervous strain, in Kenya. Then, as they were ready to depart, his "friend" hopped a plane to Arusha, Tanzania, and left John stranded with no money and a four-week hotel bill. That same day, John ran into the Interpol policeman on the street. He had to leave.

Another friend, this one from California, bought him a ticket to Arusha and gave him fifty dollars. He got a small plane at Wilson Airport, and, flying as Dr. Busingye, went first to Arusha and then worked his way south to Dar es Salaam. He had scarcely settled there when he was recognized by the police. They were asking for him among people who might be his friends—asking for him by the name of Dr. John Branion. He went into hiding in another friend's house, and did not go outside the door for a month.

But he could not keep running and hiding. He was nearly fifty years old and had serious heart disease. His friend in Dar offered to let his wife and child go with John as cover to travel to Lusaka, Zambia.

Zambia is contiguous to Tanzania, to the southwest. Zambia is shaped something like a dumbbell and Lusaka is in its constricted middle. Travel there had been difficult, but in 1973 a truck road between Zambia and Dar es Salaam was built with United States aid, so that copper mined in Zambia could travel to the port of Dar es Salaam.

On this road, dressed as an Arab in turban and jalabia, John set out from Dar es Salaam at 1:00 a.m. by bus. The bus had hard wooden seats with straight backs. He and his temporary family rode for twenty-six hours, and came to the Zambia border.

John knew that the Tanzanian guards, on their side of the border, would be looking for Dr. Branion or Dr. Busingye. But the Zambian guards likely would not. A friend diverted the Tanzanians' attention while John walked forward across the border and presented himself to the Zambians. He was accepted.

His temporary family crossed the border. Together they boarded another bus with hard wooden seats, and set out on a second twenty-six-hour ride to reach Lusaka.

January, 1978

It was ten years since Donna's death and John was still a man without a country. Back home, Jan was twenty-four and Joby fourteen. Even little Jeff would be turning eight that spring. When John called Joanna she would not put Joby on the phone. Their estrangement was complete. But there was nothing to be gained by anguish. Had he been in the United States he would be in prison; he would be no more use to them in prison than he was here, searching through Africa for sanctuary.

Zambia, which used to be called Northern Rhodesia, has a cooler, drier climate than Tanzania. Lusaka, a city of 500,000, appealed to John.

Almost at once a wonderful thing happened. On the street he ran into Elim and Habib, the two men who had helped him escape from Eldridge Cleaver. They had lived in Zambia for several years and were doing well.

They introduced him to a Dr. John Billingsley, who had moved to Zambia from Detroit and was John's age. He and John became fast friends. Billingsley let John use his car and practice medicine with him. Physicians were even scarcer in Zambia than in Uganda, and there was plenty of work. Billingsley tried to get resident status for John in Zambia. Billingsley's friends helped. Three times they got three-month renewals of John's tourist visa. But after the third time Zambia would not renew it again.

John had to leave. In the nine months of work he had earned only enough money to pay for his own plane ticket. He wanted to try West Africa. Friends told him he could enter Ivory Coast without a visa. Billingsley gave him the name of a contact in the African Bank. And the official language of Ivory Coast was French, one of John's most fluent languages. He bought a ticket to Abidjan.

His information had been wrong. He landed in Abidjan, only to be told that tourists *did* need a visa. He asked for a brief pass. He wanted to get to the African Bank. He pleaded. He reasoned. He pleaded again, all in French. It took him twenty-four hours of talking and three shifts of airport personnel, but he finally got a one-day pass. He went directly to the African Bank to ask for a permanent visa. Incredibly, the contact's brother was chief of police. The man made two phone calls, and John got a one-year visa.

But that was the limit of the luck he would find in Ivory Coast. He could not get work. The ministry would not give him a job. He sought refuge in a Catholic retreat. The fathers tried to get him a job, but nothing worked. He had to move on. He bought a ticket back to Lusaka.

When he landed in Lusaka, he had ten dollars left and nothing else. Then he was stunned by bad news. The officials in the airport said he could not enter Zambia twice in the same year. It was December 17, 1978, fourteen days before 1979. In fourteen days he could enter. The officials were sympathetic, though, and agreed to call John's friend Dr. Billingsley. Billingsley came to the airport immediately. He arranged with the officials for John to be allowed twenty-four hours in Zambia to find somewhere else to go.

Billingsley suggested Botswana. He had a friend there. The next day, John flew to Habarone, the capital of Botswana.

John liked Botswana. It is a lightly populated country, with the Kalahan Desert in the southwest supporting nomadic tribes and rolling plains in the east where herds of cattle graze. There are more cattle than people in Botswana. Here, for the first time in ten years, John saw a Howard Johnson's restaurant, an unexpected reminder of his home land.

Billingsley's friend Ben was a successful businessman and treated John like a brother. Another friend of a friend took John to see the minister of health. They needed trained gynecologists and offered John a job. They wanted only a little time to run a security check. They told him to go home and wait. "Only a formality," they told him.

They never called him back.

In Denver, Shirley felt she was putting her life together. She had never met anyone else like John, and in fact she did not expect to; but she was beginning to overcome the depression of not knowing how he was, not knowing whether he was still alive.

She had a job that supported her and Jeff. She had friends in Denver and a nice apartment. There seemed no reason ever to go back to Chicago.

Once in a while she would come upon Jeff, standing in the middle of his room, his eyes closed, spinning slowly about with one arm held out straight in front of him. He would turn until he didn't know which way he was looking, then stick out a finger, point, open his eyes, and say, "Someplace out there is my father."

Uganda was falling apart, sinking into economic disaster and civil and border wars. For years Uganda and its longtime foe, Tanzania, had skirmished on the border. Now the Tanzanian invasion forces were swelled by huge numbers of Ugandan rebels and exiles. Uganda was in turmoil. In April of 1979, Amin had fled the country.

When it turned out that Botswana would not allow John to stay, he thought his only alternative was to return to Uganda. It was March of 1980 and he was broke. There was cheap transportation being offered in Dar es Salaam to return exiles to Uganda now that Amin was out, but John did not have enough money even for that.

With the remarkable friendliness and generosity that Africans had shown him so many times before, Ben offered to advance John $200 to get him to Uganda and cover expenses.

The flight was via Johannesburg and Nairobi.

Johannesburg! Thoughts of apartheid, South Africa's economic connections with the United States, and the "invincible" South African security police went through John's mind. Every person on a flight landing in Johannesburg is checked. He was terrified, but he had no choice.

When the plane landed in Johannesburg a delay developed— engine trouble. An hour stretched to seven hours. Finally, the passengers were told they could not proceed to Nairobi until the next day. The plane, officials said, required major repairs. John and the others were transported to hotels. Officials collected the passports of all the passengers.

John spent the night in fear. A delay this long would surely give the South African security police time to identify him. Had he run for ten years to be caught now? "In the morning they told us the flight to Nairobi was ready, and we boarded and left. How they missed me, I just don't know."

In Nairobi, he was uneasy again. The face of the Interpol policeman who had tried to blackmail him kept appearing in his mind's eye. It was several hours before he could board the flight to Dar es Salaam, so the airline put him up at the Nairobi Hilton. He stayed in the room, hiding. The flight left at dawn the next morning with no trouble.

In Dar, he stayed with friends because booking a flight to Entebbe in Uganda took several weeks. Dar was alive with reporters from various news services covering the thousands of Ugandan exiles trying to get home now that Amin was ousted. John got a flight on December 12, 1979, and landed in Entebbe that same day.

Tanzanian troops were controlling security and immigration at Entebbe airport. The Tanzanian officer who inspected John's Ugandan passport happened to be a man with a splendid memory. He remembered that John had been thrown out of Tanzania years before. He saw that the page that must have been stamped persona non grata was missing from the passport. John had removed it seven years before. The guard also saw that John's passport had been falsely renewed in Zambia, where there had been no Ugandan representatives. He detained John and was sending for the police when a Ugandan Immigration Officer who had been a friend of John's intervened, keeping the passport but allowing John to leave the airport.

John got a job teaching at Makarere University. "There was no medicine. The country was pauperized. There weren't even bandages. People coming to the hospital for surgery had to buy their own dressings and bring them in. They had to bring their own mattresses. When test tubes broke, there weren't any to replace them."

The Ugandan government had still not given him a new passport, and this left him vulnerable, but there was nothing he could do about it and he enjoyed teaching. He even began to think of sending to the United States for his family.

But his old enemy, his heart, was stalking him again.

"In 1981 I started getting chest pains again. My blood pressure was up. You can't get drugs in Uganda, you just have to treat yourself as best you can. I'd work two hours and teach, then go home and lie down an hour, then go back and work.

"It was getting worse and worse. Shortness of breath. Sharp chest pains whenever I exerted myself. I thought it was time for me to give up. It was the end. I would just die, in Uganda."

Shirley said, "I had completely lost touch with him. There were no reports coming back from anyone. The last I knew, he was going to Switzerland for open-heart surgery. I believed he had died on the operating table.

"Jeff asked quite often where his father was, why his father wasn't with him. For years I had always told him he couldn't be here, but he wanted to be. And that maybe some day he *would* be.

"Now I thought we would never see him again.

"Suddenly, he called. Out of nowhere. It was spring, I remember. The spring of 1982. He had called Jan, in Chicago, and she called me to ask me whether it was okay for her to give him my phone number. Of course it was okay.

"He said he was dying and he wanted me to come to Uganda and bury him."

Shirley needed time to think. She wanted to see John; if he had been near, she would have gone immediately.

"I didn't have the money for the air fare. Two air fares, Jeff and me. I was making a regular salary, but it's hard to explain to somebody in Africa that what you're making here doesn't go far. What I was earning a week, here, you might earn in Uganda in four months. But that doesn't mean you have any money left over. I'd get my salary check and by the time I paid rent and bought food, it would mostly be gone. The money was gone.

"And I thought the FBI would follow us to try to find him. Besides, Jeff was in school here. What would life in Uganda be like? I'd heard about Idi Amin, and even though he was gone, it wasn't a stable situation. And to take a child into a place like that. . . .

"But I couldn't help thinking. Jeff had asked all these years where his father was. What if this was his last chance to see him? Besides, John was the only man I ever loved. Well, I just sold everything I had that I could sell, and put the rest in storage in Denver, and we bought tickets and went to Uganda."

"John was very sick. He had chest pain now even when he wasn't exerting himself. A few weeks after we arrived John had a heart attack. He didn't tell me about it at first; he just didn't come home from work, and I went and found him lying down at school.

"There was nothing we could do, medically. There was no medicine to speak of there, and we had no money to send him someplace else.

"But I started talking to him. I told him my experiences with positive thinking, and the way I'd converted all the fear and tension I had been having. I told him about using the right side of his brain to help heal himself, and about going to deeper levels of consciousness.

"Well, you can imagine! Doctors just *do not* believe in things like that. He thought it was just so much talk. I'd tell him and tell him and I'd say 'Look at me; I'm applying this.' And he'd nod, but you could see him think it was just my imagination.

"And if we'd been anywhere else, he might have gone on resisting it. But there we were—out of reach of medical intervention, out of reach of basic medications. He was going to die. That was all. If he didn't turn it around somehow, he was going to die.

"I told him I was not going to allow that.

"He had a lot of anger. At the Browns, who he thought sabotaged his trial or pushed for his arrest. At the United States legal system. Never before, in all the time I'd known him, had he been an angry person. Now he was angry at life. And it was one of the things that was killing him.

"And stress. He'd been through so much."

John rested and worked, and slowly his thinking changed. Shirley insisted that he meditate three times every day. Jeff was going to school and adapting well. Shirley was learning to cook Ugandan style and use Ugandan foods. Shirley and Jeff were both learning Kiswahili rapidly. They had a pretty house on the school grounds with a garden in back where they grew tomatoes and beans.

John gradually began feeling better. He was eating virtually no fat. Ugandans eat less meat than Americans, and the meat they raise is far less fatty. Shirley gave him fresh vegetables, fruit, grains, and legumes. John himself started cooking again, as he had liked to do with his father and Donna in the old days.

The political situation in Uganda had not improved as much with the ouster of Idi Amin as the foreign press suggested. Obote, who had returned to power, had not been able to eliminate the tribal rivalries, even though the random violence had decreased. John admired a man named Museveni. Museveni had "gone to the bush," as Ugandans say when a person is fighting from a position in the country, but John constantly predicted, "Museveni will come back."

John and Shirley made friends at Makarere, including a woman named Fatima. Fatima was originally from Zanzibar, but had married a Ugandan and was working in African radio. In 1987, Fatima described to me the situation as it had been in Uganda:

"When I first met Shirley and John and Jeff they were a mystery to me. I liked them very much, but I wondered what their story was. Why were these educated Americans living and working in Uganda, in what was really the middle of a war? Why would as skilled a physician as John Branion be working here with no supplies? Life was not secure here. Kampala, the capital, was a war zone.

"John was working with wounded men, and doing surgery under terribly difficult circumstances. Old, old equipment. And never enough medicine. He delivered babies, too.

"Coming from a culture, as I did, where life was practically over when a person reached the late forties, Shirley and John were inspiring. In Africa, you feel you've done what you've been meant to do by the time you reach middle age. People die at fifty-five.

"And of course, in African and middle eastern cultures, the position of women is very inferior. In many places, women are still chattels. They can't even receive birth control in some places unless their husbands go along to the clinic and give permission.

"It was good to see a couple who loved each other. A peaceful couple. Shirley and John spent *all* their time together, except when John was actually working. There was a tremendous sense of peace in their house. John was very devoted. Shirley was very much in love with him. And Jeff was doing well in school. He was a very intelligent boy, and very able to make friends. I was proud of him, just to watch him. It was very inspiring.

"And they both liked to cook. At their house, you would be served the *best* meals."

Shirley became pregnant.

"I thought about how John had never had the chance to actually raise his children," she says. "He loved children. He was very good with them. He had never seen a child of his grow up from birth to adulthood. Joby had been taken away from him. Jan grew up with him at first, but he lost her in the late teen years. And Jeff—with Jeff he'd missed all the middle years. I thought we could live there in Uganda always. And he could bring up his child.

"I was apprehensive because of my age. I was forty-three then, and the chances of complications were higher. And then, there was just no medicine in Uganda. But I thought I had the world's best obstetrician right there."

John, who had been quite serene since Shirley and Jeff arrived, had developed a sense of impending disaster. He fought it. It was a negative thought, so he put it out of his mind.

Suddenly, everything broke. One evening, he didn't come home. In Uganda, nobody stayed outdoors after sundown. It was too dangerous. There could be killers in the dark. But now it was after dark, and where was John? Shirley paced and looked out the window. She tried not to let Jeff see how worried she was. John was always home by now. Dinner was started. She looked out again, but there was no one coming up the walk.

Fatima recollected: "Shirley and I found him in the police station in Wundegeya, near Makarere University. He was being held in the jail there. We found him, but we couldn't do anything to get him out.

"They have a system in Africa where you take food to a relative in prison. Shirley was allowed to take food in to him, but she couldn't get him out. John was apprehensive. He thought they were going to ransom him back to the United States.

"Then after a couple of weeks, Shirley took him food one day, and he wasn't there any more. He'd been taken to Entebbe Airport and put on an airliner. There was a sheriff from Cook County aboard. The next thing we knew he was gone. All this had happened in a period of fifteen days or so, and the stress on Shirley was terrible.

"John had managed to smuggle a note out to Shirley via a maid in the hotel where they had kept him overnight in London on the way home. Shirley went to everyone to complain and ask for help. Everyone! She was magnificent! She went to Obote's daughters! She went to judges, magistrates. Obote knew about John, but he still let it happen.

"Some other people and I helped arrange a press conference for her. The press is controlled in Uganda, but there are reporters from outside, foreign and other African press, sometimes people from Nairobi. Shirley was wonderful. She told them, 'I thought slavery had been abolished in Africa. But here you see, black men are still being sold.'

"Naturally, she was implying there had been a payoff. Well, there probably was, one way or another. But that finished her in Uganda. Two hours later the security forces deported her and Jeff."

October, 1983

On Saturday, October 1, 1983, the headline of the City section of the *Tribune* was: "Convicted Wife Killer Who Fled Found in Africa."

"'We have word from the State Department that the Ugandan government has decided to expel Dr. Branion and is prepared to turn him over to our representatives,' said Greg Ginex, Chief of the Criminal Prosecutions Bureau in the Cook County state's attorney's office.

"Ginex said detectives from the Cook County Sheriff's fugitive section are expected to leave for Uganda on Wednesday to be on hand when police surrender Branion at Entebbe Airport.

"'If all goes well, the long-sought fugitive should be back in this country, headed straight for prison by week's end,' Ginex said.

"Upon his arrival in Chicago, Branion will be greeted by two old acquaintances: former homicide detectives Michael Boyle and John Mannion, who went on to law school and became assistant state's attorneys.

"Now, as prosecutors, they may get a chance to prosecute their old adversary again—this time for jumping bail."

A day or two later, the mission was complete. The *Tribune* headlined: "Fugitive Wife-killer Arrested in Africa."

The story said Branion "was arrested in Africa Wednesday by the Cook County Sheriff's Office, and by nightfall was in a London jail awaiting a flight to the United States.

"The twelve-year odyssey of Dr. John Marshall Branion, Jr. ended at Entebbe Airport in Uganda, whose former dictator-president Branion had served as a private physician until a new regime took over and declared Branion officially out of favor with the country.

"'Good morning, doctor. We have a warrant for your arrest,' said Sheriff's investigator Michael Blackburn as Ugandan police escorted Branion to the hatch of an airliner where the Cook County lawman and his partner, investigator Albert Roth, waited.

" . . . Although Branion maintained his innocence, police established a motive of marital discord and, using a stopwatch, demolished an alibi in which he claimed he could not have been present when 'an intruder' entered the home and fired the fatal shots.

" . . . Keating said he understood that Uganda's decision to expel Branion was reached last month at 'diplomatic levels' between Washington and the Ugandan capital of Kampala.

"In Chicago, Branion's trial attorney, Maurice Scott, said he had obtained a copy of the court file of the case—at the 'request of a mutual friend' he did not identify—but said he has no plans to represent the physician.

"'I don't know of any legal remedy available to him, short of a petition for executive clemency,' Scott said. 'I feel he is innocent; I did then and I do now.'"

A photograph appeared in the October 14 *Tribune*. Titled "Fugitive Arrives from Africa," it shows John Branion in beard, dark glasses, denim jacket and handcuffs.

The same day the Chicago *Sun-Times* ran a close-up AP photo. Titled "Twelve-year Flight Ends," it says Branion "spent seven of his twelve years as a fugitive serving as personal physician to former Ugandan dictator Idi Amin."

And on Monday, October 17, the *Tribune*'s story was: "Bail-jumper killer meets 'old friends'"

"Dr. John Marshall Branion, the convicted killer who jumped bail in 1971, looked thin and haggard to a few 'old friends' who were waiting to see him as he made his first appearance in Cook County Criminal Court in more than 14 years.

"'Every story has an ending' said Michael Boyle, an assistant state's attorney who was one of two Chicago homicide detectives who gathered the evidence that helped to convict Branion in connection with the 1967 murder of Donna Brown Branion, his socialite wife.

"'I heard one time Branion perished. I had been told he was killed in the revolution' that banished Amin from power, Boyle said.

"'I'm here to see an old friend,' quipped John Mannion, Boyle's partner in the 1967 investigation. 'He looks like he had a rough time. He's thinner.' Like Boyle, Mannion graduated from law school and joined the Cook County state's attorney's office in the years since Branion's disappearance.

"'Everybody gets old. We've all got gray hair now,' Mannion said."

PART FOUR

The Struggle

· CHAPTER TWENTY-SIX ·

A cold Saturday morning, the twenty-third of November, 1985. I got up at 6:00 a.m. in order to have time to drink two cups of coffee slowly. Then I called Shirley Branion to let her know I was leaving. It was almost an hour's drive from my place north of Chicago to her place south of the Loop, and we had arranged this call so that she would have time to get ready. Most of the way to her house, it was still dark.

She was ready when I rang the doorbell. We left Chicago at 7:15 with 280 miles to drive to southern Illinois, where Dr. John Branion then lived—in the Graham Correctional Facility. at Hillsboro, Illinois, a maximum-security Illinois state penitentiary.

After we were past the refineries and factories surrounding outer Chicago, we were in open, flat country that had once been prairie. We saw wide fields with corn stubble and now and then a broad marsh with open water in the distance. Huge flocks of Canada geese were migrating south. It was just a few days before Thanksgiving and just a month short of being eighteen years since John's first wife, Donna Branion, was murdered.

It was a five-hour drive, not counting the stop for hamburgers. We considered getting food at a McDonald's drive-through window, but instead we went inside so that we could stretch out. All the way to Hillsboro, Shirley talked about the case and her husband John and her children, Jade and Jeff, and I asked questions.

Jeff, John and Shirley's son, was nearly seventeen. "Jeff was away in France last summer," she says, "in the Experiment in International Living program. He and John speak French together sometimes."

"So Jeff's a junior this year?"

"Mmm-hmm. The Harvard recruiter asked him to apply. John's so proud of him."

"How long since he's seen John?"

"Three months. August. That's the last time Jade saw John, too." Jade, who was one and a half, was growing so fast John was missing everything—

all the milestones, the first word, the first step. She was born three months after John was imprisoned. "We just can't get down to the prison. It's too far. I can't afford to fly. And even if you take a bus to Springfield or St. Louis, you can't get to Hillsboro without a car. I ride with friends, if they'll take me. But it's hard. You can't dump two children on friends. A baby for five hours in a car—"

"Yes, I know."

"Let alone if she gets carsick."

"And by the time you get there, she'd be so tired she'd sleep or cry through the whole visit," I said.

Shirley had just gone back to college a year and a half before, when she was able to find a good person to take care of Jade. She was studying television and film.

"I was a nurse for nearly twenty years," she said. "But that was enough."

John and Shirley had been doing research on John's case, finding witnesses to where John had been when the murder took place. In the years since the crime, he had forgotten much of what he did that day, who he had been with at the hospital while Donna was being murdered. Even on the day of the crime he could not remember much of what he had done that morning; the earlier events of the day were blasted out of his mind when he came home with his son and found his wife dead on the laundry room floor.

"How did you locate these witnesses?"

"John called some of the hospital people from prison. He figured they must have seen him at work that morning."

"How does he pay for calls?" I knew he earned about a dollar a day working on the prison newspaper.

"He can't. He can only call people who'll accept calls collect."

"Can he call any time he wants?"

"No, the phones are on every other day. And he can't call during work periods."

"Does he call you?"

"Once a month. I can't afford anything more than that. Long-distance collect adds up too fast. We have an arrangement. He calls either the first or second day of the month, depending on when the phones are turned on."

"He's a doctor. Why is he working on the newspaper? Why not the infirmary?"

"He lost his license when he was convicted. They won't even let him work as an orderly."

"What a waste."

We got to Hillsboro about 1:00 p.m. It was a small, scattered-looking town, with not much sense of "center." Signs along the roadway read, "PENAL INSTITUTION DO NOT PICK UP HITCHHIKERS." We had a reservation in what seemed to be the only local motel. It was small and clean, but there was no restaurant. As it turned out, we wouldn't need one. We would stay all day in the prison.

We took just enough time to sign in, then headed directly to the prison.

A chain-link fence about ten feet high and topped with rolls of barbed wire surrounded the compound. The long drive leading to the front entrance was flanked by wide stretches of meticulously groomed grass, brown now in November. A few flakes of snow were just beginning to blow through the air when we arrived. In front of the entry were remnants of what must have been flower beds in summer, carefully dug under. There was not a gum wrapper nor a soft drink can nor any other litter, nor so much as a branch of a tree out of place. Plenty of free labor, I thought.

We parked and locked the car. I had brought a tape recorder but had been told I couldn't take it inside, so I left it in the car. I figured we might find out more later about how strict or lenient they really were.

Shirley knew the procedure. We went to the entry desk, where we gave them our driver's licenses to keep until we left. A woman in a guard's uniform checked our faces against our drivers license pictures and punched the license numbers into a terminal. I assumed that if there were any outstanding arrest warrants on us, they would soon know.

We also signed the visitors' book with the name of the person we were visiting, his number—L34569 in John's case—and our relationship. Most visitors wrote "wife" or "friend" or "freind." The one just before me wrote "granny."

Then we sat and waited.

Whether they were processing our driver's licenses, telling the interior guards that L34569 had visitors, checking to see whether we were on John's visitors list (if we weren't, we wouldn't get in), or just letting us know who's boss, they took quite a while for it. We talked and watched the next shift of guards arrive. Most of them had a characteristic walk, these prison guards. It seemed derived from decades of watching actors in western movies, with an extra touch of Dirty Harry. Feet farther apart than usual, especially when they stopped and stood for a moment. Arms held a few inches out from the sides, to allow for the invisible two-gun holsters. Shoulders moved as a whole chunk. Gunslingers.

Then we were admitted. The admission guard handed us a locker key with a number on it. We went to the locker and put in it everything they didn't want us to take inside. Keys. Wallets. Bulky outer clothing that could contain drugs. Books. Pens and pencils, even sheets of paper. If we had guns or knives or bombs, this was the place to leave them.

We could take in twenty dollars. At Hillsboro you met your prisoner in the canteen, and you could use the money for coffee, sandwiches, candy, and so on from the machines. The prisoner was not allowed to buy anything himself, but his visitors could buy food for him.

We entered the room where women visitors were searched. The female guard had us take off our shoes and jackets, patted us down and checked inside our shoes and the bottoms of our feet. I was amazed at how cheerful and courteous to the guard Shirley was through it all. In the same situation, I think I would have been resentful. Silent, maybe, but resentful.

The woman who searched us stamped our hands with a dye that showed up under ultraviolet light.

Passed through, we entered an "airlock" exit from the admissions area. We walked through sliding entry doors, which the guard operated on word from the woman who searched us. When we were inside this vestibule, the sliding doors closed behind us. Not until they were closed did the guard open the sliding exit doors on the far side.

We crossed a featureless courtyard that was totally enclosed by blank walls and walked into another airlock entry. Once admitted to the corridor, Shirley showed me the way to the guard's booth. There a male guard looked at our hands under ultraviolet light. The stamp mark glowed purple.

From there we approached a booth in the guards' area, where we changed a twenty-dollar bill for coins.

We entered the canteen and signed in with a guard who sat on a platform overlooking the whole canteen area. Then we waited for John to arrive.

To go to see visitors, a prisoner runs through a full strip search.

I had never met John, or talked to him. I liked Shirley. I liked the fact that she just wouldn't quit. But John Branion himself was the important unknown. I had serious doubts, from the documents Shirley had brought in, that he could have killed his wife. But doubts are not certainties. It was very important to me to find out what sort of person he was.

We talked and waited for the prison system to produce him.

Shirley had spent months and months trying to find an attorney to take John's case. Howard Savage, who had been hired by John in 1969 to undertake his appeal, was now a judge and couldn't resume the case. Savage did not hold out much hope to Shirley that any efforts in the courts to free

John would work. Shirley had been to several lawyers, but they usually said one of two things: "Get $10,000 together and we'll see what we can do," or "There's nothing anybody can do for him except appeal to the governor for clemency."

My husband, Tony D'Amato, is a professor at Northwestern Law School in Chicago. His fields are international law and jurisprudence, the philosophy of law. Shirley had read a newspaper article describing a case in which Tony and others had succeeded in getting a man out of a Mexican prison. With that much information, she started to ask around about him.

Tony is a scholarly sort of person who likes to write articles and rarely takes cases, possibly one or two a year. Most of those are international law cases.

When Shirley telephoned him, she said her husband was in prison for a crime he hadn't committed. Tony told her he'd talk with her, but that it wasn't really his field. She came to his office.

"Has Dr. Branion appealed the conviction?" he asked.

"Yes," she said. "The appeal was denied."

"Illinois Supreme Court?"

"Yes. Denied."

"Did the attorney appeal to the United States Supreme Court?"

"Yes. They wouldn't hear the case."

"What date was that?"

"1971."

"1971! When was the murder?"

"1967. December 22."

"But—that's eighteen years ago. What was the sentence?"

"Twenty to thirty years. I know what you're going to ask. He didn't start serving the sentence until 1983. He was free on bond from 1968 to 1971. When the Supreme Court wouldn't hear the case, he knew he was going to prison. He went to Africa instead. He was there twelve years."

"Oh, Lord."

"He'll be sixty in January. He's had four coronaries and bypass surgery. He's in prison for killing his wife and he didn't kill her. He'll die there unless something is done."

Tony was appalled. "Then he's exhausted all the ordinary state appeals."

"What can you do?"

"You know, we have two coexisting systems in this country. The state courts and the federal courts. You could try a post-conviction motion through the state system."

"How often does that work?"

"Maybe a chance in a thousand. And the state courts take years."

"He doesn't have years. His heart's not good enough."

"The federal system is faster, usually. You could ask for a writ of habeas corpus."

"How likely is that to work?"

"I don't know enough about this case. But it's very, very rarely granted."

Shirley said, "But he's innocent."

"What papers do you have?"

Shirley had with her a copy of the decision of the Supreme Court of the State of Illinois. She also had with her six affidavits: three of them showed that Dr. Branion had left the hospital at least a few minutes later than the jury knew. These were from the hospital lab technician, Robert Wadley, the pharmacist, LaHarry Norman, and the nurse who circulated patients into the clinic examining rooms, Betty Adger. One affidavit was from a Cottrell Meadors, an acquaintance who saw Branion in the car with his son at a time that made the witness think he could not have been home killing Donna. And two of the affidavits showed that the night before the murder Maxine Brown, the friend who was to come to lunch, had been asked to lunch by both Donna and John Branion, not by John alone over the phone and at the last minute, as the Illinois Supreme Court decision stated.

In fact, as I read it, there were several points in the Illinois Supreme Court decision that raised questions. It said that Mrs. Kentra, the next-door neighbor, heard the sounds about 11:30 and Dr. Branion left the hospital about 11:30. Then how could he be in the apartment killing his wife? How far was the apartment from the hospital? And Mrs. Kentra had said she heard the sounds about twenty minutes after 11:05. Wouldn't that make it 11:25?

It said that Dr. Branion picked up his son at nursery school and then visited Maxine Brown's office with the child, and that the police patrol car was called at 11:58. That was twenty-eight minutes. Could the murder really have been squeezed in? Or to put it another way, how long did the murder take—only the time required to fire four shots?

Then there was the sentence: "When the police found, a month later, a box of .380 caliber bullets designed to hold 25 bullets, with exactly four missing, the evidence was convincing." This is a strong statement.

If the four rounds of ammunition that were missing from the box in the closet were really important evidence, why didn't Dr. Branion get rid of the box during the month between the murder and the day he was arrested? A stupid person might not think of it. An emotional person might forget it for the moment. But this was a bright person who had a month to do it.

It said that Donna Branion was killed with a rare Walther PPK. I knew the Walther PPK was anything but a rare gun in 1967. In fact, it was the dernier cri of guns. It was the James Bond gun, made popular by both the Ian Fleming books and the Sean Connery movies. My guess was they sold so fast they'd be hard to keep in stock. I didn't know whether this was important, but it undermined my faith in the Illinois Supreme Court's statement of the facts.

The case obviously was circumstantial. Circumstantial evidence is in some ways the best sort. It is much more reliable than eyewitness identification, for example. But it does have to fit together and be substantial. In this case it was thin. No one saw him at the scene. No evidence put the gun in his hand.

Motive, means, and opportunity. For motive they had Dr. Branion's affair with Shirley. How urgent was that? Why couldn't he have got a divorce? Did he even want one? Surely, if every man who ever had an affair killed his wife, the number of women in this world would be pretty small.

Means: he apparently owned a gun or guns. If a man has a set of steak knives and one of them is used to murder his wife, to what extent does that prove he killed her? The problem with the gun as proof was that it was available to anyone who entered the house.

Opportunity? That was the real question. Did Dr. Branion have the time to kill his wife?

Shirley had no money to spend on the case and Tony had no time, or very little. He had classes and was in the middle of writing two books. But I had just finished a project, a long novel, and I had not started anything new.

Tony, Shirley, and I talked about the difficulties. Did she want me to start research, on the understanding that we didn't know whether there was enough for a legal case? What if all that came out of it was a short magazine article?

"That would be better than what we have now."

"What if it looks to me like John is guilty?"

"It won't. And the more you find out, the clearer it's going to be."

Tony was well aware that most felons claim they are innocent. Cautiously, he said, "The first thing we need is a transcript of the trial. Either the trial attorney or the appeal attorney would have it."

Shirley said, "No. They say they haven't. I've been to both of them."

Dr. Branion was a professional man, and as a professional he realized how much work this was going to be. He was worried about Tony doing the work without compensation. Although Dr. Branion was indigent, he insisted in his first telephone conversation with Tony that Tony should be paid for his legal services. Tony said that he wanted to handle the habeas corpus aspect of the John's case pro bono, but that he would not object to being compensated by Dr. Branion from any future developments after the habeas matter was over. The two possible future developments were these: that I might produce a book on the Branion case, if there was enough material, and that a book could conceivably be the basis of other products like a movie or television show. Second, that if John was released and there was a civil lawsuit by the Branions against the state for wrongful imprisonment (not a likely prospect), then John could compensate Tony. John agreed to this approach.

For my part, I decided to do what I could with the case, and write what seemed possible, and if I made any money on the writing, share it fifty-fifty with the Branions after expenses. It looked at this time as if there was only enough information for a magazine article.

The plan was that Shirley and I, together, would do the research. Tony would come in later to prepare legal papers, if we found enough for that. For now he would get the court order we needed to have the trial transcript unearthed from an Illinois vault.

But—a case eighteen years old? Jurors were surely dispersed. Witnesses would have died. How many had died and how frustrating it would be I did not even guess at that time.

Was it even possible to reconstruct what had happened eighteen years before? To rebuild a picture of everything John Branion had done on the morning of December 22, 1967? And then to decide for certain whether he was innocent or guilty?

We thought at the time we were being very realistic in wondering whether we would find out enough to make a case or a story. As it turned out, we had no idea how obstructive the record-keeping departments of the state would be. Or how much material would simply be lost. Or even how irrational the judiciary could be. If we had known then, we might not have started the project at all.

Except for the guard's dais, the canteen in the prison at Graham was almost indistinguishable from the McDonald's where Shirley and I had eaten lunch. We sat on colored plastic chairs that were attached to plastic tables. Around the top of the brick walls hung paintings by prisoners. Some were really good.

We talked about the paintings and waited for John.

I expected a bitter man, and an angry man.

Shirley saw him first.

He was wearing blue prison denims and he came through the door, nodding to the guard and scanning the canteen with his eyes. He was a puckishly handsome man, nearly sixty, though he looked perhaps fifty. He had a high forehead, alert intelligent eyes, a springy step, and he was smiling broadly at Shirley. They hugged—a long minute—and then she introduced me.

"I'm glad to see you both," he said.

John must have realized that a lot was riding on what I thought of him. It is one thing to think that someone may be innocent. It's quite another to devote perhaps years of non-stop research to his case. But he didn't launch into any arguments. He seemed delighted to see Shirley and happy to have somebody from outside to talk with. We sat back down. It was 2:00.

John turned to me. "How was your trip?"

"Okay. Long."

Shirley said, "I wish you were closer to Chicago."

"I'd like to meet Tony," John said. "But getting all the way down here— I know he doesn't have the time."

"Well, you can call him collect," I said. "How do we go about writing letters?"

"The guards here read our mail. They're supposed to just open it and look it over for contraband."

"What kind of contraband?"

"Drugs. They're supposed to open the letter and look between the sheets of paper and hand it on to you. But we know they read it, because some of the guards taunt the prisoners with what they find out from the mail."

"Is it okay if we write you about what we're finding out?"

"Have Tony write. Mail from attorneys isn't supposed to be opened by the guards. You write "legal mail" on the envelope and I have to open it and shake it out in the presence of a guard. But they aren't supposed to read it."

"Okay. What about mail you send us?"

"That is the stupidest thing! We're supposed to be able to send out mail unread. But they make us leave the envelope open and they seal it before they take it to the post office. Which means, of course, they can read it if they want. It doesn't make any sense! We're certainly not able to send out any contraband. It's stupid! There's no reason for it. A few of the guys have gotten together to ask a court to declare our right to seal our mail."

"Including you," Shirley said, wryly. She knew John's tendency to say what he thought.

"Yeah."

We talked about Donna. "I didn't kill her," John said, almost wearily. "I loved her." He put his hand over Shirley's. "Shirley knows."

We talked and talked and talked. The case, the kids, John's flight to Africa. What to do now. We walked over to the bank of food machines for coffee, then later to find some dinner. There was a sandwich machine and a hot meal machine with little cans of stew or spaghetti which you took to the microwave to heat. John had been avoiding fat in the years since his heart attacks and coronary bypass surgery.

"Everything here has fat," he said. "Fat and salt. I'm supposed to be in the diet line—high fiber and low fat—and they keep dropping my name from the diet list. And here. Look at this. Ham and cheese. Sausage and biscuits. Butter. Egg salad. Potato chips. People shouldn't eat this stuff."

"This machine has apples."

"Oh, okay. What do you want in your coffee, Barbara?"

He wanted to pay, he wanted to treat us, but of course he didn't have any money. He couldn't even touch money. So he settled for carrying everything back to the table for us.

"I'll be sixty next month," John said. "Almost everybody in here is under twenty-five. Most of them never finished high school."

I thought: who is a European-trained physician who speaks five languages going to talk with in a place like this? I asked, "Do you have some friends here?"

"Oh, yeah. Several. I had one kid, he always wanted to talk about things. *Loved* to talk. He was just so damn bored. He was in for just a year. Burglary. Terrible family background. His father beat him. You know the sort of thing."

"Yes."

"But he was going to go straight. He promised me. We talked about what he would do. What kind of job he could get. He had some training as a cook."

"Great."

"Well, but he was back in three months. Another burglary." John shook his head. "He really had me fooled."

John laughed ruefully at himself for being so gullible. And then admitted he was still talking with the kid.

"Maybe this time," he said.

I had not expected this sort of gentle, ironic humor.

At the moment we were talking, his trial judge, Reginald Holzer, was coming to trial himself for extorting money from attorneys. After eighteen years of subtly asking attorneys who had cases before him for "loans" which were never repaid, Holzer had been caught by a federal probe.

"Do you think they'll retry my case because Holzer was corrupt?" John asked.

Wishful thinking. "I think they should. But the system doesn't work like that." I remarked that Tony thought a corrupt judge was the worst thing that could happen to a judicial system.

"Sure. Still, you have to feel sorry for him," John said.

"For Holzer? Why?"

"From the story, he was living in a Michigan Avenue apartment, that went for $2,750 a *month*. Spending, spending, spending. That's crazy. There wasn't any need for that. He didn't even really need the money he extorted. Not to live on. He just couldn't help it."

"He should have helped it."

"No, I don't know. You have to feel sorry for him. It was an addiction. Money to him—he must have been a lot like a junkie."

I had long since resolved that I would ask John Branion questions to find out how he thought and what he was like. But as far as deciding whether he could have killed his wife, I would use only information external to him—police reports, trial testimony, independent witnesses.

"John, how about some hard questions?"

"Okay."

"The police say they didn't find any signs of break-in at your apartment. And they say there was this special burglar-bar on the back door. How would somebody get in?"

"Donna used to leave the back door unlocked in the daytime so Maxine Brown could come in and visit. They were best friends. Maxine lived in one of the upstairs apartments. But I don't think that day she would have; Maxine was at work that day. What I think happened is Donna opened the front door to somebody who said he was a delivery boy. It was Christmas, just before Christmas, you know."

"They say you knew Donna was dead because you saw lividity on the body, but there was no lividity yet—"

"I said cyanosis. I don't know why they thought I said lividity. But the point was, I knew she was dead. Her color was bluish. You can't mistake it if you've seen enough dead people."

And he was a doctor. No doubt he had seen dead people.

"Did Donna know you were having an affair with Shirley?"

"Donna knew. We just didn't talk about it."

"How long had that been going on?"

"Six years."

Six years! It didn't sound very urgent to me.

232 · THE STRUGGLE

"I see you gave the police a .380 when they asked for a gun. Why not the Walther PPK, if you had one?"

"I don't think it went like that. It was confused, you know. There was Donna, dead, and the children—Jan came home from school a little after 12:00, because it was the last day before Christmas. There were police all over the house. One of them asked me for a gun and I gave them one. And later—about 3:00—they took me to the police station. I don't think they asked anything about the gun then. They asked what I did all morning and things like that. Then I went home, and they came to the house in the evening and that was when they asked for the .380, I think. But in the afternoon I hadn't even looked for anything—whether anything was missing."

"That's two guns you gave them. And the Walther PPK was a third. How many did you have?"

"About thirty."

"Wow. Why so many?"

"I had been collecting guns for quite a while. I had several antique guns that I really liked. I found one of the antique guns was missing that night. And five hundred dollars we had ready to go buy Christmas presents. I had some rifles and shotguns. I used to go goose hunting in Canada every year."

"Did you keep any of them loaded?"

"Yeah." His voice sank. He was not proud of it.

"Where did you keep them?"

"One near the front door and one near the back door."

"Was one of those the Walther?"

"I don't think so. I think it was in the den on the closet shelf. I think one of the ones near the door was the Hi-Standard. That was why I thought of it when the cop asked for a gun. You know, the guns—they were up on closet shelves, where Joby couldn't get at them."

"Still—"

"I know. Don't say it. *I'll* say it. If I hadn't kept them around this probably never would have happened."

We left at 8:00, after six hours of talk. Our backs ached from the plastic chairs. Probably John's was worse, because he had arthritis in one hip, but he didn't say so. Shirley and I stayed overnight at the motel so we could come back to see him in the morning. We talked about what we would do next—get the transcript, find the hospital records, find other witnesses—not knowing how difficult the task would be.

While we went back to the motel, John returned to a cell which was seven by ten feet in size. There was a window ten inches wide and four feet high in the far wall. He had a steel bunk, a steel chair, a steel clothes bin, a steel sink with a steel mirror and a toilet. The door was solid—no bars—but there was a glass panel in it six inches wide and two feet high. From this panel a guard could see all parts of John's cell. There was no privacy. Out in the common room, prisoners shouted and screamed. At 10:30 p.m. his cell door was locked. It would not be opened again until 5:00 a.m. and there was no way for him to call out. He worried that if he had a fifth heart attack in the night, he could not get help.

CHAPTER TWENTY-SEVEN

The Daley Center in downtown Chicago is a twenty-five-story building housing the circuit courts, judges' chambers, Cook County records, state's attorney's offices, jury empanelling rooms, and so on. It is named for Mayor Richard J. Daley, who was for decades Chicago's big boss. The building is as square, functional, and undecorative as was the irascible mayor.

Tony telephoned the records clerk at the Daley Center for the transcript of John's trial. "We'll look for it," they said and they took down the file number.

A week passed. Tony called back.

"We're looking for it."

Again a week later.

"We're checking the warehouse."

And again.

"Don't keep calling. Give us a little time."

He waited a little while, then started calling twice a week. They were still looking for it.

Tony said to Shirley and me, "I'm beginning to picture a filing system where they file papers by pitchfork."

He kept on calling.

Thanksgiving passed.

We asked the Department of Corrections to transfer John to a prison nearer Chicago, like Dixon, so that his family and attorney could visit him. Tony was working unpaid and could hardly fly to St. Louis and rent a car to drive to Hillsboro, spending a day and considerable money. The Department of Corrections responded that John was "properly placed."

Still no transcript. Without the transcript of the original trial, any appeal was well nigh impossible. There was far too little information in the decision of the Illinois Supreme Court to base a case on. Finally, Tony started to pay personal visits to the clerks at the Daley Center. He got to know the manager and three or four others. But he got no transcript.

Tony said, "Let me into the warehouse to look."

"We couldn't possibly do that."

"My client is in prison. I can't pursue his case without the transcript. It'll save you time if I look."

"I'll go look myself. But we can't let you in."

We assumed that when we got it, the transcript would tell us everything—what the alibi witnesses for the defense said, what John Branion had said about the gun, the pathologist's testimony, maybe some mysterious, convincing evidence of John's guilt we didn't know about that had decided the case for the jury. Everything.

This was important, because the reasons given in the opinion of the Illinois Supreme Court for upholding John's guilty conviction were extremely odd.

This opinion, like most court opinions, was relatively short, possibly fifteen pages if it had been in typed form, and was written by the majority, that is, the judges who decided against Branion, with Mr. Justice Burt delivering the opinion.

It states that Mrs. Kentra heard "a commotion" at about 11:30, and that about fifteen or twenty minutes later saw Dr. Branion come out on the back porch. It says "Mrs. Kentra saw the defendant's face and he did not appear to be agitated." I would later find that she had not said any such thing. It said "the defendant claimed" that he picked his son up out in front of the nursery school, that he could tell his wife was dead because "he had observed lividity in her legs."

It says, "It was further established, through the testimony of Dr. John Belmonte, that Mrs. Branion died as a result of four gunshot wounds to the head, neck, and shoulder." It says Dr. Branion "made no mention" of a Walther PPK when questioned by the police and that he "told the police nothing was missing from the apartment."

Toward the end of the opinion, the judges say that the state proved to the jury Branion could have been at the scene between 11:30 and 11:58 and that Mrs. Kentra described the commotion as taking place "shortly before Dr. Branion came out of his back door after the murder."

Lastly, the judges described what they considered the "most telling evidence." First, the murder was committed with a "rare" Walther PPK. Second, "Exactly four bullets were found in and around the body, and when the police found, a month later, a box of .380 caliber bullets designed to hold twenty-five bullets, with exactly four missing, the evidence was convincing."

In addition to the internal discrepancies, like that about Mrs. Kentra's times, there wasn't much here to prove Branion's guilt. Was that all the proof the state had?

There was a reference in one of the appeal briefs to a rope mark on Donna Branion's neck. There was nothing about it in the Illinois Supreme Court decision. We needed to know exactly what the pathologist had actually said. We needed that transcript.

Christmas came and passed—still no transcript. Tony called the capitol at Springfield, where the Illinois Supreme Court is located. Could it be in their vault? They weren't sure, but didn't think so. January came and John Branion turned sixty in prison. His blood pressure was rising. His children wanted to see him. We again asked the Department of Corrections to transfer him. Still no movement.

Shirley and I took Betty Adger to lunch. She was the nurse in charge of the clinic at the Ida Mae Scott Hospital. She was twenty years older than she had been when Donna died, but she was pretty and vivacious and the events were as clear in her mind as yesterday. I could understand this; it was the day something shocking had happened to a close friend. It was very much like the way people remember where they were when President John Kennedy was shot. She could not understand how John was convicted.

She called him "Branion."

"Branion was so good with patients. He took *time*, you know? And he was a happy person. It never made any sense that he had killed Donna."

"You knew Donna?"

"Oh, sure. Donna and Branion and Shirley, too. They were all doing okay. There wasn't any *stress*. Branion was happy and Donna was happy and Shirley was happy. There wasn't any reason for Branion to kill Donna."

"You said in your affidavit that you offered to testify at the trial."

"I sure did. I talked with Scott, John's lawyer. I was on the witness list. I was waiting out there in that room where they keep witnesses—I think it was five days. And they never called me. That last day, when they said we could go, I thought they meant go for the night and come back the next day. I couldn't believe it when they said the case had gone to the jury. I just couldn't believe it."

Shirley had obtained a copy of the autopsy protocol. While we were trying to get hold of the trial transcript, I was working on that.

When an autopsy is performed, the autopsy physician dictates his findings into a microphone as he works and the words are then transcribed by a secretary. As a result, the form is full of misspellings and run-on sentences, making it very difficult to tell when the description of one wound leaves off and the next begins. However, it was obvious that there were many bullet wounds in Donna Branion's body, probably thirteen. How could they have been produced by four shots? I asked John when he telephoned. He did not remember anybody ever bringing up the number of wounds or questioning the four-shot theory in any way.

How did thirteen wounds fit with the Illinois Supreme Court statement that the four missing bullets, combined with the "four shots" fired at Donna Branion, was "convincing" evidence of guilt?

A bullet striking a human body will ordinarily make either one or two wounds: one, an entrance wound, if it lodges in the body; two, entrance and exit wounds, if it passes through. This is also called a "through-and-through" wound.

Occasionally, a bullet will make more than two wounds. This can happen in a couple of ways. If two body parts are lying in the path of the bullet, the bullet may pass through both. This often happens when a person raises a hand to defend himself. The bullet may enter the palm of the hand for instance, exit the back of the hand, then enter the chest and exit from the back. Making four wounds. But this only happens with body parts that can be interposed.

In the case of Donna Branion, this seemed unlikely. The wounds were in the central body. One entrance wound was in the right eye, four in the base of the neck or upper chest area in front, one or two in the right shoulder or upper arm. It didn't seem likely that the one or two entrance wounds in the shoulder or upper arm were caused by bullets that had struck the chest first, because there was no wound in the right chest wall where they could have exited before striking the arm.

One bullet had remained in the right upper arm, so it may have produced only one wound.

Dr. Belmonte had also noted that he thought the wounds of the back were exit wounds.

A second way a bullet can make more than two wounds is by fragmenting. This often occurs after a bullet strikes a bone. But Donna Branion's body had been fluoroscoped; there were no bullet fragments left in the corpse, and there probably would have been if any bullet had fragmented. Some of the resulting pieces would be small, and with little mass they would have little momentum and lack the force to exit. Also, ammunition fired from an automatic like a Walther PPK is usually jacketed, which means it would resist fragmentation. And in addition, the Court's opinion suggested the bullets had been ballistically analyzed, which suggested that they were found intact.

I plotted the wounds on a standard autopsy silhouette, something the coroner apparently had never been asked to do. I could not make the wounds line up with four shots. It seemed to me very unlikely that Donna

Branion had been shot as few as four times. To me it looked like seven shots would have been needed to produce those wounds.

Another line of thought was suggested by the autopsy protocol. Dr. Belmonte said that Donna had bruises and lacerations on her upper and lower lip, bruises on the cheekbone, a bruise around the neck with a 3/8-inch depression seven inches long, and a bruise under the jaw on both the right and left sides. This strongly suggested a fight. Somebody had hit her in the mouth, and probably punched her on the jaw more than once. Donna had defended herself. And then, judging from the deep mark around the neck, she had been nearly strangled. The Illinois Supreme Court opinion hadn't even hinted at such a situation.

Plus, when she was finally shot, she must have died very quickly. Dr. Belmonte described damage to her left and right carotid arteries and left and right jugular veins, the top of the left lung, and damage to the aorta. He said, "The left chest cavity was brim full of blood." She would not have lived long with this massive hemorrhage.

I started to ask around for a qualified pathologist to study the report.

Jan Branion, John's daughter, had the clippings of newspaper stories that came out at the time about her mother's murder. They had been cut out of papers and saved by Sydney Brown, her grandfather. Shirley brought them to me and we photocopied them all.

From them, I started to create a picture of what the police had said publicly about Donna's murder. Now I needed any records the police department would give me about their investigation.

The elevators at the Chicago Police Department are cramped. Or maybe they just seemed that way to me; I am five feet one and I was riding an elevator with eight or ten large Chicago policemen. I felt like a kindergarten child in a crowd of adults. All the cops seemed to be over six and a half feet tall and weigh at least two hundred and fifty pounds. The uniformed officers had shiny black shoes, shiny black leather belts, dark blue uniform pants with blue shirts, and were decorated like walking hardware stores—handcuffs, flashlight, gun in leather holster, walkie-talkie, and assorted metal whistles and buttons and badges. The plainclothes or administration police wore civilian garb—shiny black shoes, dark blue pants, light blue shirts, and carried their guns in black leather holsters in the small of their backs. But no hardware store.

The Chicago Police Department on South State Street was located in a crumbling area of town where the sidewalks cracked and tilted. It was surrounded by parking lots and bars. The area was gentrifying spottily, with several sleek, trendy buildings on cleared squares of land. Older, once-elegant, now shabby buildings stood around them. It was like a patchwork quilt with tattered brocades and glittery space-age fabrics interspersed.

The Police Department building itself had a modern but disheartening facade of dun-colored stone. Its backside, however, resembled a tenement with its many fire escapes.

Lt. Glyn occupied a glassed-in office in one corner of the detectives' room. He represented the records department. About six feet tall, he wore the requisite shiny black shoes, dark blue pants, and a light blue shirt. Gun in leather holster in the small of his back.

Tony had filed a Freedom of Information request with the Chicago Police Department. They had denied it, saying FOI requests or no FOI requests, they didn't let just anybody see their files. This despite the fact that the case was nearly twenty years old. Tony argued. They finally agreed. We wondered whether they didn't automatically resist at first in order to cut down the number of requests they had to fill.

Even if that were so, Lt. Glyn was completely gracious. He gave me an unused desk next to a five-eleven woman in blue shirt and dark blue pants with a gun in the small of her back. He handed me a stack of papers in a folder marked "permanent retention file." In fact, he had even ordered the negatives of the photos taken of the crime scene, the bullets in the boxes, and Donna's body in the morgue, and had them made into eight-by-ten prints for me to inspect. I could Xerox them but I couldn't take any out of the building.

The file was thirty or so pages of closely written or typed reports, so I studied the photos first. I fanned the prints out on the desk. There was Donna, eighteen years dead, lying on the floor of the utility room, her shadow reaching down to the present.

Donna lay on her back, her shoulders partly turned to the right. Her head had fallen against a paper shopping bag, which in turn was shoved against a wooden chair. The bag had partially crumpled forward over her head. Around her upper right arm was the cord from an electric iron. Her sweater was pushed up, showing her abdomen. Her skirt was pushed up, showing her thighs above the tops of her stockings.

In the next photo, the bag had been pulled away from her head. Longer views of the utility room showed laundry equipment, a thermos, an ironing board lying on its side, and a large table tipped over. The metal legs of the table at one end had been broken off and lay on the floor. One of Donna's slippers lay where the utility room opened into the kitchen.

There were two spent pellets and two empty cartridge casings visible. After studying the written reports, I realized that the photographs had been taken after Helen Hudson and Dr. Helen Payne from upstairs had looked at the body, Dr. Payne presumably having examined Donna closely. They had been taken after Officer Catizone had felt for a pulse, and at least one casing had been moved between the first couple of pictures and the last two. The two visible pellets were not fragmented, not even deformed.

A single bullet, before firing, called a "round," is composed of three principal parts. There is the *pellet*, which is a cylindrical piece of metal composed of lead and other alloys. The ammunition used in automatic handguns usually contains a lead pellet coated with copper or brass—the "jacket"—which makes it less subject to being deformed or fragmented when it strikes a hard object. The pellet fits into a *cartridge casing*, which is usually brass. Between the pellet and the base of the cartridge casing is the gunpowder or *explosive charge*. When the explosive charge is detonated by the firing pin of the gun, expanding gases force the pellet out of the cartridge casing and out of the gun.

The two types of handguns most common in the United States are the revolver and the automatic. A revolver is named for its rotating chamber, which holds the rounds of ammunition. The revolving cylinder turns after each firing, bringing a fresh round into place in front of the firing pin and at the rear of the barrel. The spent cartridge, after firing, remains in its chamber and a new chamber is rotated into place.

In an automatic, however, the rounds are loaded into a container called a magazine, which in most cases fits up into the grip or handle. "Automatic" is a misnomer for semiautomatic. A true automatic fires off all the loaded rounds on one trigger pull. The gun commonly called an automatic chambers one round at a time, pushed up out of the magazine by a spring. The round fits into the chamber, where it is struck by the firing pin when the trigger is pulled. It is called semiautomatic because the recoil of the expended gases that force the pellet out of the barrel are directed in such a way as to chamber a new round and kick the now-empty cartridge casing out of the chamber. This is called ejecting the spent cartridge. In some automatics the casing is ejected straight up into the air. In most, it is ejected upward and to the right.

Therefore, at the scene of a crime, when casings ejected from an automatic are found, their position will tell something about the crime—where the assailant was standing, for instance, and possibly where the victim was, as well. I looked in vain for any diagram of the positions in which the pellets or cartridge casings had been found.

I turned to the police reports. Officer Catizone's report said there were three pellets and four spent shells, or cartridge casings, *under* the body. He was the first officer on the scene and looked at the body before any other policemen or technicians had moved it, even before Cleary and Kersten from the crime lab photographed it. His report was filed that same day, before any opinions had hardened in any official's mind about who had committed the murder and how it had been committed.

If the spent cartridge casings were found under her body, Donna must have been standing when they were fired. But if the two or three pellets were found under her body, either they were fired after she had fallen to the floor or they had ricocheted and fallen to the floor and she then collapsed onto them. The simplest explanation was that four shots were fired at her while she was standing. With the assailant standing in front of her at nearly point-blank range, the expended cartridges would fly out of the gun up and to *his* right, strike the wall, and fall to the floor. Then she collapsed from the wounds, fell to the floor on top of the casings, and the last three shots were fired at her where she lay.

But that makes seven shots.

The Court's opinion said there were four shots. If you accept a four-shot theory, the assailant must have fired at her as she lay on the floor, then picked up the four expended cartridge casings, which would have fallen on her body or nearby, *and raising her body, pushed them underneath.* Or alternatively she was shot standing, collapsed on the four casings, then the pellets, which had passed through the body and fallen somewhere behind her, were pushed underneath her.

Which is absurd.

I must have appeared distressed, because one of the detectives came over, looked down at what I was examining, and seeing the picture of Donna, lying in a pool of blood, said, "Yup. That would be enough to ruin anybody's morning."

There was a report in the folder from the police crime lab. I paged through it until I found the clothing report. There were powder burns on the clothing. That confirmed the notion of point blank range. I had read that the prosecutor accused Branion of standing over his wife and shooting her as she lay on the floor. Would there have been powder burns if she had been lying down and the assailant standing?

The perforations in Donna's sweater generally corresponded to the wounds, except for one thing: there was a perforation in the left sleeve, where no wound was mentioned on the body. Had a bullet passed through the sleeve without touching Donna? And if so, where did that bullet go?

Studying the photographs, other questions suggest themselves. John had told me the hall and Jan's and Joby's bedrooms were carpeted. Why no photographs of the hall carpet? The blood in the back bedroom and the blood in the kitchen, added to the finding of the body in the utility room, made it clear that Donna was either forced or dragged down that hall.

Scuff marks or drag marks would have been useful to give an idea how long that struggle took and how many assailants there were. Evidence like that, once lost, is lost forever.

There were photographs of Donna and John's bedroom. The closet doors in this room were on sliding tracks. One of them had been pushed or bumped off its track and lay backward against the clothes. In front of this door on the floor were two small, round pools of blood.

Why no photographs of the smear of blood on the kitchen wall? Kersten had taken a sample of it for analysis. It was right there in the crime lab report. Well, possibly they took fingerprints from around it, and that might be good enough. I searched the report for mention of bullet ricochet marks on the walls. Or for a mention of their absence. No luck.

Since Donna Branion evidently struggled with her killers, I searched through the police reports for a statement of John Branion's physical condition. Was he scratched or bruised? Was there blood on his clothing? But there was no mention of any such evidence. And yet the police must have been looking at the victim's husband with the greatest suspicion.

Also in the file was a slip of paper. It said that a police officer had picked up fingernail scrapings, as well as blood samples and some body-orifice swabs from the Cook County Coroner's Office. The evidence had been delivered to the Chicago Police Department. Then where was the analysis of the fingernail scrapings? It could tell the color of the assailant's skin, whether he or she wore makeup, or it could contain fibers from his or her clothes. I looked back at the lab report. Not there. Either they were never analyzed or the analysis was lost or thrown out before the report was written.

Both Officer Catizone's report and Detective Boyle's contained lists of the wounds in Donna Branion's body. Catizone listed twelve, not knowing that what looked like an abrasion on her right eyelid was really a gunshot entrance wound. Boyle listed thirteen. This confirmed the autopsy protocol. And yet the opinion of the Supreme Court of the State of Illinois said that Donna had been shot four times. It was hard to see how.

Also in the permanent retention file was the statement Theresa Kentra, the next-door neighbor, had made to the police the afternoon of the murder. For some reason, hers had been taken down and typed up, while John Branion's wasn't.

All this material would have to be taken home and studied. The department let me Xerox it.

I spent the next four weeks combing the police reports and lab reports. From the police reports, I was able to make a chronology of Dr. John Branion's morning on December 22, 1967, especially the critical period between 11:30 and 11:57. What was more important, the data came from independent witnesses interviewed by the police, not from John Branion's memory of that day. (See appendix for complete chronology.)

Shirley located a transcript of the inquest on Donna Branion. It answered some questions and raised a few others.

Michael Boyle testified to thirteen wounds in Donna Branion's body. He also said that four shell casings and three spent pellets were found under the body. A fourth spent pellet was found in her body at the morgue.

He said, "We made a diligent search of the victim's apartment, consisting of seven rooms, found no signs of disarray or forced entry. The front door of the apartment entered into the living room and secured by two locks. The rear door of the apartment is located in the kitchen, and was also secure." When Deputy Coroner Smith pinned him down on whether the doors were locked, he said, "Shut and locked."

He said the investigators had found no strange fingerprints, but when Smith pursued him about exactly which surfaces had been printed, he said only, "All the doors."

Was it possible that they never fingerprinted the plug ends of the cord found wrapped around Donna Branion's arm? Or the appliances near her body? The metal edges of the tipped-over table? The faucets where an assailant might have washed off blood stains?

By now it was February of 1986. The transcript of the trial seemed to have vanished into the bowels of the state. The records clerk at the Daley Center never found it, despite the fact that the state is required to keep it in order to be fair to the defendant; without a transcript an appeal is virtually impossible. But Tony had an idea. We knew that the case had been appealed to the Supreme Court of the United States. If so, somebody must have sent a transcript to Washington. The Supreme Court had denied certiorari, which means simply that they declined to hear the case. But Tony reasoned that they must have looked at the records, including the trial transcript, to make that decision. If so, they might have neglected to send the transcript back. Tony called the Supreme Court building in Washington. Somebody there agreed to look for a Branion file.

Shirley and I had coffee in the cafeteria that served the Northwestern medical school and law school. The windows overlooked Lake Michigan. It was a cold winter day and the lake was frozen as far as we could see. The windows made low thumps as gusts of wind coming over three hundred and fifty miles of lake struck them.

I said, "I need to talk with Maxine Brown."

"She's dead," Shirley said. "She died of cancer, about ten years ago, I think."

"I'm sorry. Well, I should see Nelson Brown. If we can't get a transcript, I need to know what he said at the trial."

"He's dead, too."

"How?"

"He was found outside their family bank one morning. It was near Easter in 1983. Multiple stab wounds and the fan belt of a car wrapped around his neck."

Suddenly, I felt chilled. "Like Donna," I said. "Multiple bullet wounds and the mark of a rope around her neck."

"Yes."

"And I suppose people asked—"

"—where John was." Shirley nodded, patiently. "He was in Uganda. So was I. He wasn't brought back here until August of 1983."

I was filling in a picture of John's life.

I dropped in unexpectedly at the pharmacy of LaHarry Norman. In 1967 he was the pharmacist at the Ida Mae Scott Hospital. In the office of his pharmacy, along with his own golfing trophies, he had four or five of the trophies John had won when he was racing his Corvette. Norman told me that John always let him know when he was closing the clinic for lunch, so Norman could go to lunch too. He says that once a week or so he went home to lunch at John's and Donna's.

I met with Billy Hooks, John's longtime friend. He had gone Christmas shopping with John and Donna the day before Donna's murder. And he had been at the party on the last night of her life.

John told me about the kinds of illness he used to see at the clinic. His specialty was obstetrics, but when he took clinic duty he saw anything and everything that walked in. There was a lot of hypertension, diseases of poor diet, lack of exercise, poverty.

A transcript existed! It was in the vault of the Supreme Court in Washington. The catch was that they would not send it to Tony directly, even though Tony was John's attorney. It was technically the property of the Supreme Court of Illinois, and therefore it had to be sent to the capitol of Illinois, Springfield, and Springfield could send it to Tony.

I talked constantly with John on the phone, taking notes of everything. His memory of the day Donna died and even the many days of the trial was flickery. Details came and went. He might remember a detail, and then

246 • THE STRUGGLE

not be able to guess exactly where it fit in. This was especially true of the trial. It apparently was so painful that he did not recall most of it. He had been too successful in putting it out of his mind. Events farther in the past were different. They were sharp and clear.

"John," I said one day, "you know I don't believe that everybody who is having an affair necessarily kills his wife. If the figures are right, half the wives in this country have had affairs and three-quarters of the husbands. But I think if you are saying that the situation between you and Shirley and Donna was stable, people have a right to ask how that could be."

"Well, Donna knew about Shirley. Donna was—it was important to her that forms were observed. Her family was concerned with respectability."

"But are you saying she didn't *mind*?"

"Donna wasn't as worried as a lot of people might be about what was actually happening. She was concerned with how it looked. And she liked her home, and things."

"She said it was all right?"

"No, no. You don't understand Donna. She didn't even talk about it."

Over the next several months, I continued to ask him about Donna's reaction to his affair. He seemed really to believe that Donna accepted the situation. He and Donna had arguments, he said, like every other couple. But they always made up again afterward.

It is impossible this long after her death to guess what Donna really thought of this situation. For his part, John may have been approaching this issue the same way he approached so many things, with more optimism than was warranted. It may be that if Donna hadn't come right out and said she was hurt, he thought that meant everything was fine. Friends have told me, though, that for as long as Donna lived, she and John continued to do things together as husband and wife, as a family, and that probably reflects an underlying solidity in their marriage.

· CHAPTER TWENTY-EIGHT ·

The law school buildings at Northwestern University have a medieval air. They are made of gray stone blocks with mock flying buttresses, pointed Gothic windows, stained glass, and heavy wood panelling inside, on which hangs engravings of long-dead judges in long white wigs. The main hall is three stories high and hung with purple and white banners. You could play *Camelot* there and not spend a cent for scenery.

Tony's office is on the third floor. The ceiling is high, the windows tall, narrow, and mullioned, and the room inside is lined with wooden barristers' bookcases. Shirley, Tony, and I sat in his office. The transcript had arrived. It was 830 legal-sized pages and weighed nine pounds. We couldn't have been more pleased if it were a baby.

It had been repaginated four times as sections and appeals were added, or as it went to various courts. The first thing we did was to Xerox four copies. Shirley Branion, Tony, Tony's secretary Joanne Garcia, and I sat on the floor with piles of transcript that had been Xeroxed in sections, putting them together in order. But the fact that there were four numbers on every page had confused the Xerox shop and some of the parts were mixed. One of us was going by the numbers in the top right margin. Another was going by the bottom left. Some of the numbers were unreadable. The ones on the bottom right were light blue, and therefore did not photocopy well. When we discovered what we were doing, there was groaning and stamping around and a lot of laughing. We couldn't be dampened much, now that the transcript had come.

It was going to answer all our questions. What about fingerprints? When did Theresa Kentra hear the shots? How did they drive that route and get such short times? How this? Why that? Was there a mysterious fact we didn't know about that forced the jury to convict? We got everything straightened out by dusk. Shirley and I each carried a copy home with us.

Reading and then rereading that transcript over the next couple of weeks was an eye-opening experience. And very depressing.

The picture that emerged from the trial was not at all what the Illinois Supreme Court opinion had led me to expect. True, having seen the police reports had prepared me to find that some of the opinion was wrong. But the reports contained in the permanent retention file ended with the day of John's arrest. It was four months from then to the trial. Evidence might have turned up.

But it hadn't. There were no surprise witnesses that put John Branion at the scene of the crime. There was no new lab report, nothing that put the gun in his hand or a scratch on his face. Nothing.

What was more upsetting, the trial transcript for the first time revealed that Dr. Branion's words at the police station the day of the murder were never clearly transcribed and could have been misunderstood or distorted. And that Donna's own brother confirmed John Branion's version.

And as to the four-bullet theory of the crime, it was a notion that appeared for the very first time in the prosecutor's closing argument, was never addressed at the trial, never asked of Dr. Belmonte, never testified to or debated at all.

And most important, Dr. Belmonte had stated that the bruise on Donna's neck would have taken fifteen to thirty minutes of continuous pressure to produce.

Most Americans believe that a person prosecuted for murder has to be proven guilty beyond a reasonable doubt. They envision the prosecution painting a consistent and coherent picture of the crime. They think that the accused has had his day in court.

Most Americans realize that sometimes an accused person is incapable of doing anything to help himself at his trial. He may be unintelligent, mentally ill, whatever. And if he is also poor, he may have to be given a court-appointed attorney. Many Americans realize that in these cases, the accused may not receive the kind of justice they wish everyone had. But most of us tend to believe that, on the whole, relevant information comes out at a trial.

I had been exposed to the same ideas. What's more, I had read hundreds of detective stories and true-crime books in which justice triumphed through a combination of thorough research and rationality. In detective novels, the police officer or prosecutor carefully assembles the time factors and decides who had the time to commit the crime. He takes the evidence and deduces who is guilty. He does not lose fingernail scrapings. He does not fail to collect fingerprints. If the deceased fought with the killer, he does not fail to notice whether the accused is scratched.

For example, I realized that John Branion was being accused of lying when, and if, he said he had picked Joby up out in front of the nursery school. Not one person had told the jury this accusation was ridiculous—that going into the school and spending five minutes there was five minutes of solid alibi. Nor had anyone made the point that John had not even tried to claim that time. What possible good would it have done him to "lie" himself out of time spent?

The more I looked at the transcript of the Branion murder trial, the more uneasy I became about criminal justice in the United States. The Illinois Supreme Court opinion sounded so authoritative. The trial contained similar information, but it was often either extremely doubtful, unfounded, or in some cases disproved. The original documents, such as the police reports, were even less probative of guilt. It was as if the "proofs" became more and more transparent and faded away, the farther back toward the original source one explored.

As if that weren't enough, the time element, taking only the *prosecution's* own evidence from the trial, proved that he did not have nearly enough time that morning in December to kill his wife.

Dr. John Branion was a highly educated man, and he had a private attorney of his own choice. And yet the presumption was that he was guilty. And nobody, it seemed, had ever tried to make coherent sense of the actual, physical evidence.

When I first started working on the Branion material, I had resolved to stop all research once a month and, using everything I had accumulated to that date, see if I could formulate a reasonable scenario in which John Branion had killed his wife. I would give full weight to all the police materials and would use absolutely nothing Branion himself had told me, unless it was confirmed by an impartial witness. That way, I believed, I would not be misled by my sympathy for the anguish of the Branions themselves.

By the end of January, 1986, after three months of collating reports, I phrased my monthly "Could He Have Done It?" report in a different way.

In this reconstruction I would leave aside the actual amount of time available to Branion. No counting of minutes. I would simply *picture him doing the crime as it was known to have been done.* I would see if it were plausible.

So—Dr. John Branion has decided to kill his wife, using a clever time alibi. He leaves the hospital, goes directly home, and lets himself in the front door. Has he parked near the apartment in order to gain time, or a couple of blocks away so that his car won't be recognized by the neighbors? Remember, most of the people in that building knew him and his car. Well, never mind that.

He lets himself in with his own key and finds Donna immediately. Instead of keeping the gun hidden, then suddenly shooting her, he chases her into the back bedroom. Why? Well, maybe she suspected something. He hits her and knocks her into the closet door. Why? Why not shoot her then? He drags her down the hall and holds a cord around her neck for fifteen to thirty minutes. Why? By then it's 11:50 or 11:55 and too late to go get Joby.

Well, try it this way. It was not planned; it was a crime of last-minute fury, irrational. He goes home, not meaning to kill her, but meaning to discuss something with her that they couldn't discuss in front of the children at breakfast. He has decided they will talk about it now, before he picks up Joby and before Jan gets home. It escalates into an argument, then into a fight, then to murder.

But for an argument, there is certainly no time.

All right, he goes home intending to kill her. He has the gun in his pocket, having taken it to the hospital with him in the morning to save time and kept it in his car while he worked.

He walks in. Why doesn't he shoot her immediately? Why not make it quick and preserve his clever time alibi? Shoot her instantly. Leave immediately. He's in a hurry. But instead he fights with her, holds her by the elbow, marches her from room to room?

Well, possibly she sees his intent and fights with him. But he has a gun. Well, maybe he doesn't have the gun yet. Maybe he meant to pick it up at home, but she sees murder in his eyes and fights back before he has the gun.

But he's almost six feet and weighs 210, an ex-football player who spends his spare time wrangling horses. And she's five feet three, 135 pounds, an unathletic homebody—and he couldn't knock her out quickly?

Never mind that. He decides to march her into the utility room and put the cord of an iron around her neck and hold it there for fifteen to thirty minutes.

Why?

Then he drops the cord, picks up his own gun and shoots her with it several times.

Why? Why not strangle her while he has the cord around her neck? The cord, unlike the gun, would not be associated with him.

He leaves the house, goes to get Joby, where he enters the school unrumpled, even takes off his own coat in full view of the teachers, helps Joby on with his outer clothes, visits Maxine's office unrumpled, and then is seen by Cottrell Meadors a bit after that, driving along in the car with Joby, talking to Joby pleasantly, heading home.

After the police come he tells the officers that Donna used good sense in admitting people to the house, instead of saying that she was careless. He says that none of the doors were standing open when he got there, instead of saying one was. He forgets his late patient, forgets to mention seeing the administrator Leonard Scott on his way out of the hospital, forgets to cite the five minutes he spent inside the nursery school. Doesn't mention that it took William Payne a little time talking with John before he called the police. Does not try immediately, that afternoon, to claim anything is missing from the apartment.

No matter how I picture it, it doesn't make sense.

"I should tell you about a case I had," Jim Doherty said. "We got it on appeal. A man who was convicted of murder, even though the dead woman left a suicide note in her own handwriting."

"Had he coerced her?"

"No. She had been depressed for quite a while. And the man had no reason to coerce her. He hardly knew her."

A man had picked up a woman and they had gone to a motel together. Late in the night, while the man slept, the woman wrote a note, saying "I killed myself" and signed it. Then she put the muzzle of a shotgun in her mouth and pulled the trigger with her toe, blowing the top of her head off.

Because he was sleeping very soundly (they had been drinking), and also because it was muffled in her mouth, the man did not hear the shot. When he woke up later and found her dead, he panicked. He left the motel and, running away, tried to get rid of the shotgun. Both he and the gun were later found by the police.

The pathologist misinterpreted the injuries to the body. Though the roof of the woman's mouth was gone and there were powder burns inside, he believed that she had been shot in the forehead from in front. The prosecutor argued that the woman's arms were too short for her to have reached the trigger if she held the gun out in front of her. Therefore the man must have shot the woman in what might have been a suicide pact, and then not gone through with killing himself. Despite the unlikelihood of a suicide pact on the part of two people who hardly knew each other, the man was convicted.

Doherty found two independent pathologists to look at the evidence.

The evidence of the body made it clearly suicide, they concluded. And to confirm, the blood and tissue was on the motel ceiling. Doherty got a reversal, and the man was freed.

The pathologist for the state had been the man who signed on second in the Branion autopsy, not Dr. Belmonte but his assistant.

Tony and I had gone to meet Jim Doherty, Cook County Public Defender. Professor Jim Haddad at Northwestern Law School said Doherty was a lifelong friend of Dr. John Branion's father. Doherty had a photograph of John's father in his office, Haddad said. We called Doherty. He was interested in hearing about what had happened to his old friend's son after his conviction, and he wanted, I think, to give us some advice.

The Cook County Public Defender's offices were a warren of rooms and cubicles and secretarial anterooms. We arrived after the end of the work day and there were still papers everywhere. Doherty took us into his own large office. On the wall, ten feet from his desk, was the photograph of John's father. And under it a poem to the man, written by Doherty after Branion's death.

"That was a great man," Doherty said.

Doherty, now in his sixties, must have been much younger than Branion, Sr. Doherty had brought in three of his associates to talk about the son of his old friend.

They had read the Illinois Supreme Court opinion. They started asking questions.

"What about these four rounds of ammunition missing from the box in his closet?"

"Donna had thirteen wounds," I said. "They can't have been made with four bullets."

"Says the pathologist told them four."

"He didn't. He was never even asked."

"What about calling and inviting this Maxine Brown home for lunch at the last minute?"

"He didn't. John and Donna both asked her at a party the night before."

"What about denying he had a Walther PPK?"

"He was never asked about a Walther PPK."

"They also say he told them he only had one gun—"

"They asked for a 9 mm in the afternoon. He gave them one. They asked for a .380 in the evening. He gave them one and when they asked if he had any other .380s he said no. The Walther is a 9 mm."

"What about going into the nursery school, when he said he didn't?"

"Going in took him *longer.* He spent five minutes doing it. And we don't even know he said he didn't. Probably he just wasn't specific."

By now, late winter of 1986, I had a good diagram of what John Branion had actually done that morning of December 22. I had brought along several Xeroxes of it. One of the younger men said, "This is very convincing."

There are two parallel justice systems in this country, state and federal. Certain crimes like counterfeiting and kidnapping that involve the crossing of state lines are federal crimes. A person arrested for these crimes is tried in a federal court.

Most crimes, like assault, robbery, and most murders, are state crimes. A person arrested for them is tried in a local court, and if he appeals he appeals to the state appeals court, then to the supreme court of the state. After that he may appeal to the United States Supreme Court, which may or may not grant a hearing.

To re-enter the state courts at this point, we would have to ask for post-conviction review of the case.

To take a case previously in the state system into federal courts, you need first to have exhausted all state remedies, and second, to have an issue of constitutional importance. You petition for a writ of habeas corpus. Habeas corpus dates back to early English law and the Magna Carta. It charges that whoever is holding the person in question is doing so illegally and must bring him before a judge.

In the United States, it is mostly for constitutional violations that an attorney turns to habeas corpus and argues that the state, actually the prison warden in this case, is holding the prisoner illegally. The state then defends the action of the prison warden in holding the man.

Doherty and his associates and Tony threw back and forth which was better for John Branion—to go into the federal system or back through the state system.

"You have to go state first," somebody said. "Or the feds will throw it right back to state court."

Tony said, "If we take prosecutorial misconduct as an issue, they'll say it was decided by the supreme court in 1971."

"What about ineffective assistance of counsel?"

"Sure. Scott never interviewed the alibi witnesses. He didn't time the route, and so on. But—"

"They'll say Scott was a private attorney of Branion's choice."

"Yes," said Tony.

"And not *totally* ineffective," somebody else said.

A lot of voices:

"You know how many incompetent lawyers are out there?"

"They'd have to reverse half the criminal cases—"

Somebody wrapped it all it up: "They almost *never* reverse for incompetence of counsel."

"But the statute of limitations has run out on post-conviction review in the state courts," Tony said, meaning the case had gone past the time frame when it could still be appealed.

"Because he fled the country."

"Which, they'll argue, was his own fault."

"So we have to go federal," Tony said.

"But if you go federal, they'll throw it back."

"We can argue innocence in the federal court," Tony said. "The state court will say it's res judicata," already judged.

"If you go state post-conviction first, and lose, you can go federal after that."

"Two bites at the apple."

"And if you go federal," somebody else said, "they'll just send it back to the state court anyway."

"And if you go federal and lose, you've lost forever."

There was a pause. Then somebody said, "Of course, we all know that the state courts would rather die than overturn an Illinois Supreme Court decision."

"So the best you hope for is the Illinois Supreme Court to reverse itself."

"How long do the state courts take?" I asked.

They all looked at each other.

"Take two or three years to get a state court, that's a lower state court, to rule on it."

"And then?"

"Another couple of years for the Supreme Court of Illinois to rule."

"Branion is sixty," I said. "He's had four heart attacks and coronary bypass surgery. He doesn't believe he'll live that long."

For two hours they batted it around. State post-conviction motion or federal habeas corpus.

"State courts want you to let them clean up their own mistakes."

"Sure. But they don't admit they make them."

"They'll never reverse."

It was late when we left and long since dark. The lights of the Loop were cheerful outside the big windows. As we left, Doherty gave me an account he had written of his suicide case. And he warned us about the Branion appeal: "A case like this will break your heart."

While the research was going forward on John's case, we kept on trying to get him transferred to a prison closer to Chicago, so that his family could visit. Hillsboro was five to seven hours by car, and off the beaten track for bus, train, or air.

We heard that the Illinois State Penitentiary at Dixon had emergency buzzers in the rooms, in case an inmate got sick in the night. After seven months of trying everything—calling state representatives, reasoning with the Department of Corrections about his medical condition, Shirley writing letters direct to the director of the Department of Corrections, appeals to friends of friends who may know somebody—suddenly he was simply transferred to Dixon, no reason given.

He was informed a few hours before so that he could let his family know where he was. But he was not told the exact time of the move. The inmates were transferred in a prison van in manacles under armed guard, but the DOC kept the time and route unknown lest somebody try to hijack the transport and free the prisoners.

Dixon had been a lower-medium security prison, but had just recently been "upgraded" to high-medium security to handle the system's overflow. A new wide perimeter was bulldozed around the buildings and a high fence with barbed wire installed.

It was otherwise very much like Hillsboro, but John now had a buzzer in his cell. In the few cases he knew of, when prisoners got sick, the guards responded very, very slowly to the call for help. But it was better than nothing. Also, he could get his medication here once a day, and time the dosages himself.

And it was just 120 miles west of Chicago. While the vast machinery of the criminal justice system chewed its way through the appeal, Shirley and Jade and Jeff could visit John.

April, 1986

For a while I kept the files on the Branion case in an upstairs office. But it got so that when we were discussing it, which was almost every day, I spent too much of the time going upstairs for papers. So the file box moved down to the living room. After a few weeks it became two file boxes.

By April, I had a clear enough narrative account of what happened on December 22, 1967, plus a chart of the time required by all the events of that morning, an analysis of the probable number of bullets fired, and a background of the Branion family. Tony took these materials to Tom Geraghty, the head of the Legal Clinic at Northwestern Law School. The clinic was a department of the law school. Its purpose was to provide law students with some practical experience—under supervision—in working up cases, filing them, and taking them through trial.

Tom looked over the materials. After a few days he got back to us that he'd like to use the case for his students and would like to work on it personally.

We had been given the name of an independent pathologist who might look at the autopsy report and see if my conclusions were right. We approached him and then sent him the materials. But his examination was cursory and he wanted $350 to work up an affidavit.

We decided to drop that line.

Dr. Belmonte never testified that four shots could have made those thirteen wounds. There was no testimony to that effect—it was Tuite's invention. And in a way, whether the person who shot Donna had found a loaded gun or loaded it from the box—neither scenario really proved that it could or couldn't have been John Branion. We decided to argue that the four-shot theory was unfounded.

"To me the only really probative thing about that box in the closet," I told Tony, "is that if John had used the bullets from it to shoot Donna, he would have got rid of it."

Shirley and I had been talking about the affidavit of Betty Adger, the nurse on clinic duty at the Ida Mae Scott Hospital. Betty had said she entered the morphine prescription for the emergency patient in the drug book, the procedure mandated by law for dangerous drugs.

"Where do you suppose that drug book's gone?" I asked Shirley.

"The hospital closed several years ago."

We drove past the building, which was empty of tenants, run-down looking. Shirley wrote down the name of a realtor, whose sign was on the side of the building.

During the next few weeks, I hunted for jurors. We wanted to know about the photographs of Donna dead being shown to the jury when they shouldn't have been. There were half a dozen questions we'd like to ask them. We didn't even know their names until we got the transcript, and when we did get it the transcript didn't include any record of the voir dire, the one point in the proceedings when the lawyers ask the jurors where they live and where they work.

Eight of them were women. If they were married, and we didn't even know that, they would most likely be listed under their husband's names, making it even harder to find them. Armed with the Chicago phone book, I started making calls.

Meanwhile, Shirley had talked with the hospital building realtor. He said there were no records in the basement. He didn't want to give her the owner's name.

We had some very common names among the jurors, and a few unusual ones. Most of the unusual ones had no listings in the Chicago phone book, regardless of first name. I tried the North Suburbs book. Still nothing.

One day at last I located one. I called a number and found a juror's sister-in-law. She told me she remembered the trial—and that her brother-in-law died a few months after it.

At the Chicago Public Library I tried the West Suburbs Directory. Then the South Suburbs. No luck. But they had microfilm of Chicago phone books for every year decades back. At least I could find out where the jurors lived at the time, then go to the addresses and ask neighbors if they knew them.

The microfilm was faded, washed out by the passage of years. Whole sections were almost impossible to read. When I'd done all I could, I had found the address of only one juror, one of the men.

I went to the address. The windows of the first floor of the building were boarded up. There was a metal accordion grate over the inner lobby door. The outer door hung by one hinge and beckoned slowly in the breeze. Inside the lobby the floor tiles were broken and the dozen brass doorbells hung down on frayed wires.

When I rang the bells, nobody answered.

Shirley telephoned the city tax bureau, figuring to get the name of the owner of the Ida Mae Scott Hospital building. But they didn't want to give out the information.

A friend of ours, Joseph Mahr, owned and ran a detective agency in a Chicago suburb. He sent a man to check out the hospital building. He didn't see any records in the basement, either.

Meanwhile, Shirley had found a woman friend who lived near the building. She had heard that the file cabinets were emptied into the base-ment and sold. She said there was a flood in the basement several years ago in the spring. Afterward, there were boxes of soggy paper stacked out on the curb for the refuse trucks.

July, 1986

At home we were beginning to forget what we used to talk about before the Branion case. Tony was spending almost all his research time on the question of whether to go federal habeas corpus or state post-conviction. This was library research, case research, so he was not focussing on the autopsy or the physical evidence at this point.

Tom Geraghty talked by phone with the prosecutor, Patrick Tuite. Tuite was willing to give us some sort of statement about a conversation he had with Judge Holzer when Holzer was considering a verdict in Branion's favor. We didn't know quite what it would say, and Tom and Tuite were finding it hard to get the time to meet.

It could be another point in the appeal brief.

The most basic question of the case at this time, whether to go for state post-conviction or a federal habeas corpus, was still hanging fire. The only person who could really make that decision was John himself.

Tony and Tom and two of the students piled into Tom's car and drove out to the prison in Dixon. The canteen there was sunnier and more open than the one at Hillsboro. There were glassed-in booths where prisoners could meet privately with attorneys. They laid out the pros and cons for John.

State courts like to be allowed to "clean up their own mistakes." But a lower state court may not want to overturn an Illinois Supreme Court decision. In fact, hardly anybody ever expects them to do it, for any reason. So—the best he could hope for, probably, would be to go to state court, then appeal to the Illinois Supreme Court to reverse its 1971 decision.

"How long," John said, "would that take?"

"Two or three years to get a lower court to rule on it. The Illinois Appellate Court might take another year, maybe two. Final appeal to the Illinois Supreme Court might take another year or two."

"Then—as much as six years, maybe," John said, trying to keep calm.

"Yes.

"Plus, the statute of limitations has run on post-conviction for you. It's ten years, and the case was fifteen years ago. For post-conviction, you also need new evidence."

"But we've *got* new evidence."

"Not really. It's new to us. But Scott could have got the emergency patient information from the witnesses if he'd interviewed them. The bullet wound analysis could have been done by an expert at the time. Scott could have timed the route. They can argue it was available to the defense with reasonable diligence."

"What about Tuite's conversation with Holzer?"

"Tuite could say he'd have told about it if anybody asked him."

"Incompetence of counsel?"

"Scott was a paid attorney of your choice. They're not going to be sympathetic."

"All right, then—what about going federal?"

"It's a faster process. Months instead of years."

"What else?"

"We can argue your factual innocence. At the state level that was res judicata, already decided by the Supreme Court. Also, we have a better chance of using the Tuite conversation with Holzer and Holzer's extortion attempt. They're real habeas corpus issues. And there is no state habeas corpus in Illinois. We can tie the incompetence of counsel and prosecutorial misconduct issues into the overall picture of your innocence. And they help explain why you were convicted in the first place."

"Then what are we waiting for?"

"You have to be warned, John. If we lose through the federal system, that's it. We've lost forever. It's one bite at the apple instead of two. You can't go back to the state courts."

"I understand that."

"Also, we could go to the federal court, fight for several months to try to get them to accept jurisdiction, and then they might deny it. So then we'd *have* to go to state court and we would have lost all that time."

John said, "And if we do get into the federal court, and they decide against me, and it goes up to the U. S. Supreme Court, for all we know they might not even hear the case."

"Right. It happened to you before. And neither court is going to like the fact that you fled the jurisdiction. They're going to hold that against you."

"Mmm-hmm. You know, I've talked this over with Shirley. She and I've agreed. Something that takes five years or more—I just don't think it's going to come in time for me."

"It's your decision. But once it's in motion it's an irreversible decision."

He was quiet for a minute.

"Federal," he said.

· CHAPTER TWENTY-NINE ·

Early in our involvement in this case, Tony heard from contacts in the state's attorney's offices that prosecutors at the time of the trial had an entirely different theory of the Branion case. They said that the state really knew John Branion could not have been home early enough or long enough to kill Donna. But the prosecutors believed he hired somebody to kill her, and therefore felt justified in nailing him. The word was "right man, wrong theory".

Was there ever any evidence that he had hired an assailant?

I looked into it every way I could through the case papers, and either Tony or I talked with both prosecutors. They never claimed that there was any other evidence whatsoever. We never heard about any independently, in four subsequent years of research. There was apparently no large sum of money withdrawn from Dr. Branion's bank, and no word among his acquaintances that he had ever looked for a killer.

In addition, as Tony argued to another state's attorney, if Branion had hired a killer he would have had to have suggested some pretty foolish moves. First, to have the killer use Branion's own gun. Second, not to tell the killer to get Donna at a time when Branion was out of town, at a medical conference or other meeting. Third, to kill her at a time of day when Branion himself would be home soon after. Fourth, to kill Donna at a time when Branion would come upon the murder with Joby by his side.

Well, maybe the assassin could have gotten the wrong day. But it still seemed unnecessarily stupid. In addition, when Donna died, John lost Donna's future inheritance of the Brown fortune. So why not just get a divorce?

It is very difficult to prove a negative. But to me the strongest proof against this cold-blooded hiring of a killer was that he had forgotten on the day of the murder to tell the police all his alibi witnesses of the morning— the nurse Betty Adger, the pharmacist LaHarry Norman, technician Robert Wadley, hospital administrator Leonard Scott, the late emergency pa-

261

tient, and the extra time he spent in the nursery school. He just didn't act like a man covering up.

July, 1986

We had driven Branion's route, the one the police said could be done in six minutes, and never got it below eleven minutes. But now our frustration over the difficulty of finding other records turned our focus back to it. Tony said, "What if the police minimum driving time is impossible?"

"You mean the six minutes?"

"Sure. We've said Branion couldn't have done it because of traffic, because of the snow, all of that, but what if the actual distance can't possibly be covered in six minutes? Detective Boyle said they did it at—"

"—at thirty miles an hour, stopping for all traffic signals."

We grabbed a city map and spread it out on the floor. Grabbed a ruler. There were a lot of turns and corners and we knew we were not being exact.

"It looks like about three miles," I estimated.

"Three miles at thirty miles an hour is six minutes."

"But of course that's without slowing down to turn, stopping at stop signs, red lights."

"Maybe we've got 'em."

What we needed, though, was an expert.

Tony made some calls and was lucky enough to find Thaddeus Aycock at the Northwestern Traffic Institute. Aycock was a senior consultant and lecturer in the Accident Investigation Division and was once an Acting Training Officer for the Georgia State Patrol. He had testified as an expert in numerous state and federal courts. He agreed to do a study.

Aycock and his wife first drove the route, using the trial testimony given by Boyle of the route he travelled. They took the route past the Branion home to "kill Donna," as the police did. They got six different times, ranging from ten minutes and forty-two seconds to thirteen minutes and forty-two seconds. And this was in the summer with no snow. It was July 13, no particular holiday, no particular crowds.

Then Aycock calculated the theoretical minimum driving time, given the distance, turns, and traffic signals. He would take the length and shape of the route alone, as if there were no other cars on the street. Of course, in real life, there would always be some obstructing traffic and some pedestrians.

The actual distance proved to be 2.8 miles. He allowed deceleration time at each turn and signal and acceleration times afterward. Because this was the theoretical minimum, we asked him to imagine that all nine stop lights along the route were green. The mathematical chance of nine successive stop lights being green is one in 512.

Aycock's theoretical minimum time—seven minutes and five seconds.

"We've got 'em," I said.

Tony hoped so, but he knew the state would claim that a 1986 run doesn't prove anything about 1967. One of the students, Tina Rainville, was assigned to ask the traffic department if any of the stop signs or lights was new. After several tries, she found out that as far as anyone knows they are approximately the same, but the department did not keep the kind of records that really answered our question.

"But look, the most likely thing is that one or two of the lights used to be stop signs. It rarely ever goes the other way; they don't take out lights and put in signs." This was an area of town that was already fully built up well before 1967. Eventually, we found one light that had been a stop sign in 1967.

Since the police said they stopped at all signals, they must have stopped at all stop signs. Since we called the lights green for our minimum time, any light that was a stop sign in 1967 would add time to the trip. I checked Aycock's sheet. His total time required to come to a stop was 6.87 seconds. His time to accelerate again was 6.07 seconds. One would have to subtract from their total of 12.94 seconds whatever time it would take to travel the same distance at thirty miles an hour, but it would seem that any light that was then a stop sign would add at least another six to eight seconds. Seven minutes and twelve seconds.

Which meant that Detective Boyle had testified to an impossibility.

I had kept on trying to find a forensic pathologist who would analyze the autopsy for us. But one or two said there was not enough information—in fact were distressed at how skimpy the autopsy was—and the others wanted a lot of money. Since the four-bullet theory had never proved anything anyway, logically, John and the lawyers decided simply to cast doubt on it, but to base the appeal on the impossibility of John committing the crime in the time available.

One of the problems, too, about looking for more than a few months for any one piece of data was John's health. We were very conscious of the fact that his heart was failing. There was always a trade-off between taking more time to perfect the evidence and the real risk that he would die before the brief was even filed.

John himself was in favor of hurrying, although he was also aware of the need to get our facts down cold. All we could do was to consult with him and try to balance the two needs.

August, 1986

Tony, Tom Geraghty, and some of the students spent weeks combing the transcript for ammunition. At one point, Tony had accumulated twenty-five counts of either prosecutorial error or ineffective assistance of counsel. Part of the problem now was determining which was which. For instance, Tuite claimed in his opening argument that John Branion could not have seen from the skin of his wife's legs that she had changed to a color of death, because she was wearing black mesh stockings, but in fact the stockings were a medium-light open mesh and skin was visible above the top of the stockings. Was that prosecutorial misconduct? Or was it ineffective assistance of counsel on Maurice Scott's part that he had not reviewed the photographs and so could not object?

The second level of this issue involved how many of these counts to include in the actual brief. Was the stocking argument too trivial? Would, say, fifteen items of incompetence of counsel and twelve of prosecutorial misconduct look like a laundry list? Tom thought it would. He argued for limiting the list to a few of the strongest arguments.

And what about Tuite's appeal to the prejudices of the jury? At a time just after the riots of April, 1968, he asked the jury to convict Branion in order to "send a message to the punks on the street."

Was this an appeal to racial prejudice? And should we argue it, if so? Again, Tom said no. If it was an appeal to prejudice, it was not explicit enough. Prosecutors made arguments like that all the time. And judges currently were not very sympathetic to arguments on the grounds of prejudice.

Tom suggested sending a private detective to talk with the court reporter who worked with Judge Holzer. The man was living in another state. He might remember something about the judgment notwithstanding the verdict that Tuite said Holzer was going to grant. Tuite said he heard Holzer dictated the memo to somebody.

The detective reported back that the former court reporter was living in an exclusive section of town and seemed very unhappy to see him. The court reporter also denied any knowledge of the judgment notwithstanding.

I called the present Cook County court reporters' office at Tom's suggestion. I wanted to find out whether any other reporters worked regularly with Holzer, and whether any of them were known to have worked for him on the days most likely to matter, the first week of June, 1968.

One of the reporters had known John's father. He was very helpful and searched the morgue where they kept the old court machine tapes and notebooks. Nothing. He got some names of retired court reporters and checked on them. Nothing. No sign of the memo.

In August, Patrick Tuite's affidavit came in. He described hearing about the rumor that Judge Holzer was going to grant the motion for a judgment notwithstanding the verdict, then asking a court reporter and being told, "It doesn't look good for the prosecution."

Tuite said he went to Judge Holzer without Maurice Scott present. Tuite asked Holzer whether he intended to set aside the verdict of guilty. Holzer said yes. Tuite then argued that Holzer should let the Appellate Court decide. Judge Holzer told Tuite that he didn't want John Branion in custody, waiting for an Appellate Court decision.

Later, one night, Judge Holzer called Tuite at home. He said that he wanted Tuite to ask for a one-week postponement before ruling on Branion's request for a new trial.

Tuite said, "But I'm ready to proceed."

Holzer insisted that Tuite ask for a postponement.

Now, twenty years later, Pat Tuite said that he thought Judge Holzer may have been trying to pressure Branion for corrupt reasons.

This communication between a judge and a prosecutor outside of the presence of the defense attorney is called an ex parte communication, and is forbidden. Tuite's description of it agreed quite closely with the affidavit of John's old friend Bill Hooks, who testified to Nelson Brown's telling him of making a $10,000 payment to Holzer.

Judge Holzer had finally been caught. In 1986 he had been indicted as a result of the federal probe into judicial corruption in Chicago, codenamed Greylord. He now faced a prison sentence.

· CHAPTER THIRTY ·

On November 20, 1986, the petition for writ of habeas corpus for John Branion was filed in U.S. District Court. We also filed an application to proceed in forma pauperis, which meant that John could be exempted from paying filing fees and having his brief expensively printed.

We had the issues down to four grounds.

Ground one—Dr. Branion was denied a fair trial because of the prosecutor's ex parte communication with the trial judge.

Ground two—Dr. Branion was deprived of the right of due process of law because no rational trier of fact could have found him guilty beyond a reasonable doubt. (According to habeas practice, we had to present all the evidence in a light most favorable to the prosecution.)

We argued that in fact there was *no* evidence to support a conviction. Uncontradicted evidence by the state's own witnesses made it impossible for Dr. Branion to have committed the crime. We cited the time the police said it took to drive the route, added reasonable minimum times for stopping and starting the car, and so on. We included a table of what John provably did that morning.

Then there was the time consumed by running out the back door and calling for Helen, testified to by their witness Mrs. Kentra, the time to go upstairs and call Dr. Payne, verified by Detective Boyle. And so on.

We argued that their witness, Dr. Belmonte, said the strangulation part of the crime alone consumed fifteen to thirty minutes. We argued that the state introduced no evidence whatsoever linking Dr. Branion to the murder. We argued that the state's theory of guilt was inconsistent with the evidence it presented—a violent crime, with blood, evidence of a struggle, and so on, that left Dr. Branion uninjured, not disheveled, and with no extra time to change his clothes.

We argued that the victim's thirteen wounds were inconsistent with four shots being fired and that no one had ever testified that four shots killed Donna Branion. And we argued that Mrs. Kentra testified that she heard the sounds before 11:25, while Dr. Branion was still attending patients at the hospital.

Ground three—Dr. Branion was denied a fair trial because his defense counsel failed to provide him an effective defense. His defense counsel failed to investigate the alibi, to find out about the emergency patient, and to interview witnesses such as Wadley, Norman, and Adger; failed to investigate police driving time (here we included Thaddeus Aycock's study of the route and time); failed to investigate material facts about bullet wounds; failed to refute the assertion that the Walther PPK was a rare gun; failed to show that the "Joby lie" was actually a point of exculpatory evidence; and failed to develop the negative financial motive—John's loss of the Brown fortune through Donna's death.

Ground four—Dr. Branion's right to a fair trial was violated by the misconduct of the prosecution. The prosecutors had deprived him of his right not to testify or have his not testifying commented on by accusing him of getting Nelson to testify for him; attempted to shift the burden of proof to the defendant, asking, "What does he want us to believe?" and suggesting a scenario and belittling it; and argued a scientific impossibility to impeach Belmonte, the prosecution's own witness.

Our petition concluded: "No rational trier of fact could have concluded that four distinct instances of starting, stopping, and parking the car could have been accomplished in no time whatsoever."

We knew that we might be thrown out of federal court on grounds one, three, and four, and conceivably all of them. That was the immediate danger.

We specifically mentioned that John had fled the country, because the government would surely mention it if we didn't.

"They're going to come down hard on it," John said.

"Everybody sure thinks they will," I said.

"What I thought at the time, there was no justice for me here. I thought there was no justice for any black man in this country."

People had told John that if he had simply gone into prison, he could have been out by now. Even some of his family members wished, now, that he had done that. Certainly the state was going to argue that he should have surrendered to his sentence.

Is a person morally obligated, I wondered, to go to prison for a crime if he knows he didn't commit it?

Then the procedural hurdles and legal skirmishing started. Nothing is quick, nothing is simple in the law. And much of the maneuvering seemed to be designed to avoid dealing with the issues.

December 3, 1986: Our motion to file in forma pauperis was granted. This meant Branion, as a pauper, would not have to pay filing fees or have his brief expensively printed.

The judge assigned was Susan Getzendanner. Appointed by Jimmy Carter, she was the first woman on the federal bench. She was considered somewhat liberal. We were cautiously pleased.

I had never been able to locate Dr. Belmonte, the pathologist, in any Chicago-area phone book. Shirley, the ex-nurse, suggested calling the county medical association. I did. They had two Dr. John Belmontes. I picked the younger one to call first.

He was at the hospital. I tried again later. He was in surgery, but they would put a message on his beeper.

It turned out he was waiting to go into surgery. I told him why I had called and he remembered the Branion case well. But he had not followed the outcome of the case.

"He was acquitted, wasn't he?" Dr. Belmonte asked. I imagined he might well have thought so, because of his own evidence.

"No."

"Let's see. Copper-jacketed ammunition for a .38 automatic, wasn't it?"

"Yes!" I was amazed that he remembered. He talked a bit about the case.

Then I asked, "How many shots would you think would cause that number of wounds?"

"I remember thinking at the time it was about seven."

We were also going to enter a motion for John to be released on bond, pending the outcome of the appeal. The primary grounds were his ill health and our claim of a prima facie case for his innocence. And that he had a family waiting for him. It was not very likely to be granted, with his history of fleeing the country. But at worst it would present his stable family situation and his precarious medical condition.

Dr. William Buckingham, a widely known professor at Northwestern Medical School, agreed to look over Branion's medical records from the prison. He concluded that the diet he was getting in prison was likely to make his heart condition worse and that he needed an expert workup in a major cardiac care unit.

The legal wrangles started. The government was trying to get the case sent back to an Illinois court. However, sometimes it seemed as if they—or the system—were just dragging things out.

January 7, 1987: The government's motion for an extension of time to January 9 was granted. A status hearing was set for January 22, 1987.

January 9, 1987: The government filed a motion to dismiss our petition for failure to exhaust available state court remedies.

January 23, 1987: We filed Branion's motion for release pending hearing for habeas corpus.

February 5, 1987: The government's response in opposition to the motion to set bond was filed.

February 18, 1987: Our reply to answer brief was set—due March 4, 1987.

February 20, 1987: Branion's motion to set bond was denied. Well, we hadn't expected it. Branion's motion to amend the petition was granted. Parties were directed to file a brief memorandum—Branion on February 27, government on March 10.

March 3, 1987: The government responded to our motion to strike.

March 11, 1987: Notice of motion, government's instanter (in person) motion for an extension of time to respond to the motion to strike an affidavit.

March 11, 1987: Branion requested clarification of the court's order.

March 11, 1987: The government filed for an extension of time to respond to the motion to strike. Branion's motion to strike and the government's motion for an extension of time to respond to the motion became moot.

March 11, 1987: We filed a motion for clarification. The motion for clarification was granted. The Government is to file the first brief on the issue of culpable negligence by March 23, 1987. The answer brief to the motion is due March 30. A status hearing is set for April 16 at 10:30 a.m.

April 1, 1987: Branion filed a memorandum of law.

None of the government's responses or arguments concerned any of the substantive points. They did not argue about facts. They did not disprove any factual claim we made. Their briefs were about procedure, about the meaning of language in the law, and about past cases that backed them up or why the cases we cited should not be the precedent which controlled the outcome. These things devoured time.

Meanwhile, John's physical condition was deteriorating. He had other health problems besides his heart, including hypertension and severe arthritis in one hip.

Dr. Charles Hahn, who did John's coronary bypass operation, was visiting from Switzerland. He was in Chicago for a world cardiology convention.

Shirley met him at the airport and they drove out to Dixon to see John. A couple of days later Tony and Shirley and I had lunch with him. We chose a Chinese restaurant because cardiologists usually approve of Chinese food. Sure enough, Dr. Hahn ordered the vegetarian stir-fry. And plain, not fried, rice.

He did not believe John would live very much longer in what amounted to captivity. "He needs a thorough workup at a top cardiology center. He may need another bypass. John thinks he's reasonably well because he isn't having much heart pain right now. But that isn't diagnostic. If parts of the heart muscle are dead, they don't feel pain."

Tony explained how slowly the justice system works in the United States, and asked Dr. Hahn for a written medical assessment of John's condition to add to any further request we might make for release on bond.

April, 1987

By now, the article I had originally thought of writing on the Branion case was expanding into a book. Jeff had been accepted by Harvard, Yale, and Duke. Sentiment was drawing him to Duke, where his stepbrother, Joby, now lived. Joby, who had been a football star there as an undergraduate, was now an admissions officer. It would be nice to know somebody at school and Joby had been telling Jeff all the good things about Duke. But finally he decided to go to Harvard.

John wished he could be at Jeff's high school graduation. Jeff was to be valedictorian. We asked John if he'd like us to request the court to let him travel to the graduation. No telling whether they would grant it.

"No. They'd send me in manacles, if they did it at all. It would be too embarrassing for Jeff."

But John hoped more than anything else to be out of prison in time to spend Jeff's last few months at home with him before he left for college.

Finally, on May 26, 1987, came some good news: The government's motion to dismiss the habeas corpus petition on the ground that Branion had failed to exhaust his state court remedies was denied. In other words, Susan Getzendanner had turned down the motion to throw us back into state court. This was a major victory.

We could easily have lost on three of the four grounds. We won on all four.

Not that anything moved faster.

May 26, 1987: A status hearing was held and continued to May 27, 1987.

June 6, 1987: The government was given leave to file a motion to reconsider. They were given until June 15 to file an answer and their motion for summary judgment. Our answer brief to their motion was due June 30. Their reply to our answer was due July 7. A status hearing was held and continued to July 14.

June 8, 1987: The government's motion to alter the May 19 opinion by deleting the res judicata section in the last two pages was granted. The government's motion for an extension of time to June 22 to file answer was granted. The briefing schedule was to stand.

June 22, 1987: The government filed its answer to the petition for the writ of habeas corpus and motion for summary judgment.

July 6, 1987: Branion filed a reply to the "answer and motion for summary judgment."

July 15, 1987: The government was given to July 27 to file a reply in support of its motion for summary judgment.

July 15, 1987: The government's motion to strike was filed.

August 5, 1987. A short status hearing before Getzendanner. The parties handed in briefs.

August 6, 1987: The government's motion to strike was denied.

The Branion case was constantly with us. Tony was constantly in court or readying something for the court.

But the early skirmishing was over. The date for Getzendanner to rule was August 19. John was very hopeful, despite the fact that everybody had warned him that cases like his rarely ever win.

On August 19, the ruling was reset to August 20.

On August 20, that date too was stricken. We were told we would be notified by mail.

Judge Getzendanner had three possible alternatives. She could deny Branion's petition, leaving him in prison. She affirm his petition and set him free. Or she could order a hearing.

On August 31, 1987, we heard she had ruled on the Branion case. Not knowing her decision, we rushed to get the opinion. The bottom line: Branion's petition was denied.

Saddened as we were, we started to read it, and within a few pages, we could hardly believe our eyes. She agreed with us. She concluded that the murder would have taken more time to commit than Branion had between 11:30 and 11:57.

In the months that she'd had the petition, Judge Getzendanner had evolved an alternative theory. If Branion didn't do it after 11:30, he must have done it before 11:30.

How? He could have left the hospital earlier than 11:30, she said. Evidence to the contrary was "hearsay." When Detective Michael Boyle testified Branion said he had left the hospital at 11:30 and that he "was initialed" in the hospital records as having treated a patient at 11:30, and when Boyle said he interviewed the patients and talked to the last patient—all hearsay. The jury could disregard it.

Even if "was initialed" meant independent verification? Yes, here was a footnote. Even if the jury believed that the notation in the hospital records were made by someone other than Branion, they still could have disbelieved it as hearsay and therefore unreliable.

Tony and I were aghast. What could she possibly believe about the way the prosecutors work? I asked, "Does she really believe that the police took *Branion's* word for where he was all morning? With Theresa Kentra testifying to hearing the shots around 11:20, they would have *loved* to show that the principal suspect left the hospital by then."

All right, then, how did she get around the neck bruise? If Branion left the hospital before 11:30, and the murder was committed at 11:25 when Theresa Kentra heard the shots, then he had to start the strangulation process at 11:10, which means he left the hospital at around 11:00.

"I find Tuite's comments," she said about the prosecutor's claim that a bruise can form after death, "to be error, since *his* theory of bruise formation was not based on any evidence in the record. But the error is harmless. The trial judge's instruction (to disregard all statements made by counsel on personal opinions of fact which are not supported by actual evidence) cured this error and made it harmless."

On ineffective assistance of counsel, she noted that Scott had failed on all of the points we had raised in our petition. However, since none of these claims were raised on direct appeal, she wrote, "I may not consider them myself on collateral review." The only one of the points which might suggest Branion was "probably" innocent would be the first point. "If

Branion really did leave the hospital *after* 11:30 a.m., then it is quite likely that Branion could not have done everything he is acknowledged to have done and also killed his wife."

But she discarded the affidavits of Betty Adger, LaHarry Norman, and Robert Wadley. "All three of these affidavits were sworn out in 1985. This is extremely stale evidence . . . I could not trust the present memories of events that are twenty years old."

And she was not pleased with Branion himself: "The reason the only evidence now available regarding these events is so old is that Branion himself chose to flee to Africa rather than to serve his prison term as was his legal obligation."

The thirteen bullet wounds? She said that a bullet might have passed through more than one body part.

The final blow here was something we had known all along—something that gave John Branion sleepless nights of regret. "This is not to say," she concluded,"that had a jury been presented with these additional facts it would still have found (Branion) guilty beyond a reasonable doubt."

"How can she suggest John could have done it before 11:30! He was never accused of that," Shirley said.

Tony said, "Is a defendant obligated to answer a case that was never brought by the prosecution? You'd have year-long trials. People would be trying to answer every wild scenario any appeals judge could ever dream up years later."

Jeff was crushed and angry. It was August 29. A week later he left for his first year at Harvard.

Now somebody had to let John know. He had been so optimistic. We were all worried about what it would do to his health. I called the chaplain at the prison. John was in the room with him. Knowing the word could come any minute, he had gone to the chaplain's office.

"I have bad news for him," I said.

The chaplain had been worried, too. "He's been telling me he was going home."

Then I talked with John. What was there to say?

"Can a judge just make up something?" he asked. "I mean not even the prosecution ever suggested I ran out of the hospital in the middle of the clinic!"

"We're going to ask her for a reconsideration. She can't have read everything carefully."

September 9, 1987: Branion's attorneys were given leave to file a motion for reconsideration. We spent hours raking through the transcript. We argued everything for Judge Getzendanner again, trying to cover every point she'd brought up, and we paid particular attention to her conclusions. In particular we argued that the court erred in substituting its contrary-to-fact theory for the prosecution's theory.

"If the jury can disregard the prosecution's evidence and substitute any speculation of its own," Tony wrote, "habeas corpus would be meaningless."

Because Getzendanner had said some bullets might have passed through more than one body part, we felt she could not have read our argument about the bullets. We repeated it. We explained about the bullet wounds all being in the central body. We argued that the court should have held a hearing, where all of this could be tested. "A court should not substitute its speculations for analytical evidence."

We heard that Getzendanner was going to retire into private practice. Would that make her more hasty in her decision? Or would it make her more courageous, less worried about being reversed by a higher court?

On September 22, 1987, she answered our motion to reconsider.

It is only hearsay, she said, that Judge Holzer was going to rule for Branion before the attempt to extort money. However, Tony's argument won on the major hearsay question. She agreed with us that it was "technically correct" that Branion's out-of-court declaration about when he left the hospital was not hearsay. It was admissible, but she found the jury was free to reject it. As for the hospital records, even though they were entered by the prosecution, the jury was not required to rely on them.

She seemed now to have read our discussion of where the bullet wounds were, because she tacitly agreed with us, not repeating her idea that one bullet could have passed through two overlapping body parts. What she came up with was even more far-fetched: Branion's argument that more than four bullets were required, she said, "ignores the possibility that the bullets may have deflected off walls causing multiple wounds."

Motion to reconsider denied.

CHAPTER THIRTY-ONE

"Getzendanner," Tony said, making a horrible joke, "is off the wall."

"Wait, wait," I said. "Belmonte said the wounds of the back were exit wounds. To get four bullets to make thirteen wounds and exit out the back, three of them would have to go around and come in again and exit again."

Tony said, "Bouncing off three or four walls to do it."

"Without losing momentum."

"And going back in from the front," Tony said "*through the assailant.*"

And two of the bullets would have had to get under the body somehow. A slow right turn in mid-air while she was falling, diving down to hit her after she fell?

When the decision from Getzendanner came down, *Chicago Lawyer* magazine, a monthly newspaper devoted to Chicago-area courts and law news, wanted to do an article on the case. We had not sought out publicity up to then because it angers some judges, who see it as "trying the case in the media." But right now we were not in court, and John Branion made the decision to go ahead. We felt, too, that possibly an article might produce some information. Somebody out there might know more about what had happened to Donna Branion. It was even possible that somebody out there knew who had killed her. We could always hope.

The manuscript of my book had grown to a 300-page narrative. I took it to Rob Warden, the editor of *Chicago Lawyer*. He had known Patrick Tuite and Susan Getzendanner and Reginald Holzer and others for years. He was able to get interviews from most of them. Holzer wouldn't talk, but what he got from Tuite rocked us back on our heels.

Tuite said the defense "had a witness who made it impossible for Branion to have done it. He was a guy who said he stopped Branion on the street and talked to him for about five minutes. There wasn't five minutes to play with under our theory and he (Scott) didn't call him.

"He was on their list of witnesses. We went out and interviewed him and we couldn't break him. He was a solid citizen. We thought, oh shit, here's a guy who's going to testify that he stopped him on the street and talked to him for five minutes. He was a solid citizen, but he never hit the stand."

The prosecution knew Branion had not left the hospital before 11:30. "Like Getzendanner's opinion said, he said he left the hospital at 11:30. We couldn't destroy that. I have always felt that he (Branion) knew who did it and he supplied the weapon . . . But you look back nineteen years and you figure it out. And I don't think, like Scott said, he'd walk in with his son and let the son see the dead body. It was never our theory that it happened earlier [than 11:30]."

Warden asked him about the four bullet argument. "You'd have to look at the autopsy to be sure," Tuite said, "but there was a theory that most of the wounds were caused by the four [bullets].

"If they called that other person who said he stopped and talked to him on the street for five to seven minutes, it would have—they stopped to talk, and he looked at his watch and thought it was strange to see the doctor on the street this time of day. It was near the apartment after he picked up Joby. It would have been impossible, then, that he could have done all this and been back in the neighborhood seven minutes earlier.

"Our theory was going to be that he was wrong about the time or the date. But the guy said, I was there and I remember that date because the woman was killed that day. He was a reputable guy who was not flaky or belligerent."

Immediately, we rushed out to find this mystery witness. I grabbed the witness list from my file. John always believed he had talked to a woman outside the apartment that day, in fact he remembered her saying how Joby had grown, but maybe his memory was faulty and it was a man. Or a couple, man and woman. There were two names on Scott's witness list that we did not know. Rob Warden tried to phone them. Then he sent letters. Shirley and I drove over to the addresses, but at one there was no person of that name. The other address did not exist. Somehow, Scott misnamed the street. There was no such street.

We drove to similar-sounding streets. No luck.

I hired a detective to do a search through the usual public and private documents used for skip tracing. Shirley started asking through her grapevine, people who had known people in the old days. Hospital people. Old friends of John's. Finally she called Betty Adger and asked whether she knew either of the men or recognized their names as patients from the hospital.

No luck.

The *Chicago Lawyer* article came out at the beginning of November, 1987, when we had been working on the case exactly two years. It raised a lot of sympathetic comment. Several more people volunteered to help with parts of the work.

There was a good front page photo of John, taken at the prison, by photographer Loren Santow. The article was virtually the whole issue. In it, Rob Warden and Patricia Haller remarked: "Most important, however, Branion had no opportunity to commit the murder, which is eloquently exemplified by the present situation: A federal judge says that the murder almost certainly did not occur when the prosecutor said it did. The prosecutor says it almost certainly did not occur at any other time."

I was talking about the Branion case with Rob Warden. His office was in a building on East Jackson in the heart of the attorneys-courts axis, walking distance from "attorney row" on LaSalle Street and the Dirksen Federal Courts Building and the Daley Center, where the Illinois state courts for the area are located.

Rob Warden was a friendly, accessible, man. He was a veteran reporter, having earned his stripes in the Middle East and North Africa. His office had pale gray walls with neatly framed memorabilia, and a floor and sofa littered with piles of paper on his latest cases.

"You know, an innocent person puts his foot in it exactly like this," Warden said.

"What do you mean?"

"Well, you go down to 26th and California (the Criminal Courts Building) and watch the call on the cases. The habitual criminals know how to do *everything*. They never say a word unless their lawyer says they can. They never volunteer information. They address the judge as 'your Honor' and the prosecutor as 'Mr. State's Attorney.' They know the ropes. You take an innocent person who gets picked up by the police, and they never ask for a lawyer. Their first instinct is to try to *help* the police. They don't just answer the question, they elaborate on it."

"John says he thinks most of the people in prison with him are guilty."

"I agree. I'm not saying that. It's mostly habitual criminals they pick up in the first place. I just think the non-criminal who *happens* to get arrested is more likely to give the police something they can work on, something that looks suspicious to them. Something they can use in court. You know, they'll try to help, so they'll guess at what time they did something—people *never* remember exactly—and the next thing, the police think they've caught them in a lie."

I thought of John saying Donna used good judgment about who she let into the apartment. Talking about not taking her pulse because he could tell from her color she was dead. Guessing he got to the nursery school about 11:35 or 11:40. Answering everything they asked at the station. Blurting out the afternoon of Donna's death that nothing was missing from the house.

"And then the police say, 'Only a guilty person would tell the police a lie.'"

Tony asked that the case be assigned to another judge for reconsideration under a little-known rule, 52b. A couple of weeks later we were informed: "October 15, 1987 It appearing that the above captioned case requires further judicial action, Chief Justice Grady recommends to the Executive Committee that this case be reassigned by lot to an active judge of this court, since Getzendanner is no longer sitting."

On October 22, 1987, there was a hearing scheduled before Judge Paul Plunkett.

We talked one day about what it would cost if a defendant wanted to hire a lawyer to carry on this sort of case. Tony had spent possibly seven hundred hours on it by now. If a lawyer charged a hundred and fifty dollars an hour that's $105,000. Plus, they would have needed a researcher to do what I did. I had spent possibly two thousand hours, but probably half of it on writing, possibly a thousand hours on actual research. There was Tom Geraghty's time, Dr. Buckingham's, the detective's, Thaddeus Aycock's, and all the students'. A defense of this sort of case could cost $200,000 or more. I had paid my own expenses for Xeroxing, the work of the private detective, food, parking, gas, tolls, and so on for the trips to the prison, John Branion's collect phone calls, and dozens of other odds and ends.

And it had already cost two years.

Almost no defendant in prison could afford that. Imprisoned people have no source of income and rarely can interest anybody in their case. A rich person may not be able to buy a verdict, but in this country a rich person can buy research and attorney time that a poor person can't possibly afford.

"The system ought to review cases where the judge turned out to be an extortioner," I told Tony. "Automatic review and at no cost to the defendant."

We'd been told there were several judges we could have drawn who would be sympathetic to our case. Paul Plunkett, a Harvard graduate now in his mid-fifties, two years before had denied a habeas corpus petition for a twenty-three year old man he admitted was probably not guilty of the murder for which he had been convicted. Plunkett had some years before that been a partner in the same law firm as Susan Getzendanner. We were cautiously pessimistic.

The brief was filed. We included the Rob Warden interview with Pat Tuite, with its dynamite information that the prosecutor knew Branion did not have time to commit the crime.

November 13—a Friday—Plunkett held a hearing and asked Tony some additional factual questions. He wanted the answers by 10:00 a.m. Monday. In particular he wanted to know what John did between 11:50 and 11:57.

We spent all weekend combing the transcript for detailed ammunition. For fifty-five hours the word processor was never off. On Monday we had a thirty-one page brief of answers to the questions with eighteen pages of support.

November 20, four days later, Plunkett's decision came down. Branion lost again. But this time the reasons were different.

"We disagree with Judge Getzendanner . . . ," Plunkett said. "We hold that the Branion jury could properly conclude that Dr. Branion murdered his wife between 11:30 and 11:57."

Shirley and I read the opinion in the cafeteria at Columbia College. Before 11:30. After 11:30. Around and around. . . .

Plunkett wrote, "The lynchpin of Dr. Branion's argument is that it was impossible for him to have murdered his wife between 11:30 and 11:57. . . ." "It's 'linchpin,'" Tony said. "Is this a Freudian slip of Plunkett's?"

And all the same things came back to haunt John Branion. Plunkett mentioned the "inexplicable discrepancy" between what Branion told the police and the nursery school teacher Mrs. Kelly's testimony. He believed Mrs. Kelly saw Branion as late as 11:50 (though she repeatedly says 11:45 or 11:50.)

Well, then, if he believes her 11:50 time, he must believe her when she says John was in the school five minutes.

Wrong. That was in response to Scott's question, and so he doesn't believe it.

Well, we'd spent the whole weekend answering Judge Plunkett's questions, showing that the seven minutes after 11:50 weren't nearly enough for everything Branion did before the neighbor called the police at 11:57, and that therefore Mrs. Kelly's estimate must be late. What about that?

"Given Mrs. Kelly's testimony," Plunkett said, "travel and stopping times further along Dr. Branion's route become less significant."

In fact, he found a means to hold the lack of time against John: "This was a tight schedule but the jury could have concluded that Dr. Branion created it in order to establish an alibi."

With all this, we thought maybe he would simply leave Belmonte's testimony about the time it would have taken to form the neck bruise out entirely, as the Illinois Supreme Court did. But he found another way. He said, "He (Belmonte) did not testify that a shorter period than his estimate was impossible. . . . "

Then there were direct misstatements: He said that Branion discovered his wife with "some blood on her chest" and never checked for signs of life. Some blood, despite the police testimony to a pool of blood.

Branion's "statement that he had only one .380 caliber weapon was shown to be a lie." And, "All of Dr. Branion's handguns including his Walther PPK were apparently kept in a locked cabinet in the utility room." He believed this despite the complete lack of any evidence for it, because Nelson had to get a key for the cabinet to get the .380 in the evening and because there were children in the house. This was clearly contradicted by the trial transcript. The trial testimony of the policemen was that guns were visible around the apartment. The gun Branion gave them in the afternoon did not come from a locked cabinet. But it also ignores the possibility that Donna might have got the gun to protect herself.

He said the last regular patient, Robert Jordan, told police he saw Branion about 11:25 and that Branion was in a hurry. But what about the late emergency patient?

The affidavits about the emergency patient are inconsistent with one another as to exact time, Plunkett said. They also were "not supported by a single clinic record or indeed any credible explanation as to how the affiant can now recall a twenty minute time period in 1967."

Also, "None were called at trial. A logical inference is that they were not prepared to say then what they say now."

What about the thirteen bullet wounds?

He halfway agreed with us. But even if so, it didn't matter. Plunkett wrote: "Even assuming that more than four bullets killed Mrs. Branion and only four shell casings were found, it simply means that the police missed the other shells or they were removed by the killer. Either hypothesis still allows us to conclude that Dr. Branion's innocence is not 'probable.'"

We were staggered.

Plunkett produced his own time chart. It allowed seven minutes altogether for *all* the driving and parking and stopping and starting and getting Joby out and in. Since the police minimum was six for just the drive alone, one could conclude he believed one minute was enough for starting the car at the hospital, parking and getting out at home, going into the apartment to kill Donna, coming back out, starting the car, stopping and getting out at the school, getting back in with Joby and starting up, stopping at Maxine's with Joby, getting out, getting himself and Joby back in, starting again, stopping at the house and getting out with Joby. That's eight instances of stopping and parking and getting out and going in somewhere or the reverse. Eight of these in one minute is seven and eight-tenths seconds each.

"Doesn't Plunkett realize that Branion could try to speed as fast as he could, but if there are cars ahead of him driving slowly or stopped at stop signs and lights, he couldn't make the trip any faster?"

Tony said, "He's allowing less than Belmonte's minimum time for the neck bruise. He allows fifteen minutes for everything that happened in that apartment. All the hitting, bruising, dragging, strangling, shooting."

Plunkett added: "The delay of nearly twenty years . . . was caused by Dr. Branion's flight from this country while out on bond."

Probably no one would claim that the criminal justice system never makes a mistake. You hope it does pretty well on the whole. But the most reassuring thing would be to be able to believe that when it finds a mistake, it corrects it.

I wondered what we could argue next. "Getzendanner says he can't have killed her after 11:30. Plunkett says he could have. Getzendanner says if we could prove there were more than four bullets, it would be an important difference. Plunkett says it wouldn't matter a damn. It's like plugging one hole in the dike with your finger and it breaks out some place else."

December, 1987

We were trying to trace the gun. Maybe we could find out who actually killed Donna.

I called the Bureau of Alcohol, Tobacco, and Firearms and asked if a Walther PPK with the serial number 118274 had ever surfaced in a felony. They put me off twice. Tony said tell them to send us their Freedom of Information Act forms. I did. Then the "special agent in charge" said that the best way to trace a gun was to go to your local police station and ask them to ask NCIC to do a national trace.

Our local detective said he couldn't do it without a subpoena from the state's attorney. They thought they might be legally liable in some way if they gave out that information. I couldn't imagine how, but it seemed to be a problem for them. The state's attorney, of course, was on the opposite side.

Tony and the detective struck an agreement. The detective would query NCIC. Whatever he got he would send down to the state's attorney. He would then tell Tony only whether the gun had turned up or not. Then Tony could try to get the state's attorney to tell him about it, if it had turned up.

Like with everything else we'd done, the system seemed designed to make it difficult for the average citizen to get any information about anything. Surely nine out of ten people would give up somewhere along the labyrinth.

Several days later we heard that the gun has never turned up. Another dead end.

We had sent the ballistics information and the autopsy report and a dozen other documents to another independent pathologist who was willing to look at them pro bono.

Two weeks later, he wrote that there was not enough information to make a conclusion. He asked if there were autopsy photographs of the actual bullet wounds. He wanted to see if they looked like entrances or exits.

I telephoned him, since I was the only one who had seen the actual police photographs. There were two photographs that showed wounds close up—one of Donna's face, and one of her shoulder. Both photographs had been made before the wounds were cleaned, so you see only caked blood. I had checked the negatives I was given to see whether there were pictures that had not been printed. There were no others, and there were no photographs at all of her back.

"No autopsy photos?" he said, astounded. "I can't believe that!" But then he told me he had heard about the mistake made by the second autopsy surgeon when he was doing the case Doherty worked on of the woman who blew her head off with the shotgun, and I felt he really could believe it, he was just outraged.

I started to tell him of the other things they didn't do. Analyzing the fingernail scrapings, taking fingerprints. But I only got as far as their not diagramming the position of the spent cartridges, when he said again, "I can't *believe* they would be so sloppy!"

"Well, could you make an estimate of the *probability* that all these wounds were made by four shots?"

He said, "I doubt if there's enough here."

He promised to call early the next week.

Tony and John talked on the phone. There was always an underlying air of pressure because of John's deteriorating health. He had now been diagnosed as suffering from cardiomyopathy, a progressive degeneration of the heart muscle, in which it becomes flabby and pumps inefficiently. This is not curable, except by heart transplant.

Tony agreed to start working on the brief for the U.S. Court of Appeals for the Seventh Circuit.

I picked Shirley and the children up downtown one Saturday morning in December, 1987, about two years from the time she and I first drove to Hillsboro. Jade would be four soon. Jeff had just come home for Christmas after his first four months at Harvard.

John found that he was often depressed around the Christmas season, especially around the twenty-second, the anniversary of Donna's death. We wanted to visit him on the twenty-second, but there were problems, so we went just a couple of days before.

We drove out to Dixon, two hours of driving, and got there at 10:00 a.m. It was important to arrive before 11:00. At 11:00 they start a "count" of prisoners and you might wait over an hour before your prisoner was allowed into the canteen to see you.

At Dixon there was a large canteen, with another area separated from the main room by glass panelling, where the mentally ill or retarded prisoners met their visitors. About half the inmates at Dixon were in this category, but they didn't have as many visitors, and their special room was smaller. There was also a small room glassed off from the rest for families.

It had a few torn children's books, some dominoes, a beanbag game, and plastic balls. But Jade liked to sit in the main room and go to the canteen window for microwave pizza.

We stayed as long as we could, consistent with not getting back into Chicago too late.

"I was thinking this morning when I crossed the yard," John said, "that I was out in the woods. It smelled like it. In my head I *was* out, just for a while, walking along, and I could have walked on forever. And then, maybe it was the cold fields that the wind was blowing over, I don't know, I was back fishing with my dad. I've been thinking about him a lot lately, even though he's been dead twenty-five years.

"He was in the boat with me that last trip when we caught that muskie," he said. "I had the rod, you know, he wasn't well enough to fish. But it was the first time we ever had a muskie on of that size. And the first time ever that we caught one.

"I was playing that fish, but he'd make a motion with his shoulders, like helping me. Body English, you know. And we played it, and we played it. And then, there it was, in the boat. Thirty-five inches. Wow! The look on his face! I mean, I reeled it in, but we *both* caught that fish."

When it was time to go, about 4:00, we made a game for Jade to make it easier for her to leave. We told her she could work the magic door. You walk up to it and it slides open. It was the airlock entry-exit, and it was actually operated by a guard in a booth on the far side across a hall. After the first one slid shut behind you, the one on the far side magically opened. Jade could make it work just by walking up to it and waving her arms. But Jade wasn't falling for this.

"Daddy come too," she said.

· CHAPTER THIRTY-TWO ·

After three years of this, and what seemed at times like many wasted hours, we had to ask ourselves why we were pursuing the case. Winning was unlikely at the beginning, statistically speaking, and now seemed hopeless.

But an injustice is something that gets hold of you and won't let go. You feel every day, while you are outside and free, that a man is in prison who is not guilty. Often when John would telephone us, one of my children would answer the phone. He knew them both by name and would ask what they're been doing lately and how things were in school. They'd tell him and then later come to me and say, "I felt awful saying I was going out to a gymnastics contest when he's shut up in prison."

Citizens of the United States are brought up to believe our criminal justice system works rationally, and that when it makes a mistake those wrongs can be righted. The longer we pursued the Branion case, the more Branion's own version of what had happened proved to be true. His innocence was based on a simple two-part argument: the shots were heard at 11:20, when he was clearly at the hospital; if the shots had never been heard, he still didn't have time to commit the crime after leaving the hospital. The more the courts resisted looking at the facts, and the more they fixed on strained interpretations or perverse misunderstandings to hold Branion in prison, the more outraged we were. At the very least, they could have ordered a hearing.

This wasn't the way the justice system was supposed to work.

From the District Court, Tom Geraghty and Tony, now joined by Jon Waltz, a nationally known expert on evidence, took the case to the United States Court of Appeals for the Seventh Circuit. A whole new brief drafted according to the Seventh Circuit form had to be written. They made sure to tackle everything that the lower courts were so persistent in misunderstanding. There was a page limit here, too, which made selection a problem. Briefs must be no more than fifty pages. Because the Branion case was so complicated, had so many different proofs of innocence, and because so many misstatements had been made by courts below, Tony and Tom asked for an extension of the limit to a hundred pages. Even this would mean picking and choosing.

Meanwhile I spoke on the Branion case at a meeting of a Sherlock Holmes club in Chicago. After the talk, Dr. Douglas R. Shanklin, who happened to be in the audience, came up to me and said he would look at the autopsy protocol and other data and see whether he could tell us how many shots had struck Donna Branion. Shanklin, I learned later, was a physician licensed to practice in Illinois, Florida, New York, and Tennessee, was board certified in anatomical pathology, was experienced in forensic pathology, a professor of pathology at the University of Tennessee, had testified as an expert witness in fourteen states, and had several times taken over as Associate Medical Examiner in the Eighth Judicial Circuit in Florida during absences of the regular medical examiner.

I sent him everything I had: the pages of Dr. Belmonte's testimony from the trial, the testimony of Detective Boyle at the inquest, the autopsy protocol, and some of the police documents from their permanent retention file. Shanklin noted that the state pathologist had determined that the wounds in the front of the body were entrance wounds and the wounds in the back were exits. Shanklin labelled and placed all the wounds on a body diagram. He concluded this "rules out absolutely any possible ricochet of bullets after body passage with re-entry. Ricocheting is doubtful in any event from the close proximity of the body of the decedent to the wall behind her."

However, while I had thought the thirteen wounds were produced by seven shots, Shanklin disagreed. He thought that jacketed ammunition like this would not have been likely to strike the arm and not exit, as one of the bullets did in Donna's upper right arm, unless it had been slowed down by passing through another body part. Shanklin, looking at the other pathways, decided that the bullet that entered Donna's left eye and then deflected off bone, taking a downward angle and exiting at the base of the back of the skull, may have struck the upper arm when the upper arm was thrown backward.

In his opinion, she was struck by six shots.

About the neck bruise, Shanklin said, "It takes many minutes for fluid to accumulate to a sufficient amount in the soft tissues adjacent to the points of pressure contact for the groove to appear. Discoloration in pressured tissues appears more slowly than that following a glancing blow which tears small veins and which produces the more common form of bruise."

Shanklin also drew imaginary lines back from the exit wounds through the entrance wounds to a point where the lines focussed, the point from which the killer likely fired. Assuming the gunman held the gun at eyesight height, he would have been five feet five or six inches tall. Shanklin thinks it is likely that the gun was held at eye level for shooting, not only because this is a common posture, but also because several of the shots were disabling or potentially fatal, and Donna would have begun to crumple if they had not been fired quickly, which suggests a well-aimed, steady shooting posture.

In 1967, Dr. Branion was five feet eleven inches in height.

By working through Christmas, Tony got the brief for the Seventh Circuit Court of Appeals done by the date it was due, February 18, 1988. Dr. Shanklin's affidavit was included. The brief for the government was due April 15.

This meant still more months for John Branion to wait.

Tony argued the case on June 9, 1988 before Judges Easterbrook, Manion, and Eschbach. The attorney does not know until he arrives in court that day which three judges of the fourteen members of the Court of Appeals will hear his case. The attorney can ask for a different panel, but may have to wait some time again for the case to be heard. Shirley, Tom Geraghty, Tony and I discussed whether to accept this panel, but Shirley had to make the decision. It was again partly a question of how much longer John's small reserve of health would last. Shirley decided to go ahead.

The Seventh Circuit allows only twenty minutes of oral argument. Seven or eight were used up by procedural questions. There was very little chance to answer potential misunderstandings of the evidence, and of course, no way of telling what they did not understand unless they asked.

We did not know how soon their decision would come down.

Meanwhile John's health worsened. His hypertension was affecting his kidney function and the drugs he was taking for his heart also put additional strain on the kidneys. His arthritis was worse, but he tried to keep to a minimum the drugs he took to relieve the pain. And his life continued its dreary prison round.

I asked him once to write down what a day in prison was like. He responded with a long letter.

Every day his door was unlocked at 5:00 a.m. Whatever the temperature, it felt chilly in the featureless room. It was seven by ten feet in size. John always got up immediately. He liked to shave, wash, dress, and be wide awake before the other prisoners started to crowd the hall.

At 5:30 the loudspeaker announced, "Chow lines walking." The loudspeakers were everywhere. There was no escape from them. The voice echoed, metallic and sharp, off the bare walls in the hall. Now all the inmates had to hurry into the common area to form a line. From here they would march single file to the commissary. During the four coldest months of the year it was still dark at 5:30, and they walked the distance in total darkness.

"Because I have so many medical problems," John wrote,"— hypertension, gout, and diverticulosis besides the coronary artery disease—I am permitted to eat 'on the diet line.' Translation: I am not obliged to eat in the regular line; I get to eat in the diet line instead. To dispel any notion that this is some sort of 'perk' or good deal, let me add that the wait is most often longer on the diet line than on the regular chow line. Having advanced to the front of the line, I get to 'place my order.' This is a real joke, because no matter what sort of diet the doctor orders for an inmate, everyone eats the same food. For instance, a man on a soft diet should receive a diet that is antithetical from one on a high-fiber. Yet both of these inmates will come away from the diet line with identical trays.

"After receiving a tray I go to sit down. All the tables have four seats welded to them, and you have to take seats in the order the guards tell you to. I will always have three people to eat with, but almost never a trio of my own choosing.

"I am permitted twelve minutes to eat.

"The guards tell you when your eating time is up. I possess no 'slow eating permit,' so I have to get up and leave the dining room or be issued a disciplinary citation for disobeying a direct order. If I haven't been able to finish my food, that is my own misfortune, and no cause for an appeal for more time. I should have eaten more quickly. It makes you tense. You eat in a state of continual tension."

John was usually back in his room by 6:20 a.m. Every day there were seven "counts." The count was an actual, visual body-count check of every inmate in the prison. The prison held eight hundred men. All movement of inmates in all parts of the prison halted until the count cleared and the actual count matched the total numbers of inmates incarcerated. John had to stay in his housing unit until the clear. Usually this was about 7:20. Then the loudspeaker announced, "Medication lines walking."

Now he walked to the health care unit. This was not so bad in good weather, but if it was raining he was slowly soaked as he crossed the blank fields. Inmates were not allowed rain gear.

At the health care unit he handed in his card and again waited in line. He was getting allopurinol for gout, hydrochlorothiazide for hypertension, nitroglycerine for angina pain, and other pills, totalling nine. As often as not, the nurse miscounted. Sometimes he received the wrong medication entirely, and when he did, unlike most prisoners, he recognized the difference. It was the only time his medical training was any use to him.

Back to the housing unit. There was no stopping or chatting allowed along the way. It was now 7:30.

At 8:00 he was sitting, tired and dazed, trying to warm up. The loudspeaker jarred him. "School lines walking." Inmates attending classes formed up in the common area of the hall. John went too, because he was working on the newspaper and moved out to work at the same time.

At 11:15 the loudspeakers announced lunch lines. It was exactly like breakfast, eating fast. After lunch, he took the quarter-mile walk for medication and was back in the housing unit by 11:45. He tried to relax while the count went on. At 12:30 the loudspeaker called them back to work.

John had exercise—at his request—from 3:00 to 3:45. He wanted to try to keep strong. The exercise consisted of permission to walk around a large circle, the perimeter of a dandelion field approximately half a mile in circumference. The track was bare, worn clear by many feet over many years.

At 3:50 he had to be physically in his room for the 4:00 p.m. count. At 5:00 the loudspeaker said, "Chow lines walking." Dinner, like breakfast and lunch, was twelve minutes. He was back in his room by 5:30.

He took his shower early, so that he could watch the "MacNeil/Lehrer News Hour" at six. It was his favorite program, but most of the other inmates didn't want to see it. And then he wrote letters to Shirley. He numbered his letters to her. This was partly a habit from the days in Khobar prison in the Sudan, when his letters were destroyed, though he knew that these, while they might be read by guards, would not be destroyed. It was also a way of marking time.

During the long evening, the prisoners were allowed to move about their own housing unit and go to the "common room" where there was a television set, a clothes washer and dryer, and a telephone. Twenty-five inmates shared this housing unit and equipment.

He wrote, "The inmates bicker constantly over what program to watch, or who gets the telephone or who gets the dryer. Sometimes the arguments get violent. The only people they can argue with are each other. If you argue with a guard you get a disciplinary citation. Most of them sit around talking about their own criminal exploits—bragging—or they make grandiose plans about their ambitions of what they're going to pull off when they're released. I can't take this talk, and I spend most of the time in my own room.

"But a lot of the time it's just too noisy to read or even write a letter. The men scream and shout in the halls. The inmates believe they have an inalienable right to make noise. They're so starved for meaningful recognition that they just yell.

"Any time between 8:30 and 10:30, the loudspeaker announces medication lines. You never know when, so if you started to watch a television program, you could be interrupted any minute. Anyway, then it's back out into the cold. At 10:30 the guard locks me in my cell. It will stay locked until five the next morning.

"In the morning I get up, to repeat the procedure. Everything. Prison is nothing if not predictable. Every day is the same. *Exactly* the same."

The decision of the Seventh Circuit Court of Appeals came down on July 29, 1988. Branion lost.

Easterbrook wrote the opinion. It contained the usual collection of errors, like calling the Walther PPK a "rare gun," assertions of one side of disputed testimony, like "nothing was stolen" from the apartment. And "Although a physician, he did nothing to investigate her condition or assist her. He told police that he knew from the lividity of Donna's legs that she was dead."

The Walther PPK "could not have been stolen by an intruder on December 22 for the family's weapons cabinet was locked when the police arrived."

Easterbrook wrote, "Branion married his mistress shortly after his wife's death." Easterbrook said that the jury was entitled to take this damaging fact into consideration. But the jury could not have known about it, because the marriage took place five months after the trial was over!

Easterbrook even threw in rumor, apparently from some newspaper: Branion "fled to Africa where . . . he journeyed to Uganda and became Idi Amin's personal physician during 1972-1979."

Easterbrook then concocted a scenario that mocked the prosecution's own evidence: "Time can be squeezed out of Branion's account quite easily. Suppose the clock at the hospital was a few minutes fast. . . . Add one minute to grab Joby and one minute to meet Maxine Brown. . . . "

As for the bruises: "Branion, a physician, knew how to inflict this kind of injury in minimum time. . . . A physician planning murder would have inflicted a kind of injury that looks like it took longer to inflict than it did." This was even more bizarre than Getzendanner's notion of the bouncing bullets. Leaving aside the fact that Easterbrook had absolutely no reason to think such a mysterious deception was physiologically possible, it depicted Branion calculating how to strangle Donna in just such a way that some unknown pathologist will be precisely astute enough to think that such a bruise could take a long time to form and precisely stupid enough not to think it could be faked!

Easterbrook did not claim Branion was necessarily guilty. "It would be nonsense to pretend that this is a simple case or that Branion's guilt is obvious. There is no direct evidence of guilt—no powder residue on Branion's hands or blood under his fingernails, for example. Doubtless a physician knows how to clean his hands thoroughly . . . The two district judges who looked at this record came up with different, and inconsistent, theories of how and when Branion committed the crime, if he did."

But "Careful, rational jurors could have believed that the evidence about the Walther PPK and Branion's failure to approach his wife's body, coupled with his lie to the police about the lividity of his wife's legs, swamped any doubts about the time sequence."

Like Getzendanner, he was huffy about Tuite's chat with Holzer. "Ex parte contacts of the sort to which Tuite admits are forbidden. We were dismayed to learn that an experienced prosecutor, now a respected private attorney, would drop in on a judge to hold a private conversation about the merits of a case. Such lobbying violates the due process clause of the fourteenth amendment."

But he didn't think it was very important. Even though Tuite's affidavit made it clear that Holzer was going to overturn the verdict and changed his mind after Tuite's visit, Easterbrook said the visit did not "work to his (Branion's) actual and substantial disadvantage. . . . "

And of course, like Getzendanner and Plunkett, Easterbrook chided Branion for fleeing the country: "Branion fled to Uganda instead of pursuing his case in the ordinary way."

CHAPTER THIRTY-THREE

Tony asked for a rehearing by the full panel en banc, that is to say, all the fourteen justices of the Seventh Circuit. This request required another set of papers, more work, and another wait. But he didn't want to leave any stone unturned. On September 2, 1988, the request was denied.

We were now three years and thousands of hours beyond where we had begun.

The only chance left was the Supreme Court of the United States. Not everyone realizes that the Supreme Court, unlike other courts, does not have to hear a case just because the attorneys appeal. The Supreme Court actually is three different courts in one. It is a court of original jurisdiction: for example when a state sues another state. It is an appeals court: for example when the government appeals a case where a lower court has declared a United States statute unconstitutional. And it is a certiorari court, in which mode it will hear appeals of individual cases. Agreeing to hear such a case is called granting certiorari. Four out of the nine justices must think the case is of interest or importance to the general public or legal system for certiorari to be granted. This is a policy decision. Justice to individuals is not particularly a goal of the Court, although they are more likely to grant certiorari in capital cases than other criminal cases.

Briefs before the Supreme Court have to be expensively printed. But they will grant an exception if the litigant is indigent. We first had to appeal to be granted leave to file an ordinary, typewritten brief. This was granted.

The brief was ninety-one pages, including the supporting documents. It took weeks to write, as it had to be in the form the Supreme Court used, and had to develop issues they might be willing to hear. Among these was the argument that a person has a constitutional right to an incorrupt judge if he can show that the corruption of the judge affected the outcome of his trial.

It was filed on December 19, 1988.

After the ruling by the Seventh Circuit, it had become clear that the courts were extremely unlikely to respond to Dr. Branion's case. There was still the chance of a last-minute salvage by the Supreme Court of the United States, but practically speaking the chance was very small. It might have been one in a hundred.

Shirley and I believed that the only way we could help John now was to interest the public in his case. The only court left was the court of public opinion.

John himself still hoped for the Supreme Court. Although we had asked him through the years to consider asking the governor for clemency, John did not want to ask for a pardon. He wanted the Supreme Court to send the case back for a new trial or hearing that would prove him innocent. But he was willing for us to go to the press.

We were naive to think that the press would respond just because a man was innocent. We wrote to everyone—the local newspapers, specific columnists, national columnists, television news, national television programs, Oprah Winfrey, everybody. For a period of several months, I wrote letters every day of the week, most of which were never answered. Ted Koppel was interested in one aspect of the story, but it did not come to anything. "Sixty Minutes" replied, but said they had too many stories completed or in progress regarding innocent people in prison.

That was discouraging in more ways than one.

Shirley had written to a program that was relatively new at that time, called "Unsolved Mysteries," which had recently had a psychic on a show. She asked them if a psychic could solve a twenty-year-old murder. And she enclosed the *Chicago Lawyer* article.

Months went by. Then we had a call from Kris Palmer, a producer for "Unsolved Mysteries." She didn't say anything about a psychic, but was interested in the basic story. Could I send her the data? She especially wanted all the news clippings which I had Xeroxed years before from Jan Branion's collection, which Sydney Brown had made.

I sent her everything, including a fifty page summary of the case which I hoped put things in chronological order and made the complicated fact situation clearer. Again months went by.

In the spring of 1989, we heard from "Unsolved Mysteries" that they were seriously interested in doing a segment on Dr. Branion. They wanted me to send them the full trial transcript and other documents. They wanted Shirley to send them pictures of the family.

Still we waited, knowing that they could drop the project at any moment if it did not seem interesting to them. I was particularly fearful that they would drop it when they saw how complicated the Branion case was. It is very easy to do a show on a person who is in prison because somebody lied in testifying against him. The whole course of the avalanche of disasters that had come down on Dr. Branion was much harder to explain. It involved, in fact, ingrained problems with the way the criminal justice system works and showed flaws at every level. Would they want to deal with this?

Michael Niederman, a filmmaker and a professor of film at Columbia College in Chicago, had been interested in making a documentary of the Branion case. Crucial to this was a filmed interview of John Branion. John, of course, was eagerly in favor of it. The Department of Corrections was stonewalling Niederman. Their statement was that the proposed interview was "not in the best interests of the prisoner."

It took one full year of asking before the Department of Corrections agreed to let Niederman into the prison.

The United States Supreme Court denied Branion certiorari for the second time. It would not hear his case.

During the previous couple of years, Tony had told John that he waived any legal fees that might ever come up, but John continued to say that he didn't want to accept that. Now, with the habeas corpus door slammed shut by the courts, Tony felt that despite the enormous amount of time that he'd spent on the case, his legal work had, in a practical sense, been worthless to John. Moreover, there would be no lawsuit against the State of Illinois, no chance of winning such a case now that the federal courts had refused to release Dr. Branion on habeas. Tony told Shirley that he was waiving any and all legal fees that might otherwise come to him as a result of the initial agreement he had with the Branions. He told John by telephone that he had waived all legal fees.

With the refusal of the Supreme Court of the United States to hear the case, John Branion had no other courts he could turn to. Up to now, he had constantly said that he did not want to be pardoned, even if he could get a pardon. He didn't need to be pardoned, he said, because he wasn't guilty. He wanted to be proved innocent in a court of law.

But now, with all access to the courts closed to him, we asked him to think more seriously about it. We could petition the governor for executive clemency, possibly on the ground of ill health. John finally decided that we should try it, but he wanted to petition primarily on the ground of provable innocence, and only secondarily on the ground of ill health.

In October, 1989, Tony and Shirley drove down to the state capitol, Springfield, a five-hour drive, to appear before the Prisoner Review Board. The board hears cases, then passes its recommendation on to the governor. The board's recommendations are secret, so the person appealing has no idea whether his arguments have impressed the panel or not.

The board had announced that Tony could take twenty minutes to speak, but they let him talk an hour. He described the reasoning that proved John innocent. The board seemed composed of members of the public, rather than specialists, and one of the men was particularly concerned about the Chicago Police Department's having lost Donna's fingernail scrapings.

They reiterated that they had very little power, that the governor made the decision, and they claimed that they had no way even of knowing whether their ruling influenced the governor.

They did not say, and possibly they didn't know, how soon the governor would decide.

"Unsolved Mysteries" arrived in Chicago in October of 1988 with a large staff and took over several rooms of a major Loop hotel. They brought the segment's director, John Joseph, the producer, Kris Palmer, their cinematographer, assistant producer, and several technicians. Then they hired additional technicians and support people and equipment locally. They rented meeting rooms at the hotel to audition local talent to play the roles of John Branion, Donna Branion, Joby Branion, Mrs. Kentra, Detective Michael Boyle, and others in the past. They were very careful about accuracy, checking documents and police reports. They even hired me to provide copies of documents, check the accuracy of re-creations, and pull out segments of dialogue from the actual trial testimony, which they would use exactly as it was spoken, to restage parts of the trial. They paid me $500 for this. Except for the $25 I had once been paid to lecture on the Branion case to a writers' group, it was the only money I had ever earned from the Branion case.

"Unsolved Mysteries" restaged many of the events of the morning Donna was killed, casting actors who looked very much like the original people. They shot on location for several days, then held interviews with actual participants and witnesses in the hotel meetings rooms, then went out to the prison to interview Dr. Branion on camera—all to make the hours of film that would then be cut to make the less than twenty minutes of film eventually shown on the program. They had even rented a vintage Chevrolet that was painted to look like the patrol cars of the period. Two Chicago police officers were hired to drive up in the "patrol car" and play the first officers on the scene. They were men who had been on the department in the late Sixties and still had uniforms from that time.

The film of the Branion home was shot in an apartment building that quite closely resembled the Branion's. One of the first segments was the killing of Donna, in which she was dragged down the hall, begging for mercy, and shot in the utility room.

This scene was shot several times. During the shooting, an upstairs neighbor heard the screams and the begging for mercy and called 911 for police help. The call went out on the air, "Woman screaming for help at— " and a squad car nearby responded. It came speeding up to the building with two officers aboard. They found a 1967 police car and two 1967 vintage officers standing out in front, as if they had responded to the call.

"Unsolved Mysteries" also filmed interviews with the principal people in the Branion case. I was fortunate to be able to sit in on the interviews, because even now more information came out about the murder. "Unsolved Mysteries" had flown Betty Adger, Branion's office nurse at the Ida Mae Scott Hospital, to Chicago from Texas where she now lived. They interviewed her on camera. Her interview did not make it into the final program, but one thing she said was very important.

She was speaking about having taken Branion to see the late patient. Then she mentioned that she had left the hospital herself, after filling in the morphine prescription in the drug book. The clinic closed down for lunch, and she wanted to go out to her bank, which was located a mile or so away.

She told John Joseph that it had never taken her so long to get to her bank. It was snowing, and the streets were full of Christmas shoppers. She estimated that it took twice as long for her to drive through the streets as it usually did.

Never until that moment had I found anybody who remembered what the streets were like that very day. I found it understandable that it had stuck in her mind ever since. The idea that Branion could have hurried home to kill Donna must have seemed absurd to her at the time, and his conviction must have seemed an outrage against common sense. She said as much during the interview. She could not understand how he had been convicted.

This tied up one last thread for me. It had always made sense that it took Branion longer that day than usual to drive the route home. The area was densely populated; it was the second-to-last shopping day before Christmas, and it was snowing. But to have it confirmed was satisfying.

Unfortunately, it was just the sort of thing a court would not listen to. A judge would claim that Betty Adger could not have remembered the traffic conditions on that one day for twenty years. Judges either don't realize or don't admit they are aware that a major life event can fix the facts forever in a person's mind.

Prosecutor Patrick Tuite told John Joseph, "I always, even at the time of the trial, had doubts as to whether he actually pulled the trigger. That was our theory of the prosecution. But I always felt and still feel he was somehow responsible for her death."

John Joseph also interviewed Mrs. Kentra, the Branion's next door neighbor. She said she had always known Dr. Branion was innocent. She said she knew what shots sounded like; she had heard plenty in Europe during World War II, before she came to the United States. She said, "If Dr. Branion left the hospital at 11:30, and I heard the shots at 11:20, and I'm sure of it, I was sure then and I'm sure now, then it is impossible for him to shoot his wife."

Like the affidavits of Adger, Norman, and Wadley, a court would say this evidence is too old to be worthwhile. But we certainly wished it had all come out at the time.

The "Unsolved Mysteries" segment on Dr. Branion was to air December 19, 1989, twenty-two years almost to the day since Donna was killed. The appeal to Governor Thompson was pending. We hoped he might see the program, decide Dr. Branion was innocent, and set him free.

Two days before the program was to air, John got word through the prison mail system that the governor had denied his appeal for clemency.

The format of "Unsolved Mysteries" had each program end with an appeal to the viewers: if they had any information about the case, they were to call the "Unsolved Mysteries" telephone number, where operators would take their statements. They could call anonymously or not, and Kris Palmer had told us that if anything especially interesting came in, she would let us know. We gave them our phone number, too. If anybody wanted to call us directly, collect, we'd be eager to hear what they had to say.

I had always hoped that some day we would find out who had killed Donna Branion. It was far-fetched, of course, but not impossible that somebody who saw the program would solve the case for us.

Two of the jurors called in. One said that her son had telephoned her to say that the case she had worried about all these years was on "Unsolved

Mysteries." She had had misgivings about John Branion's guilt ever since the verdict. She also told us that one of the jurors knew or knew of John Branion and told the others he was an abortionist and a bad man. The other juror had some memories about why they voted to convict, but nothing that solved the case.

It is not permissible for a juror to know the defendant or to have an opinion about him going in to the trial. They are queried by the judge, specifically to be sure they don't bring any preconceptions to the case. Certainly if a juror had been biased and it had been discovered at the time, Branion's attorney could have argued for a new trial. We surveyed legal authorities, but none of them thought that after all these years any court would order a new trial on the ground that one juror may have lied during the voir dire.

We had dozens of calls that the gun seen on the show was not a Walther PPK. It wasn't, of course. It was a Hi-Standard. We had dozens of calls with theories about who might have killed Donna or whether or not John Branion killed her. There was nothing that helped solve the mystery.

But some support had built for John Branion. On January 22, 1990, we held a rally at the State of Illinois Building in the Loop, taking signatures on petitions urging Governor Jim Thompson to free him. Several cast members and crew from the Chicago contingent on the "Unsolved Mysteries" program showed up.

CHAPTER THIRTY-FOUR

A second airing of the "Unsolved Mysteries" segment on Dr. Branion produced another spate of two or three dozen phone calls, but none that showed the way to finding Donna Branion's killer. Meanwhile, John permitted a second appeal to Governor Thompson for clemency, this one based first on grounds of ill health and only second on grounds of provable innocence.

Again, John had to wait and see.

In the avalanche of catastrophes that had come down on John Branion, ill fortune had one more in store. In June of 1990, he suddenly had several episodes of difficulty speaking. The prison sent him to a hospital in Dixon, Illinois, where he was diagnosed as having a brain tumor.

After several days he was transferred to the University of Illinois Hospital in Chicago for more studies. The tumor was malignant.

Michael Niederman's documentary, titled "Presumed Guilty," aired on the Chicago PBS station, WTTW/Channel 11, on July 15, 1990. The host, John Callaway, had done separate interviews with Joby Branion and Shirley. His format for the show was to air the documentary itself first, then intersperse a panel of commentators and the interviews he had done. The panel was made up of the Branion prosecutor Patrick Tuite, his assistant at the time, Daniel Weil, Rob Warden from *Chicago Lawyer*, Tony D'Amato, and Dr. Frances Zemans, executive vice-president and director of the American Judicature Society.

Patrick Tuite commented on the way the justice system works. "One of the problems with the justice system is that the quality of your lawyer will affect the outcome." Even with the same facts and the same lawyers, however, he said juries are all different. "Another jury could have found him innocent." Asked which was more difficult, being a prosecutor or a defense attorney, he said the defense was far more difficult. "Jurors are prone to convict. I believe that jurors don't like to acquit."

The heart of Niederman's documentary was a timed drive along the Branion route—the one Detective Boyle said could be done in six minutes not exceeding thirty miles per hour. During this drive a time clock counted the minutes and seconds and a narration of the case continued in an inset. Going thirty miles an hour wherever possible, in excellent weather in the summer with very little traffic, it took seven minutes and thirty-nine seconds just to get to Joby's nursery school. It was 10:06 when the car arrived at Maxine's place of business. The entire drive took twelve minutes and four seconds.

The WTTW special had been well advertised and had a large viewership. We heard for several days afterward that it was being widely discussed. Three weeks after the documentary aired—Tuesday, August 7, 1990—Governor Thompson reduced Dr. John Branion's sentence to time served. The *Tribune* story on the commutation said that after his trial Branion "fled and was arrested October 12, 1983 on a Cook County warrant at Entebbe Airport in Uganda, where he had practiced medicine from 1980 to 1983 and served as Amin's personal doctor."

A spokesperson for Governor Thompson, apparently defending the commutation, told one of the news programs, "Branion isn't going anywhere." He was right. Dr. John Branion was technically free, but he never left the hospital. On September 8, 1990, he died. He had had one month and a day as an ordinary citizen without a sentence hanging over his head.

We had to ask ourselves, after it was all over, whether it was worth it. All those hours, thousands of them by the end, and all of that expense. Tony had never earned a penny on the case, and my expenses far outweighed my $525.

From our point of view, though, it was worth it. Meeting Dr. Branion enriched our lives. Beyond that, the process was an education. Learning about how the world works is always a good thing. And if we were ever involved in a court case ourselves, we would certainly never casually assume that everything would be all right; we would believe from the beginning that every single relevant fact had to be sewn up tight.

For Dr. Branion, I hope all the effort had at least this effect: he knew that people cared. Before Shirley drew us in, very little was remembered about the trial, even by Dr. Branion himself. Many acquaintances believed he was guilty simply because he had been convicted. None of the evidence about the four bullet theory, the driving time, or several other aspects of the case had ever been challenged. Dr. Branion's children firmly believed he was innocent. But the effect of all the efforts on his behalf was to show them he could be *proven* innocent. I hope this will be important to their future lives.

When John Branion was first brought back from Uganda and imprisoned, he thought he was going to rot in prison, unknown. Even though by the time he was freed he could not really enjoy it, the efforts to free him kept him aware that he was known and that many people did care. He was in prison, but his plight reached outside the walls.

And what about the other people in the case?

Nelson Brown, Sydney Brown, Vivian Brown, and Maxine Brown are dead. Oscar Brown Senior and LaHarry Norman died recently. Of the two detectives on the case, Michael Boyle went to law school, became a state's attorney, and has since died. John Mannion, his partner, also went to law school, became a state's attorney, and is now a circuit court judge in the Criminal Division of the Sixth District. He recently told a reporter, "I have arrested them, prosecuted them, and now I judge them."

Patrick Tuite left the state's attorney's office and is now generally conceded to be the leading criminal defense lawyer in Chicago. Daniel Weil, who was his second in command on the Branion case, is Building Commissioner of the City of Chicago.

Uganda has good news and bad news. After several more bloody years under Milton Obote, John Branion's favored candidate, Yoweri Kaguta Museveni, came to power and the killings stopped. However, in the years since, Uganda has been increasingly ravaged by AIDS.

The building that was Area One police headquarters in 1967 is now the DuSable Museum of African-American History.

Judge Reginald Holzer was convicted and sent to a federal penitentiary. He served just about two years and is now free.

▪ CHAPTER THIRTY-FIVE ▪

Donna Branion's death gave rise to a large number of rumors. When word got around that I was looking into the case, I started to hear a great many of them. Some were far-fetched, like the idea that addicts had broken into the doctor's home looking for drugs. If this had happened, there would probably have been more damage around the home. Other rumors, including one that Donna was holding orgies at the house, and another that a militant white cadre was killing families of civil-rights workers as a sort of intimidation attempt, seemed completely unfounded. The most likely explanation was the commonplace view that she had been killed by home invaders looking for money who hit the Branion home randomly, possibly just ringing doorbells until somebody opened a door.

However, one rumor I was told by several people couldn't be easily dismissed. It was that the Branion home had been entered by "Red Squad" men looking for Branion's records about the Black Panthers he had treated.

The Red Squad was a group of Cook County state's attorneys and police seconded to them who investigated black activist and antiwar activist people. The Red Squad was most powerful during the late Sixties and early Seventies. After they were involved in a break-in at a Panther apartment in Chicago, resulting in the killing of two Panther leaders (including Fred Hampton) and the wounding of several other people in that raid, their activities started to draw heavy public criticism and the unit was disbanded. Hampton's relatives and the other victims eventually won a judgment against the City of Chicago.

During this period, some of the Red Squad people twice broke into Dr. Quentin Young's office, probably searching for records. Young, later medical director of Cook County Hospital, was an associate of Branion's in the civil-rights movement. When he discovered the break-ins, Young called the police. Later, he found out that the police were involved. Young and several other people who had experienced similar attacks eventually won a lawsuit against the City of Chicago in 1982. The judge in the case was Susan Getzendanner. After this, the State's Attorney's Office was no longer permitted to borrow police officers for clandestine operations.

The Red Squad rumor in the Branion case was plausible. For one thing, because Branion's own car was in the shop that day and he had taken Donna's car to work, home invaders who knew something about him might have thought there was no one home. Also, because he no longer maintained a regular office except at the busy Ida Mae Scott Hospital, it could have been believed he kept his personal records at home.

If any of this is true, the invaders would most likely not have intended to hurt Donna. However, if she came out of a back bedroom unexpectedly while they were searching, if they panicked at the realization that she could identify them, or if they had restrained her in the utility room while they searched and she suddenly lurched and grabbed up a gun, the result could have been murder.

My friends and I made extensive researches in libraries and archives and made inquiries through attorneys involved in some of the cases. No clear evidence has ever surfaced to prove such a scenario. Most of the Red Squad files seem to have been destroyed.

Leaving aside rumor about why Donna Branion was murdered, it is still possible to reconstruct how the crime took place. Using the lab report, the crime scene photographs, the autopsy report, and the description of the house as the first police officers described it, I worked out a scenario of the crime that was consistent with *all* of the physical evidence and the evidence of witnesses.

At approximately eleven that morning, Donna's doorbell rang. She asked who it was. A voice said "Marshall Field, delivery," or words of that sort.

There was a peek hole in the front door, but Donna was too short to use it. However, it was three days before Christmas, so deliveries were reasonable events. Donna was expecting Maxine, John, Jan, and Joby all home in less than an hour, so psychologically she didn't feel threatened. And perhaps the callers were carrying a brightly wrapped box. She unlocked the door.

Two men pushed in. There is no particular reason why they should have been men, except that at least one of them was probably quite strong. Call them men for convenience—Assailant A and Assailant B.

Donna backed away.

She was just inside the front door, and as she backed away, she backed down the foyer into the hall.

One of them may have said, "Give us some money and we won't hurt you."

John had left Christmas shopping money for Donna on the night stand in the bedroom. Perhaps she told them she'd get it for them. Perhaps she hoped to reach the telephone in the bedroom. She backed carefully toward the bedroom.

In the bedroom, the men may have picked up the money and said something like, "This isn't enough, lady." Or at that moment she may have lunged for the phone.

One of the assailants jumped for her and grabbed her. They fell against the right hand closet door, knocking it off its hinges and into the clothes hung behind. Donna screamed and she wouldn't stop screaming. The man hit her in the mouth, splitting her upper lip. The blood from the lip dripped onto the floor in front of the closet, forming two small, round pools. Still she screamed.

Assailant A grabbed her left elbow in one hand and clapped his other hand over her mouth. His grip bruised her cheek and jaw, but it stopped her screaming. His other hand bruised her elbow.

Assailant B had noticed they were near the large bedroom window and he was afraid somebody next door might see what was happening. He said, "Let's get her out of here."

Assailant A pushed Donna down the hall. She resisted and he had to drag her along. They thought of taking her into the other bedrooms or the living room, but all those rooms had large windows, too, and the men were afraid someone in neighboring buildings might see. They marched and pushed and dragged Donna, who was scratching and fighting, into the kitchen, a distance of eighty feet from the back bedroom. She struggled, throwing one of the men to one side. He staggered and his hand, covered with blood from her lip, struck the kitchen wall and left a smear.

The kitchen windows were glass brick, which seemed safe enough. But just then they heard Theresa Kentra come onto the back porch, which was right outside. She slammed the door. A few seconds later Mrs. Kentra came back out for the rest of the seven bags of groceries she had in the car. Then she was on the back porch again, slamming the door. It was now 11:05.

The men were afraid Donna would scream and attract Mrs. Kentra's attention. They saw the small utility room just off the kitchen and pushed Donna toward it. She struggled at the utility room door, losing one of her slippers in the kitchen just short of the door.

They pushed her on into the utility room. Its window was small and high in the wall, and by keeping her close to the north wall, they could keep out of sight of it.

Assailant B said, "You hold onto her. I'll look for money."

While he was gone, Assailant A noticed the cord from the iron, which was detachable and was lying on the utility room counter. It struck him that this would be a good method to hold her still and keep her quiet without having to keep one hand over her mouth and the other on her elbow. He picked it up and looped it around Donna's neck. He said,

"There. Don't struggle and you won't be hurt."

The lengthy pressure of his grip on her elbow had produced bruises there. The cord around her neck was biting in, but he released it enough so that she could just barely breathe.

It was now 11:15. The phone rang—John calling from the hospital. But the phone rang unanswered. Perhaps the two men held their breath. Maybe Donna struggled, hoping to reach it.

Meanwhile Assailant B had found Donna's purse in the living room. She had it ready for her lunch date. He rifled it for money, and took whatever he found.

Just off the living room was John's study. Assailant B caught sight of the rifles on the den wall. He went in to look, to see whether he could steal them, but rifles and shotguns were too long to carry out of a city apartment unnoticed. He fingered them, wishing he could take them. Then he opened the den closet. There were pistols, including a Walther PPK. This was better than money. He picked up the Walther. It may have been loaded. If not, nearby on the shelf were boxes of ammunition and a clip. He loaded the clip, which held seven rounds, and pushed the clip into the gun. He checked the other weapons and picked out another one he liked. This one he shoved in his belt.

Next door, Theresa Kentra had put away part of her groceries and was taking the presents she had bought the children into the back rooms to hide.

Pocketing some ammunition and holding the Walther, Assailant B took a look around the house. He saw nothing else as portable as the money or as desirable as the guns. He went back to the utility room. It was now about 11:20.

"Let's go."

"She's seen us. She can describe us."

"I can fix that," Assailant B may have said.

Donna saw that he intended to shoot her. She struggled harder, hitting the man with her body and head. Her other slipper came off. Assailant A had tightened his grip on the cord.

Theresa Kentra, still walking around putting away groceries and presents, heard some of the next sounds and was at times too far away to hear others. She had most likely walked into a back room when the first shot or two were fired and returned in time to hear the next three and the falling table. Then she walked away to store some more Christmas presents. She therefore heard only three sounds that she later thought were shots, and the table falling.

Assailant B, standing just inches from Donna in this small room, started shooting. She twisted around and the first shot went through the left sleeve of her sweater and missed her body, but powder from the shot hit the back of her left shoulder. Her struggles knocked over the table. The gun, a semiautomatic, ejected the shell and chambered the next round. The assailant did not even need to know much about its operation.

Assailant A pulled her back and held her from the side with the iron cord. The next four shots hit her in the front of the chest, and one of them ruptured the aorta, causing massive hemorrhaging. They were through-and-through wounds, and the spent pellets bounced from the back wall and fell to the floor, some near her feet. Donna lunged backward, knocking Assailant A into the big metal table, knocking it over. Her blood pressure dropping, Donna's head started to fall forward, and the sixth shot hit her in the right eye, angled downward, came out the back of her neck and spent itself in her right arm. She began to collapse.

Another shot struck her shoulder. Assailant A dropped her. She fell in such a way that she was up against the wall of the room, mostly on her back, but slightly turned toward her right, with her right shoulder under her. Her head fell against a paper bag which collapsed and nearly covered her face. The paper bag itself was wedged up against a chair. The cord of the iron had slipped down over her right arm. She had fallen on four of the ejected cartridge casings and one or two of the pellets.

Assailant A turned to run out of the house.

B said, "No, we've got to pick these up. My fingerprints are on them."

They scrabbled around, collecting the pellets and cartridges they saw, but they were either too squeamish or too rattled to look under the body. The floor was clean and polished, except for the area where blood was pooling, and they found the pellets and cartridges quickly.

Assailant A was scratched and bloody. B was spattered with blood. Quickly, they washed off the most obvious blood in the kitchen sink. Then they ran.

The crime had taken half an hour. By the time John got home at 11:52, Donna had been dead another half-hour, and her skin was the color of death.

· APPENDIX ·

EVENTS OF FRIDAY MORNING, DECEMBER 22, 1967

TIME	EVENT	SOURCE	TIME CONSUMED
8:00	Breakfast: Dr. & Mrs. Branion, Jan, Joby.	Undisputed.	One hour.
8:30	Telephone call to Donna Branion from her sister Joyce Tyler, asking if Donna can babysit for her this afternoon.	Joyce Tyler trial testimony (state's witness)	1 or 2 minutes
8:50	Jan says goodbye, leaves for Shoesmith Elementary School.	Undisputed.	1 minute.
9:00	Dr. Branion leaves, taking Joby. It is ten degrees Fahrenheit, snow is on the ground, and it is snowing lightly.	Undisputed.	7 minutes.
9:07	Dr. Branion drops Joby off at the Hyde Park Neighborhood Club Nursery School.	Undisputed.	3 minutes
9:10	Dr. Branion drives from the Nursery School to the Ida Mae Scott Hospital.	Undisputed.	5 minutes as clocked by police; testimony at trial.
9:15	Dr. Branion arrives at the Ida Mae Scott Hospital. He will see thirteen scheduled patients between now and 11:30 this morning. During that time Dr. Branion remains always in the hospital.	Undisputed.	2 hours and 15 minutes at the hospital not including the emergency patient at 11:30.
10:00	Dr. Branion calls home, asks Donna whether she has decided where she wants to go for lunch with Maxine Brown at noon. Donna replies that she hasn't yet decided.	Affidavit of Dr. Branion	1 minute.

TIME	EVENT	SOURCE	TIME CONSUMED
10:05	Dr. Branion receives a call from Dr. Coramae Mann, saying that she is having trouble getting an airline ticket to Florida during the Christmas rush. He says he'll call someone he knows who works at American Airlines.	Affidavit of Dr. Coramae Mann.	1 minute.
10:08	Dr. Branion calls his friend at American Airlines, and is able to get a reservation for Coramae Mann.	Affidavit of Dr. Branion.	1 minute.
10:15	Joyce Tyler calls her sister Donna. Joyce notices nothing unusual in Donna's voice or mannerisms on the telephone. Donna seems in good spirits and is her usual self.	Testimony of Joyce Tyler	3 or 4 minutes.
10:30	Dr. Coramae Mann calls Dr. Branion to say that American Airlines called her to confirm her reservation. She thanks Dr. Branion for his help, and they chat a few minutes.	Affidavit of Dr. Coramae Mann.	2 or 3 minutes.
11:05	Theresa Kentra, the Branion's next-door neighbor, arrives home with groceries, looks at her kitchen clock.	Testimony of Theresa Kentra (state's witness)	1 minute.
11:15	Dr. Branion calls home again; there is no answer. He assumes that Donna is in the shower.	Affidavit of Dr. Branion.	¼ minute.
11:20	Theresa Kentra hears noises in the Branion apartment next door. She is putting away Christmas presents in a back room when she hears three sharp reports, followed by a thud as if something heavy had fallen. Thinking it a truck in the alley, she puts it out of her mind.	Testimony of Theresa Kentra	½ minute.

TIME	EVENT	SOURCE	TIME CONSUMED
11:30	Finishing with Robert Jordan, his last scheduled patient, Dr. Branion walks down the corridor to the clinical laboratory to ask about a test result for one of his patients. He talks with Robert Wadley, the hospital technician, and with LaHarry Norman, the pharmacist.	Affidavits of Robert Wadley, LaHarry Norman, and Betty Adger.	1½ minutes.
11:30½	Nurse Betty Adger comes in and interrupts the conversation. She asks Dr. Branion to see an emergency patient who is in pain, a Kenneth Morris. Dr. Branion agrees with her that Morris should not have to wait until the clinic reopens after lunch.	Affidavits of Betty Adger, Robert Wadley, and LaHarry Norman.	1½ minute
11:32	Dr. Branion goes to the office of Dr. Moore, a dentist, since the regular clinic offices were closed for the lunch hour. Nurse Adger has put Morris in the dentist's office. Dr. Branion prescribes morphine for Morris. Nurse Adger enters the prescription in the drug book.	Affidavit of Betty Adger. (She thought it took considerably longer than 2½ minutes.)	2½ minutes.
11:34½	Dr. Branion stops back at the laboratory to say goodbye to Robert Wadley and LaHarry Norman, saying that he is rushed because he does not want to be late picking up Joby at school.	Affidavits of Robert Wadley and LaHarry Norman. (Wadley and Norman thought it took longer than ½ minute.)	½ minute.
11:35	Dr. Branion, leaving the clinic, meets Dr. Scott, administrator of the Ida Mae Scott Hospital. They say a few words.	Police report of Dec. 22, 1967; officer talked with Dr. Scott.	½ minute.
11:35½	Dr. Branion reaches his car, parked in the alley behind the hospital. He gets in and starts it up.	Judicial notice of reasonable elapsed time.	½ minute.

TIME	EVENT	SOURCE	TIME CONSUMED
11:36	Dr. Branion drives from the hospital to Joby's school. His route takes him down the alley to 51st street, then east on 51st street to Woodlawn, then south on Woodlawn to 55th street, and then east on 55th street to Kenwood.	Testimony of Detective Michael Boyle (state's witness). He timed the route a month later; his fastest time was 4 minutes and his longest time was 5½ minutes.	5 minutes. It is snowing, it is 3 days before Christmas at the noon hour, and the route goes through shopping areas crowded with last-minute shoppers.
11:41	Dr. Branion finds a parking space, stops the car, gets out, and goes up to the Hyde Park Neighborhood School.	Judicial notice of reasonable elapsed time.	½ minute.
11:41½	Dr. Branion goes inside the school and finds Joby in the all-purpose room. Joby is wearing only his indoor clothes. Dr. Branion takes off his own coat, then helps Joby into his coat, mittens, and possibly his boots. Dr. Branion put his own coat back on and then walks Joby out to the car.	Testimony of Joyce Kelly, nursery school teacher (state's witness).	4 minutes. (Joyce Kelly testified that she thought it took Dr. Branion 5 minutes.)
11:45½	Dr. Branion helps Joby get into the car, locks the door, then walks around to the driver's side, gets in the car, and starts the car.	Judicial notice of reasonable elapsed time.	½ minute.
11:46	Dr. Branion drives to Maxine Brown's office. His route takes him north on Kenwood to 54th street, then east on 54th street to Blackstone. [At 54th street and Dorchester, where there is a stop sign, Dr. Branion is seen stopping his car by Cottrell R. Meadors. Mr. Meadors also sees Joby in the car.] Dr. Branion's route continues north on Blackstone to 53rd street, then west on 53rd street to Apartment Homes, Inc., which is at 1369 East 53rd Street.	Testimony of Detective Michael Boyle. He drove the route in January. Also, affidavit of Cottrell R. Meadors.	1½ minutes. Detective Boyle testified it always took between 1 and 2 minutes.

TIME	EVENT	SOURCE	TIME CONSUMED
11:47½	Dr. Branion finds a parking space, parks the car, gets out, goes around to the other door and helps Joby out, then takes Joby up to the front door of Apartment Homes, Inc.	Judicial notice of reasonable elapsed time.	½ minute.
11:48	Dr. Branion takes Joby into the office, where they see Maxine Brown. She explains that her boss has assigned her two errands to do, so she can't go to lunch. They chat a little.	Testimony of Maxine Brown (state's witness).	2 minutes.
11:50	Dr. Branion takes Joby back out to the car, helps Joby get in, closes the door, goes around to the other side, gets in, and starts the car.	Judicial notice of reasonable elapsed time.	½ minute.
11:50½	Dr. Branion drives to his own apartment. His route takes him west on 53rd street to Woodlawn, then north on Woodlawn, where he finds a parking space near his house at 5054 S. Woodlawn.	Testimony of Detective Michael Boyle	1½ minutes. Boyle testified his fastest time was "slightly over a minute" and the slowest was "less than two minutes."
11:52	Dr. Branion gets out of the car, goes around to the passenger side, and helps Joby out. They go up to the front door of their apartment. They enter the apartment and fail to find Donna. Dr. Branion calls for Donna. He looks through the rooms and finally goes to the utility room. He sees Donna's body, blood all around her in a pool, blood on her sweater. Her legs are a greyish color. Her abdomen is exposed and does not move with any breath of life. Dr. Branion reacts quickly to stop Joby from seeing his dead mother; he turns and picks Joby up and carries him to the back door.	Judicial notice of reasonable elapsed time.	1 minute.

TIME	EVENT	SOURCE	TIME CONSUMED
11:53	Dr. Branion, carrying Joby, rushes out the back door, calling "Helen" several times. They go out onto the back porch. Theresa Kentra, the next-door neighbor, hears him calling Helen.	Testimony of Theresa Kentra	½ minute.
11:53½	Helen Hudson comes down one flight from her second-floor apartment, sees Dr. Branion, goes into the apartment, and sees Donna's dead body in the utility room.	Judicial notice of reasonable elapsed time.	½ minute.
11:54	Helen Hudson goes back to get Dr. Branion and Joby, and leads them upstairs to her second-floor apartment. Edsel Hudson, her husband, is in the apartment and takes charge of Joby. Dr. Branion, satisfied that Joby is in good hands, wanders back down to his apartment.	Area I Homicide Report of December 22, 1967, interviewing witnesses.	1 minute.
11:55	Helen Hudson goes up one flight of stairs to the third-floor apartment of Dr. Helen Payne, and asks Dr. Payne to come down to the Branion apartment. William Payne, Dr. Payne's brother who is visiting in the apartment, asks if he can help and decides to go down with his sister.	Same.	½ minute.
11:55½	Dr. Helen Payne and William Payne go down two flights to the Branion apartment, while Helen Hudson goes down one flight back to her apartment where Joby is.	Same.	½ minute.
11:56	William Payne sees Dr. Branion, in a hysterical state, in the kitchen. Mr. Payne goes to the utility room and sees Donna's dead body.	Same.	½ minute.

TIME	EVENT	SOURCE	TIME CONSUMED
11:56½	William Payne goes back to the kitchen and asks Dr. Branion whether he should call the police. He asks Dr. Branion this question several times.	Same.	½ minute.
11:57	Finally, Dr. Branion says that William Payne should call the police. William Payne makes the call. The police log the call at 11:57.	Same. Also, police log.	½ minute.
11:57½	Dr. Branion asks William Payne to call Dr. Scott, the administrator of the Ida Mae Scott Hospital. William Payne makes the call.	Area I Homicide Report of December 22, 1967.	½ minute.
11:58	Officer Catizone, in a nearby squad car, gets a call to go to 5054 S. Woodlawn.	Undisputed.	
NOON	Officer Catizone arrives on scene.	Undisputed.	